Plautus: Four Plays

Casina
Amphitryon
Captivi
Pseudolus

Plautus: Four Plays

Casina
Amphitryon
Captivi
Pseudolus

Translated
with Introduction and Notes
David Christenson

Copyright © 2008 David Christenson

Cover: Three actors on the stage. Scene from a comedy (Atellan farce): Man at left wearing a slave's mask and two women. Wallpainting from Pompeii. Museo Archeologico Nazionale, Naples, Italy. Photo Credit : Erich Lessing / Art Resource, NY

ISBN 13: 978-1-58510-155-9

Table of Contents

Introduction

Plautine theater must have been a lively spectacle. A cross-section of a stratified and status-conscious society—upper and lower ranks, women and men, young and old, free and slave, rich and poor, Roman, Italian and other—flocked into open-air, temporary theaters that were constructed solely for this spectacle and then dismantled. The occasions for theatrical performances in Rome were religious festivals held in honor of a god, which might also feature gladiator contests, chariot races, and various other entertainments. The competition for an audience thus was stiff, but Plautus seems to have been a very successful comic playwright; though Plautus himself was probably of low status, and not a Roman, the comedies of this "outsider" managed to capture the imagination of the diverse and predominantly Roman crowd at the festivals. A large part of Plautus' success probably was due to the broad nature of his humor and the sheer delight of the playful and punning Latin his characters speak. But the rich social fabric of the plays no doubt also accounts for their appeal in the Rome of Plautus' day—and perhaps also for the survival of twenty-one Plautine scripts through continuous copying by hand down to the Renaissance, when they were first published in book form, as they continue to be today, in Latin editions and in translations such as this volume. Just what has made Plautine theater so engaging to so many different types of people, in both the ancient and modern worlds?

Plautus and his World

Although Plautus was a popular figure in Roman comedy and his works went on to influence Shakespeare, Ben Jonson, Molière and many other playwrights, virtually nothing certain is known about him. He is said to have been born in Sarsina in northern Umbria in 254 BCE, though the sources for this information are not entirely credible. Even his name—Titus Maccius Plautus—is suspicious. Titus may have been slang for "Phallus" (cf. "Dick" in English), Maccius apparently means "Son of Clown" (the clown is a stock character in an-

1

cient Italian farce) and Plautus or "Flat(foot)" is a nickname for actors in ancient Roman Mime.[1] It is unlikely that this mock-grandiose name was bestowed upon him at birth, but rather, he probably took it on after working in theater in various capacities and eventually achieving notoriety as a comic playwright in Rome. Plautus most likely then was by birth a slave or free person of low social status who only acquired a social identity through his success in the theater.

The twenty-one Plautine plays that survive (not all are complete) were written between c. 205 BCE and 184 BCE, said to be the year of Plautus' death. Of the four plays translated here, only *Pseudolus* is securely dated, i.e., to 191 BCE. The plays were produced during a dynamic period of the Roman Republic. The Romans had seized control of Italy, and were now setting their sights on the larger Mediterranean region and acquisition of an empire there. This brought them into conflict with not only the Carthaginians in North Africa, who under Hannibal's leadership were defeated in the Second Punic War in 201 BCE, but also with various kings and city-states of Greece. These conflicts finally ended with the destruction of Carthage and the sack of Corinth (marking the final relegation of Greece to a Roman province) in 146 BCE.

Rome at the peak of Plautus' career thus was undergoing a major cultural revolution. Roman soldiers stationed abroad and other travelers had fallen under the spell of Greece, and many had learned at least some Greek. Greeks and Greek culture were now exerting enormous influence on many facets of Roman life, and Greek philosophers, rhetoricians, artists, poets and teachers were ubiquitous in the city. Though there obviously was demand in Rome for things Greek, morally conservative figures such as Cato the Elder (239-149 BCE) railed against the reputed decadence and dangerousness of this new wave of foreign influence. Traditionalists depicted the infusion of Greek culture as a serious threat to Roman customs, institutions, public morality, and the national character itself, which they idealized as rooted in values such as practicality, perseverance, frugality and simplicity. The Greek cultural invasion nonetheless rolled on in Rome, though with considerable tension. Even the most resistant members of the elite ranks of society eventually saw the utility in creating a national literature to rival that of the Greeks as a means of enhancing Roman prestige in the Mediterranean world. Drama based on Greek source-plays (such as Plautus') debuted at Rome in 240 BCE.

Plautine comedy located itself squarely in the thick of these culture wars. As far as we know, the source-plays he adapted for the Roman stage and his Roman audience were all Greek, and all of Plautus' surviving plays maintain a Greek setting. Scholars have long argued that this geographical displacement (cf. Shakespeare's use of Italy) allowed Plautus and other Roman playwrights

---

1   For Plautus' name, see further Gratwick (1973).

to safely stage plays with characters and situations ("they're Greeks after all") that might otherwise have been deemed a threat to public morals, and therefore were unfit for elite public sponsorship. But this thesis is greatly complicated by the extraordinary degree to which Plautus Romanizes his plays. Amid all the Hellenistic aspects of the comedies, Plautus constantly mixes in distinct references to Roman institutions, customs, public officials, the geography and topography of Italy and Rome, and to contemporary events and issues. The resulting comic world of the plays is a rich and provocative jumble of both Greece and Rome, which one scholar has aptly dubbed "Plautinopolis."[2] The effect of Plautus' deliberate conflation of Greek and Roman cultures was to suggest to his audience that while the nominal Greek setting might allow for comfortable escape into a foreign and immoral land of fantasy, they were also watching characters who were not unlike themselves and who lived in a world not entirely divorced from their own. To some extent, we expect this to be the case for all drama that aims to be relevant to its audience. What is most striking about Plautine comedy's cultural amalgamation of Greece and Rome is how closely it mirrors the larger process simultaneously unfolding outside the narrow confines of the theater. And this was a process which proved to be essential in indelibly shaping Roman culture and Rome's sense of national identity.

Plautus and Ancient Comedy

Most, if not all of Plautus' surviving plays, are based on plays belonging to the genre called New Comedy, which flourished in Greece from c. 325 to 250 BCE. This was the third phase of Greek Comedy after Old Comedy, now represented primarily by the bawdy, fantastical, and quintessentially Athenian plays of Aristophanes performed in the 5th and early 4th centuries BCE. Middle Comedy, which survives only in fragments and through titles of plays, describes the period of transition to the better-attested New Comedy. Greek New Comedy no longer focused on contemporary Athenian politics and the prominent individuals involved in them, but was cosmopolitan and featured more universal themes and plots. It did away with the pervasive obscenity, elaborate costumes, exuberant music and choruses, and the satire and personal invective that had defined Old Comedy. Comedies became more domestic than political, and were now built around stock characters such as clever slaves, greedy pimps, parasites, prostitutes, young men in love, saucy cooks, braggart soldiers, etc.

The only plays of Greek New Comedy whose remains are substantial are those of Menander. The extant plays—or parts of plays, as no single play survives entirely—consist of five acts, and feature stereotypical and often highly coincidental situations involving, e.g., the reunion of children separated at birth

---

2   Gratwick (1982) 113.

with their family. Despite the unrealistic nature of some plots, already in antiquity Menander was praised for his subtlety in capturing human psychology and realistically depicting social life; Aristophanes of Byzantium, an ancient scholar, is said to have exclaimed "O Menander and Life, which of you imitated the other?" Menander's plays are much in keeping with the predominant modern trend toward theatrical realism or naturalism, and are sometimes said to be a forerunner of television sit-coms.[3]

Menander died in 292/1 BCE, well before the beginning of Plautus' theatrical career. But his plays and those of New Comedy playwrights such as Diphilus, who provided the source play for Plautus' *Casina*, enjoyed revivals in Athens and were also performed throughout the Hellenistic world by itinerant acting companies such as the "Artists of Dionysus." Parts of southern Italy and Sicily, though now under Roman control, had been colonized by Greeks centuries earlier, and the earliest Roman playwrights were probably first exposed to Greek comedy there. Though the genre they created came to be known as the *fabula palliata*, or "play in Greek costume," Roman playwrights did not slavishly "translate" Greek New Comedy to the Roman stage. The extant fragments of the earliest (i.e., pre-Plautine) Roman playwrights reveal, for instance, the addition of musically elaborate songs, or *cantica*, which do not correspond to anything in Greek New Comedy.

Native forms of Italian comedy were also instrumental in this process that is better described as creative adaptation rather than translation. These forms of popular Italian drama were unscripted in Plautus' day, and so we only know of them through later testimony or the fragments of much later scripted versions. One popular form of comedy was Atellan farce, so named because of its origin in Atella in Campania. These performances were short, largely improvised skits involving masked, stock characters such as Bucco ("Fool"), Maccus ("Clown"), Manducus ("Chomper"), and Pappus ("Grandpappy"). There were certain fixed routines and situations, probably full of slapstick and vaudeville-like comic banter. Mime was another form of popular entertainment, also unscripted in Plautus' day, and nothing like what we think of as mime today. Mime actors and actresses (a rare example of the use of female performers in European theater before relatively recent modern times) had a reputation for bawdiness. They were nicknamed "flat-foots" because they performed barefoot. The actors' costumes sported large phalli and the actresses sometimes appeared in the nude. Mime troupes likewise performed stock scenes calling for improvisation, and they seemed to have favored short, bawdy skits, including those featuring adultery. [4]

---

3   For Menander's comedy in general, see Goldberg (1980) and Zagagi (1994).

4   For popular Italian theater, see further Beare (1964) 137-58 and Marshall (2006) 1-15.

As I noted above (pp. 1-2), the name Titus Maccius Plautus betrays its origins in these popular dramatic forms, and it is very likely that Plautus had direct experience in Atellan farce and Mime before establishing a place for himself in the Roman comic scene. Native Italian drama can thus be viewed as an important transitional bridge between Greek New Comedy and Roman theater that lent Plautus' comedy much of its unique flavor—though we should not underestimate his personal contributions to the comic tradition. Just how different is Plautine comedy from Menander's? Fortunately, the discovery in 1968 of a short section (on papyrus) of Menander's *The Double Deceiver*, the source play for Plautus' surviving *Bacchides*, allows for direct comparison. The parallel texts reveal that Plautus has added much musical accompaniment to the scene; obscured an act-division and altered dramatic pace by combining what had been separate speeches in separate acts; and he has freely removed or added entire speeches. Where Menander is focused on his characters' psychological motivations and realism in general, Plautus opts for a joke and delineates character in only the broadest strokes. He also changes (and jazzes up) the names of Menander's characters, and he superimposes an entirely different and characteristically Plautine linguistic style.[5]

Plautine comedy thus represents a significant departure from its Greek models through its addition of native Italian as well as peculiarly Plautine elements. Roman New Comedy did away with the five-act structure and choral interludes of Greek New Comedy, and replaced these with continuous and relentless action, while also greatly enhancing the element of song within the plays. In Plautus in particular, Greek New Comedy's focus on character, characterization, and careful structuring of plot gives way to banter and a constant barrage of jokes, prolix sound and word-play, and more elastic and unbalanced plots in which characters at times appear to be improvising.

Plautus' Comic Theater

Roman plays were performed in connection with state-sponsored religious festivals, and, like the various other entertainments that took place in this festival context, were generally referred to as *ludi*, or "games." In Plautus' time, festivals associated with drama were held in honor of the gods Jupiter, Apollo, Ceres, Flora (an Italian goddess of flowers/flowering), and the Magna Mater, "The Great Mother," an eastern goddess introduced to Roman cult in 204 BCE. The public festivals featured grand processions, the sacrifice of animals, and public feasts. The plays were performed either in the Roman forum, a large circus (built for chariot racing), or in front of a god's temple. Of the four plays in this volume, only the occasion of *Pseudolus* is known, i.e., the festival of the Magna Mater

---

5   For detailed comparison of the parallel texts see Anderson (1993) 3-29.

(*ludi Megalenses*) held in early April, 191 BCE. State funds allocated by the elite Roman senate financed the festivals. It was the direct responsibility of Roman magistrates called *aediles* to administer the festivals and oversee the entertainments that took place during them. As this Republican office was typically held by ambitious, up and coming politicians, the *aediles* contributed some of their own funds to finance special entertainments for the *ludi* as a means of cultivating political support from the Roman populace. As the festivals approached, their specific duties included contracting for plays with playwrights and troupes. The male actors that made up these troupes typically were slaves or free persons of very low status, such as freedman (i.e., former slaves). It was extremely disgraceful for a freeborn citizen to perform as an actor, and one who did normally sacrificed his citizen's rights.

Though the Romans easily could have built grand stone theaters after the manner of the Greeks in this period, no permanent theater was constructed in Rome until Pompey the Great constructed his in 55 BCE. Later writers moralized that the Roman Republican elite regarded the theater as a place of decadence and potential civic unrest, and so fiercely resisted all attempts to build permanent theaters. Pompey crowned his theater with a temple of Venus (Victrix), probably to justify the permanent structure by ostensibly continuing the tradition of dramatic performances before a temple, and so also drama's religious associations. A more practical explanation for the ban on stone theaters is that the senatorial elite and the ambitious sponsors of the *ludi* viewed the necessary construction of temporary structures for each festival as a visible reminder to the Roman people that the *ludi* depended on their personal benevolence.

Consequently, nothing survives of the theaters of Plautus' day. There is little written testimony as to the nature of these temporary theaters and no contemporary visual evidence, and so we mostly rely on the plays themselves to reconstruct only a general layout. The action onstage usually takes place on what is supposed to be a street in front of a wooden backdrop with up to three doors, which can represent up to three houses depending on the requirements of each play. Much later artistic representations of Roman theaters depict partially enclosed porches in front of these houses, but there is nothing in the texts of the plays to verify their existence in Plautine theater. *Amphitryon* presents an anomaly, as the single stage-house/palace there must allow for action on an upper storey in order to perform the scene (11) in which Mercury harasses Amphitryon from above. There were two side wings, one of which is coventionally assumed to lead to the forum/center of town, the other to the country or harbor. There was also an altar somewhere in front of the stage-backdrop. There was no curtain in Plautus' day, and the audience sat on temporary wooden benches. The best seats directly in front of what was probably only a slightly raised stage were reserved for the senatorial elite from 194 BCE on. There is no definitive way to calculate the capacity of such theaters, but references to the crowd in prologues indicate an extremely diverse and densely packed audience, whose members comprised the broad socio-economic spectrum of Roman society. Such a simple physical layout suggests a certain degree of theatrical minimalism and stylization. Most significantly, and in stark contrast with Greek stone theaters that featured a large orchestra (i.e., dancing area for the chorus) between the stage and the audience, temporary Roman theater encouraged close interaction between actors and audience.[6]

All the actors wore masks, as also had been the case in Greek New Comedy and Atellan farce. No definitive visual representations of the masks used in early Roman comedy survive, and so we have no detailed understanding of these. Stereotypical masks were used to immediately identify a character-type to the audience. The evidence of the plays themselves, however, is ambiguous as to whether each character-type allowed for the use of multiple masks, e.g., did all comic slaves always wear the same mask? Masks do not, as is sometimes assumed by those unfamiliar with masked performances, severely restrict an actor's expressive capabilities and lend a static quality to performance. An actor skilled in masked drama can subtly animate his mask through specific gestures and careful control of his body. An audience familiar with a form of masked drama featuring stock characters brings certain expectations about each character's behavior to the performance, a factor which only further piques the audience's interest when a character diverges from the expected, as Plautine characters often do. Very few details are known about costumes, except that they too were codified to sharply distinguish character-types, e.g., an old man (*senex*) wore a white cloak and held a walking stick, while the cloak of a young man (*adulescens*) was darkly colored.[7]

Plautine comedy exploited the physical proximity of actors and audience in temporary Roman theater to largely erase any boundary between their respective spaces. One of the distinctive features of Plautine comedy is the unusual degree to which actors/characters speak directly to the audience. This is immediately evident in Plautus' chatty prologues. Here, in addition to providing background and other information about the dramatic situation, the speakers of the prologue aggressively seek to secure the audience's close attention and goodwill toward the actors and play, and often sign off with a word of encouragement or flattery for them (e.g., *Casina* 87-8, *Captivi* 67-8). The prologists also take special care to anticipate any potential anxiety or confusion on the audience's part, as when the prologist of *Captivi* repeatedly explains that master (Philocrates) and slave (Tyndarus) have switched identities, or when Mercury in *Amphitryon* explains

---

6 For speculation on the nature of temporary Roman theater, see Beacham (1992) 56-85 and Marshall (2006) 31-82.

7 For masks and costumes in New Comedy in general, see Wiles (1991).

that the play is a *tragicomoedia*, or "mythical burlesque" (50-63: cf. p. 15 below). Mercury even in effect pulls off his mask (27-8) to joke with the audience that since he and the actor playing Jupiter are actually slaves in real life, they fear being beaten for an unsuccessful performance. The speakers of epilogues (e.g., *Casina* 1012-18, *Captivi* 1023-30) similarly seek to cajole the audience into applauding for the play.

As characters, the actors are no less solicitous in striving to make their case to the audience. In monologues and monodies (i.e., solo songs) in which they regularly address the audience in the second-person plural ("you") or directly refer to them as "spectators," characters constantly try to persuade the audience over to their own points of view. Asides to the audience in the presence of other characters have a similar effect. Often, one character eavesdrops on another character who is already speaking directly to the audience, and so undermines any sympathy that character had sought to gain through his own asides. Thus, Plautine characters often find themselves in a fierce competition with one another for the audience's allegiance.[8]

So why do Plautus' actors/characters play up to the audience so much? As anyone with experience in live theater knows, actors feed off their audiences, and a real bond between the two results in successful performances. And hearty, genuine applause for pleasing an audience bears obvious psychological rewards. Plautus' actors, as actors generally, are acknowledging that the audience is an essential player in the entire spectacle we call theater. This acknowledgment of the audience's role can be viewed as another act of flattery toward them, but the unusual urgency with which Plautus' actors/characters court their audience suggests other factors are also at work. We recall that Roman actors (as probably also Plautus himself) were slaves or free persons of low status in what was a rigidly hierarchical and status-conscious society. Their continued survival in their craft thus depended on the approval of both the audience and the festivals' sponsoring magistrates. The constant appeals of Plautine actors to the audience in part may then reflect the troupe's and playwright's insecurities related to their precarious social and economic position. But this desire to please, sometimes with fawning servility, is no ground to dismiss the plays themselves as simple specimens of pandering to popular taste. The plays are too socially complex for this to be universally valid, and, as we shall see, they can offer provocative challenges to the status quo of contemporary Roman society.

Another pervasive feature of Plautine comedy is the phenomenon of metatheater (or metadrama), which here refers to any self-reflexive means used by actors/characters in a play to remind an audience that it is watching a play.[9] For

---

8   For rapport between actors and audience, see Moore (1998) 8-49.

9   For a broad treatment of metatheater in Plautus, see Slater (1985).

example, in *Casina*, after Cleostrata and Myrrhina have completed their preparations for humiliating Lysidamus in the form of a play-within-the-play featuring Chalinus in the role of Casina, Myrrhina exclaims:

> No playwright has ever devised a better
> Plot than this clever production of ours! (860-1)

In a similar vein, at the end of *Casina* Cleostrata agrees to forgive Lysidamus because "this play is long and I don't want to make it any longer" (1006). It has been argued that all theater is necessarily metadramatic, and that theatergoers are to some extent always aware that they are watching a play. It is also a commonplace that theater mirrors life, or perhaps more accurately, life mirrors theater: for example, we speak of assuming and playing roles in society, we judge behavior as (un)conventional, etc. What were the possible effects, for Plautus' audience, of so frequently being invited to reflect on the experience of watching a play? Do Plautine actors, by insistently uncovering the plays' theatrical underpinnings, merely draw attention to the fact that performance is artifice, illusion and convention, i.e., do they merely emphasize the "unreality" and theatricality of the play? On the one hand, metatheater is simply playful (the root meaning of *ludi* is "play" after all), and the immediate goal of Cleostrata's concern about the length of the play is to elicit laughs. But Cleostrata is also here expressing a deeper concern about the audience's reception of the play, and so emphasizing the audience's essential role in the overall theatrical spectacle. In this light, the extensive use of metatheater serves to remove barriers between actors and audience and to further open up their two respective worlds to each other. By intensely focusing on how the world of a play is constructed, even as it is being constructed before an audience, metatheater may also induce members of that audience to reflect upon the construction and artificiality of the social roles they play in their own everyday world. All the world's a stage, after all.

Plautine comedy presents a number of surprising inversions of everyday social life, e.g., those involving masters and slaves. In recent decades, Plautine scholars have tended to explain the social inversions enacted in the plays as examples of "Saturnalian" or festive comedy.[10] The Roman festival of the god Saturn granted temporary freedoms to slaves, who were even allowed some license to treat their masters with less than usual respect for their authority. As is the case for so many festivals, the Saturnalia featured eating, drinking, and general revelry; there is, however, no evidence that comedies such as Plautus' were ever performed in connection with the Roman Saturnalia. Anthropologists have long accounted for such festivals in which the most oppressed members of society are granted temporary license and empowerment by invoking what is commonly

---

10 See especially Segal (1987).

referred to as the "safety valve" theory. According to this view, the temporary relaxation of social restraints allows members of an underclass to periodically let off steam and thereby reduce the tensions associated with maintaining a social hierarchy in everyday life. Further, this grant of temporary license in the end is said to only strengthen rigid social hierarchies and to render an underclass more accepting of its subordinate position during the rest of the "non-festive" year.

Scholars who apply the safety-valve theory to Plautus argue that his plays would not have received the continued support of elite sponsors if they seriously threatened the Roman social order or were judged to be subversive in any way.[11] While slaves in Plautus' audience might have taken great pleasure from watching a Pseudolus outsmart his master, such theatrical inversions of the normal order of things are seen as only the product of the temporary festival atmosphere. It is true that Plautine comedy did not foment organized social rebellion—though for it to do so would be asking far too much of any comedy in the face of a system of power so entrenched as that of the Republican elite, made up as it was of very old and distinguished aristocratic families. The safety valve theory has rightly been criticized as too sweeping and overreaching, and there are historical examples of popular festive comedy creating actual social conflict.[12] There is no denying that Plautine comedy, with its focus on social inversion, as well as on food and drink, is caught up in the spirit of the Roman festivals. It seems reductive and dogmatic, however, to insist that Plautus' comedies could not inspire audiences, or at least segments of audiences, to reflect critically upon their own social institutions and the social hierarchy itself. Aided as they were by persistent devices of metatheater, some members of Plautus' audience may actually have come to see rank, status, power, and gender roles as the social constructions that they ultimately are. Though we possess no evidence for how any of the four plays in this volume were received by an ancient audience, together they seem to offer provocative challenges to Roman society of c. 200 BCE. The issues they raise are also of enduring interest to audiences today.

Challenging Convention

CASINA

As the play begins, *Casina* looks to be a typical New Comedy in that it is built around familiar characters and situations. Lysidamus, the patriarch of the household, is smitten with the sixteen year-old slave after whom the play is named. His son Euthynicus is also said to be infatuated with Casina,

---

11   A complex refutation of the safety-valve theory as it is applied to Plautus can be found in McCarthy (2000).

12   See, for example, Bristol (1985).

though Plautus has removed the character of the son (64-6) from this adaptation of Diphilus' *Klerumenoi*, or "The Lot Drawers." Comic convention requires Lysidamus, as an old man in love, i.e., a *senex amator*, to lose the amorous contest with his son: in comedy, love decidedly is for the young. By a remarkable coincidence that is not unusual in New Comedy, Casina, who was exposed at birth and taken into Lysidamus's household, turns out to be the freeborn daughter of the next-door neighbors. This will allow for a legitimate marriage between her and Euthynicus, though the revelation about her free birth and the announcement of the marriage are relegated to the play's epilogue (1012-18). In the Greek source play, the revelation of the girl's free birth most likely took place in a climactic recognition scene.

The amorous contest between father and son occurs elsewhere in Plautus, but only in this play is the son's cause taken up by his mother. Plautus has pointedly shifted the father/son competition to one between husband and wife. With rare exceptions, such as Alcmena in *Amphitryon*, wives in Plautus are stereotyped as nagging shrews who do little more than unsympathetically block their husbands' pursuit of pleasure. In her first appearance in the play (Scene 2), Cleostrata gives the impression that she most likely will fill this stock role of the "difficult" wife. The audience knows that Lysidamus is doomed to fail in his pursuit of Casina, but at this point they have no idea how precisely his failure is to be brought about. There is not yet the slightest hint that Cleostrata will assume the empowering role of comic heroine to thoroughly defeat and humiliate her husband.

In the first two scenes in which she appears, Cleostrata is portrayed as a potentially unsympathetic figure through pointed contrasts with her neighbor Myrrhina. While Cleostrata enters railing at Lysidamus's indiscretion and states her determination not to feed him (144-63), Myrrhina is first seen engaged in wool-working (164-70), a traditional woman's activity that instantly aligns her with conservative views of gender roles in the ancient world. The stark contrast in attitudes about marriage she and her neighbor Myrrhina express (174ff.) might also further alienate Cleostrata from at least the conservative males in the audience. Specifically, Myrrhina objects to Cleostrata's contention that Casina (as a household slave) is her own private property and not her husband's. Myrrhina here advocates the most conservative form of Roman marriage (*cum manu*), in which a wife surrendered all her property to her husband, in addition to transferring her father's absolute power over her to her husband. As for Lysidamus's sexual peccadilloes, Myrrhina appropriately advises her neighbor to be an obedient, and therefore tolerant, wife: "Let him lech and do whatever he wants, as longs as he provides for you at home" (206-7).

The topic of women's ownership of property was very much current in the early 2nd century BCE. As the result of catastrophic Roman losses in the 2nd Punic War, many women had inherited property and a law had been passed (*lex Oppia*) in 215 BCE to limit their expenditures on what were deemed luxury goods. An enormous controversy arose in 195 BCE when Roman women pub-licly demonstrated in support of repealing this twenty-year-old sumptuary law. Despite staunch resistance from conservatives such as Cato the Elder, who argued that the women's rebellion was symptomatic of a culturally dangerous reduction in male control over the household, the women were successful in securing the law's repeal. It is unlikely that the controversies raised by this incident had en-tirely died down by the time of the debut of *Casina*, i.e., c. 185 BCE. Cleostrata's and Myrrhina's exchange here about property and power thus touches upon what still probably were hotwire issues within the context of the contemporary culture wars.

As expected, the play features the gradual degradation and defeat of the absurdly lecherous old man Lysidamus. As his scheme to enjoy a night with Casina unravels, he gradually surrenders any semblance of control over his household. He is terrified by his slave Pardalisca's fictional report (Scene 14) that Casina is running amuck with a sword in the house, but can only plead with her to *beg his wife* to quell the chaos inside—and offers her a bribe to do so (704-12). His dependence on Olympio in the scheme eventually forces him to concede that he is, in effect, his foreman's slave (737). And cloakless and sexually disgraced as the result of his "nuptials" with He-Casina (i.e., Chalinus disguised as Casina), he desperately dashes out of his house and tells the audience that he has no choice but to become a fugitive slave (954), i.e., assume one of ancient society's low-est statuses. All of this could have been avoided if Lysidamus had asserted his absolute power over the household and claimed Casina as his own to do with as he pleased, as a Roman *paterfamilias* might have done in real life. His failure to do so results in these social inversions which can be dubbed "Saturnalian," and of the type more commonly brought about by a clever slave's machinations in Plautus.

But what is most compelling about the play is how Lysidamus' degradation is achieved by Cleostratra's gradually seizing control of the play in the manner of a comic playwright. In transforming Cleostrata from stereotypical Plautine shrew to Plautine theater's most powerful figure, Plautus skillfully re-deploys and upsets convention with the aim of making Cleostrata—and so the causes she represents—as sympathetic as possible. How exactly is this accomplished?

After Cleostrata's and Myrrhina's opening exchange on their oppos-ing views of marriage, there are no further debates on women's roles within marriage in the play: from here on, Cleostrata's rise to sympathetic figure and comic heroine is theatrical rather than ideological. First, she takes advantage of Chalinus' eavesdropping on her husband and Olympio (Scene 9) to frustrate Lysidamus' plan to free up his neighbor's house for a tryst with Casina, and even successfully turns the two patriarchs against each other (Scene 13). Cleostrata and her assistants Pardalisca and Myrrhina, who despite her initial opposition goes over to Cleostrata's side, first create the fictional account of a Casina armed with two swords raving throughout the house. Delivered as a parody of a tragic messenger's speech (Scene 14), the tall-tale not only frightens Lysidamus, but also prefigures his figurative castration at the hands of He-Casina. Next we learn from Pardalisca (Scene 16) that the two wives have devised a play-within-play, the faux-wedding and honeymoon, for which they are now costuming Chalinus to play the role of Casina. Once the sexual farce has begun inside, Cleostrata and Myrrhina emerge from the house and prepare to watch the entrance of the humiliated Lysidamus and his foreman:

> Such fine and fitting entertainment inside!
> We're out here on the street now to watch the wedding festival.
> My goodness, I've never laughed so much in my life
> And doubt I'll ever laugh like that again! (855-8)

The audience's identification with the women is furthered here as Cleostrata, Myrrhina, and Pardalisca take up the role of a model (i.e., satisfied) audience, and in this way seek to shape the reaction of the play's audience to what is about to take place onstage. Myrrhina shortly thereafter draws the connection between their efforts and playwrighting (860-1; cf. p. 9 above), and so makes it explicit that she and Cleostrata are present not just as spectators, but also as playwrights and directors at the debut of their own show.

It remains only for Lysidamus to face his wife and the humiliating consequences of his folly. He appears before her in his disheveled state (Scene 23), minus the cloak and walking stick he has lost in his obscene tussle with He-Casina. In one last desperate attempt to lie his way out of his predicament, he blames his loss of apparel on Bacchants, i.e., ecstatic female worshippers of the god Bacchus (Dionysus). Myrrhina notes the impossibility of this claim, in that Bacchic rites are no longer practiced. This very clear example of Romanization (cf. p. 3 above) is a reference to the Roman senate's emergency decree effectively prohibiting the worship of Bacchus in 186 BCE, and so dates the play to sometime after this event and before the death of Plautus in 184 BCE. Though modern historians have argued for political and other possible motivations for the senate's suppression of Bacchic worship, conservative moralists at the time apparently condemned the cult as a breeding ground for immorality, transgression of gender roles, and general social chaos. Sensationalistic reports of the Bacchants' control over male worshippers circulated, and it was even claimed that the women forced these men to have sex with each other. Cleostrata's and Myrrhine's use of He-Casina to humiliate Lysidamus through homoerotic acts ironically echoes these allegations of sexually transgressive acts allegedly perpetrated by the women in the cult. But in this play, Lysidamus has not innocently stumbled into the hands of "crazed" Bacchants; comic convention has dictated his demise owing to his status as a *senex amator*. Do his obviously false allegations here about Bacchants, who are purely the product of his desperate imagination, satirize male hysteria about the cult, now that the initial fury had perhaps died down?

That Cleostrata herself is the ultimate controlling force of the play is confirmed when she decides to forgive her husband on the ground that the play (1005-6; cf. p. 9 above) is already long enough and should simply end. This of course is a decision only a playwright/director makes. There is a further metadramatic aspect to Cleostrata's abrupt call for closure in that, as critics of comedy since at least Aristotle[13] have often noted, comedies typically end on more or less arbitrary grounds, so that social harmony and the status quo may be resumed. In the end, Cleostrata lets Lysidamus have his walking stick and cloak back (1009), and he presumably is to regain control of his household. The closing joke and call for applause of the epilogue (1015-18) likewise suggests that husbands like Lysidamus will continue to pursue extramarital affairs, which again might suggest his degradation was merely Saturnalian fun, and no one should reflect further on Roman marriage after leaving the theater (and the festival). Such a sweeping, Saturnalian interpretation of the play, however, seems untenable. First, Plautus has pointedly framed the relationship of husband and wife in the light of controversial contemporary events and issues: women's property rights at the play's opening and the predominantly female cult of Bacchus at its end. Secondly, he successfully strips away the negative stereotype of the comic shrew from Cleostrata, and instead bestows absolute theatrical power on her. Though I am in no way suggesting that *Casina* is a feminist manifesto, it is hard to imagine that at least some segment(s) of the diverse audience did not leave the theater thinking further about the politics of marriage.[14]

AMPHITRYON

Amphitryon is a truly unusual play. The gods Jupiter and Mercury impersonate the (mythic) general Amphitryon and his slave Sosia, respectively, so that Jupiter can enjoy a sexual affair with Amphitryon's wife Alcmena. Alcmena is pregnant—extremely pregnant—by both her husband and Jupiter. It is not made entirely clear if Jupiter has visited Alcmena earlier, or if he supernaturally impregnates her on the eve of her giving birth to twins, i.e., the mortal Iphikles and the mythic hero Hercules (Jupiter's son), as described in a messenger's speech (Scene 15) near the play's end.

Amphitryon is the only surviving example of mythical burlesque, i.e., a type of farce (popular in Greek Old and Middle Comedy) in which gods appear as characters and typically behave no better, or even worse than, their human counterparts. *Amphitryon* probably was the first mythical burlesque performed

---

13   See his *Poetics* 1453a36ff.

14   My interpretation of *Casina* is much indebted to Moore (1998) 158-80.

on a Roman stage, as is suggested by Mercury's uniquely long and solicitous prologue. There he first upsets the audience's expectation of seeing a more typical Plautine comedy by disingenuously dubbing the play a tragedy (51). Now that he has their attention, he explains that the play is really just an unusual type of comedy:

> Did I say tragedy? Are you frowning at that word tragedy?
> Okay, I'll change it, seeing as I'm a god:
> I'll make this play a comedy instead of a tragedy,
> Without changing any of the lines. (52-5)

He then coins the word *tragicomoedia*, or "tragicomedy" (59, 63), to describe a play that features comic figures such as slaves as well as "important people and gods" usually associated with tragedy (61-2). Mercury here creates a word to describe a mythical burlesque, and we should avoid projecting Renaissance and later notions of "tragicomedy" (e.g., as "dark comedy") on *Amphitryon*. Both Mercury and Jupiter subsequently always refer to the play as a comedy (88, 96, 868). To allay any apprehension the audience might develop about this unusual comedy, the gods appear onstage alone and speak directly to the audience (i.e., Scenes 2, 6, 9) in what effectively is a continuation of the prologue.

Much critical attention has focused on the character of Alcmena, whose deception by Jupiter disguised as her husband is fundamentally unfair. Because she expresses high-minded sentiments about patriotism (633-53), is devoted to her husband, and tenaciously defends her chastity (Scenes 5, 7), Alcmena is often sentimentalized into a tragic heroine who is made the victim of a cruel hoax. This view, however, arises from reading the play as a text without also imagining it as a comic performance. Alcmena is on the verge of giving birth to twins, and is the only pregnant character to appear onstage in extant ancient drama. She most likely wore a costume with stuffing, and the audience also knows that she is being played by a male actor, who may have hammed up the part. Her condition is often humorously referred to, as in Sosia's asides in Scene 5 (665-70, 681, 718-19, 723-4, 785-6). The gods further undermine her status as a "tragic" figure by crassly referring to her as Jupiter's "wife on loan" (498, 980-1), whose body has been "borrowed" (108, 1135) to serve Jupiter's lust (113-4) and to produce his son Hercules. Plautus even makes Alcmena into a sensualist, at least by the prim and proper standards of idealized Roman matrons. Despite having enjoyed an extended night of sexual activity with Jupiter, she complains bitterly about his planned departure in the morning:

> You barely warmed a spot on the bed and now you're off!
> You show up in the middle of the night and then take off. Is that
> right? (513-4)

Thus, though her treatment is inherently unjust, the sustained focus of the play is on the sex-farce, as when the ever-lusty Jupiter reconciles with Alcmena so that he may have sex with her one last time (891-2, 980-1) just before she gives birth. The gods also repeatedly emphasize that Alcmena is to give birth painlessly and will share in the glory of her son Hercules.[15]

From a conservative Roman point of view, the mistreatment of Amphitryon is in fact more striking than that of Alcmena. In Plautine theater (e.g., *Pseudolus*), the master of the house is not infrequently tricked out of some cash by a clever slave operating on behalf of his younger master, who is hopelessly in love. But nowhere else in Plautus, not even in *Casina*, does the *paterfamilias* suffer the degree of sustained humiliation Amphityron does in the second half of this play.

Expecting a warm and congratulatory welcome (654-8) from his wife in the wake of his successful (nine month) campaign, Amphitryon is sorely disappointed by Alcmena's lack of enthusiasm at his arrival. Her gradual revelations in Scene 5 about her evening of dinner and romance with the faux-Amphitryon leads him to the conclusion that she has committed adultery (810-11). As the stated purpose of Roman marriage was the production of legitimate children, adultery was an extremely serious matter for a husband, and, if proven, should result in divorce (849-53; cf. 928).

Mercury's primary role as Amphitryon's faux-slave is to keep the real master and slave away from the house so that Jupiter may "have his fill" (472) of Alcmena, and it is for this particular cause that Amphitryon is subjected to considerable mistreatment. In a partially preserved scene (11; cf. 997-1007), Amphitryon suffers both verbal and physical abuse from Mercury, who is posing as his drunken slave. In a more typical Plautine play, a clever slave may lord it over his master (cf. the end of *Pseudolus*), but in this atypical play Mercury has launched no scheme to earn this Saturnalian (cf. pp. 9-10 above) right of triumph. So Amphitryon is not only prevented from entering the house, i.e., the locus of his power as *paterfamilias*, but also suffers superfluous degradation from a household member who should be under his absolute sway.

Amphitryon is further frustrated in his attempts to enter his own home. In a flourish of impotent blustering, Amphitryon decides to rush the house:

> ... I'm breaking into the house and the first person I see,
> Maid, slave, my wife, her lover, my father, my grandfather—
> It makes no difference to me—is dead right there on the spot!
> No one can stop me, not Jove or all the gods united together!
> Yes, my mind's all made up. I'm going right into the house.
>   (1048-52)

---

15   See further Christenson (2001).

One of the Romans' central and most socially cohesive concepts was *pietas*, (cf. our cognate "piety"), which mandated dutiful and absolute reverence toward parents, ancestors, the gods of the state, and the state itself. While Amphitryon's claim that not even Jove can stop him obviously is meant to be humorously ironic in this context, his resolve to kill even his father or grandfather is surprising, as he in effect is pledging to destroy his patriarchal line if necessary. Flouting of *pietas* is elsewhere restricted to the machinations of the clever slave on behalf of the lovesick young master (e.g., *Pseudolus* 120-2), though it is nowhere else expressed in such violent terms as here. As if in direct response to this impious bluster, Jupiter's thunderbolt blasts Amphitryon into a death-like state of unconsciousness. When he regains consciousness, still outside his house, he slowly awakens only to doubt his own identity and literally declare himself dead (1076ff.). He even asks his slave Bromia: "Are you sure I'm your master Amphitryon?" (1082). Bromia's insistence that he is her master, her account of the twins' supernatural birth, and the revelation of Jupiter's role in all suddenly revives Amphitryon and restores his belief in who he is:

> That's not the worst thing in the world,
> Splitting up half of my good fortune with Jove! (1124-5)

Comic closure calls for social harmony (cf. p. 14 above), however swiftly and arbitrarily achieved, and so Amphitryon accedes in all here—though the metaphor of "splitting" he uses here frequently has obscene connotations in Latin (see *Amphitryon*, n. 62). Some Renaissance and later adapters of the play could not resist highlighting that Amphitryon, despite being blessed with divine favor, technically is a disgraced cuckold.[16]

Though domestic harmony is restored by divine fiat at the play's end, and Amphitryon is finally allowed to enter his house in order to reconcile with his wife, the fact remains that no other Plautine *paterfamilias* is so completely divested of all his power and its perquisites. In the course of the play, Amphitryon is made to believe that he has lost his wife's affection and his control over her sexuality (and so, possibly, the paternity of their child); he loses control of his household and slave, flouts *pietas*, and is excluded altogether from his own home throughout the play; and, finally, he experiences a death-like state from which he emerges with real doubts about his identity as the *paterfamilias*.

What sorts of reaction(s) might this thorough dismantling of patriarchy have provoked in a Roman audience? According to the universalizing safety valve theory, those who might have been most oppressed by a *paterfamilias* (his children, wife, and slaves) could take special delight in Amphitryon's temporary

---

16 For a brief outline of the many post-classical adaptations of *Amphitryon*, see Christenson (2000) 71-5.

powerlessness, and thereby recharge their batteries to face further domination by him in their everyday lives. Since the Roman social hierarchy was vertically complex, and free citizens were normally outranked by some of their fellow citizens, some fathers themselves might similarly have enjoyed the temporary degradation of a figure so near the top of the Theban social ladder. But other Roman fathers, especially the more prominent ones, might have left the theater with increased insecurity regarding their position of absolute authority in the household. Though some comfort could be taken in Jupiter's special status as a god with supernatural powers, this does not entirely erase the fact that a more powerful male has invaded Amphitryon's house, seduced his wife, taken over the household, and stripped the *paterfamilias* of his identity. And the overall emphasis of this mythical burlesque is on the humanness of the gods, especially Jupiter's lustiness and his deceitfully slick ability to charm Alcmena (cf. Scenes 3, 7) in order to fulfill his all too human desires. Anthropomorphized to the extent that Jupiter is in the play, it is plausible to see him as representing the ultimate alpha-male in the Roman hierarchy. But even if one denies to *Amphitryon* this capacity to expose vulnerability in a highly competitive male society such as Republican Rome was, this is a play that still has much to say to audiences about the nature of patriarchal systems of power.

CAPTIVI

Like *Amphitryon, Captivi* advertises itself as an atypical comedy from the start. In a visually arresting opening, the prologist stands beside the two prisoners of war, Tyndarus and Philocrates, who may already be in slaves' chains, as they will be when they first appear in the play (Scene 3). The prologist explains that the play is set in Aetolia (Athens is the usual setting for New Comedy) before the house of Hegio, an old man whose son Philopolemus has been captured in a war against the Eleans. In the hope of ransoming Philopolemus back, Hegio has been buying up Elean captives. He has just purchased Philocrates and his slave Tyndarus, because he has heard that Philocrates comes from a wealthy and influential family in Elis. By an incredible coincidence typical of New Comedy, Tyndarus is actually Hegio's son who as a boy was abducted by a household slave. The slave had fled with the boy to Elis, where he was sold to Philocrates' father. The prologist repeatedly emphasizes (4-5, 21-2, 49-50) the unusual circumstance of a son being enslaved unknowingly to his father.

Tyndarus and Philocrates have devised a scheme to secure the latter's release. They have switched identities (and, presumably, costumes and masks) in order to trick Hegio into releasing Philocrates, whom Hegio believes to be a slave, so that he can negotiate the exchange for Philopolemus in Elis. The prologist informs the audience that their ploy will succeed (40-3), and also that Tyndarus will unknowingly rescue his brother (i.e., Philopolomus), but he does not explicitly reveal how things will turn out for Tyndarus. Apart from the element of deception, the plot described here is most unusual. The fact that a slave and his younger master are plotting against an old man occupies somewhat familiar Plautine territory, in so far as the clever slave's deception of his elder master on behalf of his lovesick younger master is commonplace (cf. *Pseudolus*). But there is no love-interest in *Captivi*, and the fact that Hegio is now the master of both Philocrates, who will briefly play the role of his clever slave, and Tyndarus, who is actually his freeborn son, thoroughly complicates that standard plot.

The prologist in closing highlights the uniqueness of the play:

> It really is in your best interests to pay attention to this play, since
> It's not the same-old-same-old you see in other comedies.
> They'll be no dirty lines not worth repeating;
> Here you'll see no greedy pimp, no nasty whore,
> No bragging soldier; and don't you worry
> About that war between the Aetolians and Eleans.
> All the battles will take place offstage.
> It'd be downright wrong for a comic
> Troupe like ours to suddenly go tragic on you! (54-62)

The prologist comically overstates his case for the play's "purity" here, but nonetheless makes three important programmatic points regarding the unusual language (55-6) of *Captivi*, its unusual plot (57-8), and its unusual tone (59-62): (1) While there is a fair amount of sexual innuendo and scatological humor in Plautus, there is virtually no explicit obscenity. But, as becomes quickly apparent to a translator, the language of the play overall is plainer and much less exuberant than is usual in Plautus, and serious ideas are sometimes expressed without being comically undercut—the lines of Ergasilus being exceptional in this respect; (2) The plot is quite unusual and mostly lacks the usual cast of characters belonging to Plautus' demimonde: there is no greedy pimp (cf. Ballio in *Pseudolus*), there are no prostitutes (of either the nasty or nice variety), and there is no braggart soldier (cf. Harpax and his Macedonian boss in *Pseudolus*)—again the comic parasite Ergasilus presents the noteworthy exception; (3) While no one will mistake *Captivi* for a traditional tragedy, the ethical issues raised by the play, the high-minded sentiments and actions of (esp.) Tyndarus, along with the real torture he experiences during the play, mark the overall tone as more serious than usual for Plautine comedy—with scenes involving Ergasilus yet again proving to be exceptional. War remains in the background, but we hear nothing about battles, as we might in a messenger's speech of a true tragedy. The otherwise superfluous mention of tragedy seems intended then to signal that the play will feature serious themes and issues not normally treated in comedy.

In the midst of what is a serious treatment of the ethical issues surrounding slavery, Ergasilus clearly stands out. Though some critics have argued for integral connections between his role and either that of other characters or the play's central themes themselves,[17] most have viewed Ergasilus as an "inorganic" character, not essential to the plot and one whom Plautus adds to his source play in order to provide comic relief. It is in fact reasonable to regard Ergasilus as the embodiment of festival itself.[18] Ergasilus is utterly obsessed with feasting and excess, as he is a truly Gargantuan figure capable of inhuman levels of consumption. The language he uses is no less excessive than his appetite for food, as is evident from his opening monologue, where he begins by explaining why he is nicknamed "the call-girl" (69). With the loss of his primary patron Philopolemus, however, Ergasilus is now enjoying only a "Festival of Famine" (468). Beyond being a kind of personification of festival itself, he is also the one character who most insistently makes Roman allusions (90, 156-64, 489, 492-5, 813-22, 881-5), and thereby encourages the audience to connect the world of the play with their own.

There is, then, a serious side to Ergasilus. The loss of Philopolemus seems to coincide with a general breakdown in host/parasite relations, so that the parasite's traditional services (e.g., arranging for a prostitute) are now rejected (461-97). Even clever dinner conversation, the parasite's mainstay, is no longer valued, and the parasite is left with nothing to offer in exchange for his coveted meal. If we can believe Ergasilus, the problem is not uniquely his: "I wasn't the only parasite pointlessly on the prowl in the forum" (491). The theme of reciprocity in social relations, we shall see, is paramount in this play, and so the situation parasites allegedly face reflects that central preoccupation. And does the audience itself identify with Ergasilus' frustration at their own "Festival of Famine" (468), i.e., the fact that they too have been served up something less lavish than the comic fare they have come to expect from Plautus? For Ergasilus, the return of feasting (Scene 13) coincides with the return of Philopolemus, i.e., the event that restores proper familial relationships between Hegio and both his sons. Curiously, though, the feast the famished Ergasilus enjoys "like a hungry wolf" (912) is not communal, as might be expected at the end of a comedy such as this (cf. the end of *Pseudolus*). Nor does the epilogue call for communal feasting, and so here we find one more unsettling element that sets this play apart from others in the Plautine corpus.

Before examining the play as a whole, some general background about the institution of slavery is necessary.[19] The main sources of slaves in the Roman world were prisoners of war and persons kidnapped by pirates or brigands. Children exposed by their parents at birth might also be taken up by strangers and raised as slaves (cf. *Casina*). According to the oldest Roman law code,

---

17   Most notably Leach (1969).

18   For festive comedy (or carnival) in general, see Bakhtin (1984).

19   For Roman slavery, see Bradley (1994).

The Twelve Tables, a Roman *paterfamilias* could even enslave his children up to three times. Chance and circumstance, not membership in a targeted underclass, determined who was enslaved in antiquity. Thus it very often was the case that formerly free persons became slaves. Slaves had no legal rights, and Roman law went so far as to insist they had no parents; the Roman agricultural writer Varro (in)famously referred to a slave as a "tool with a voice." Despite some support for the notion of the natural equality of slaves and free persons from Greek philosophers from the 5th century BCE on, a supporting ideology of slavery evolved, according to which slaves were assumed to be the inferiors of their owners in character, morality, appearance, etc.

The lot of Roman slaves varied greatly. Slaves of the household, especially those born there, usually had it best. They might develop close relationships with their owners and families, and even be treated like a (free) family member. When Tyndarus' true identity is revealed, Philocrates assures Hegio that his son has enjoyed this kind of humane treatment:

> ...We were together since childhood,
> And I can assure you he had a proper and respectable upbringing.
> (991-2)

Philocrates curiously had earlier told Tyndarus that he was "like a second father" to himself (238). At the other extreme of servile treatment was confinement to the mill or the mines, where only death brought an end to debilitating labor and squalid living conditions. This is precisely the type of brutal sentence the livid Hegio passes on Tyndarus when he learns that he has been deceived. Tyndarus fortunately is rescued from the mines, and vividly describes the horrors of his confinement there:

> I'd seen lots of paintings of the tortures in the underworld,
> But none of these can capture the living hell
> I was in at the stone-quarries. (998-1000)

Tyndarus further characterizes his emergence from the stone-quarries as a form of rebirth when he bitterly and ironically responds to Hegio's address to him as his "long-lost son" (1006):

> ... You're pretending you're my father and I'm your son
> Because, like a parent, you've brought me into the light of day.
> (1007-8)

Probably very few slaves in real life escaped the living hell of forced labor in the mines. For those slaves who found themselves in more fortuitous circumstances, however, Roman slavery offered a ready mechanism for social rebirth: manumission. Roman slaves could possess their own money and property, and so could purchase their freedom from their masters, or they might be manumitted for loyal service in their owners' wills.

In the play, Tyndarus and Philocrates must not only accept their new roles as Hegio's slaves, but also adapt to their reversed roles as master and slave, respectively, if their scheme is to succeed. In their first appearance in the play (Scene 3), they appropriately lament their new status as Hegio's slaves, as also their chains to the Guard, who ironically—and correctly—assumes that they both formerly were free (196-7). Philocrates there echoes the supporting ideology of slavery (i.e., that slaves are morally inferior) by quipping, "So at least we aren't the only cowards" (262), upon hearing of the capture of Hegio's son.

In launching the ruse against Hegio, Philocrates adeptly assumes the character of the clever slave of Plautine comedy, as Tyndarus' commentary on his master's deceptive actions indicates:

> The old man has entered the barbershop and is about to be clipped.
> And not so much as a towel to keep his clothes clean!
> Hard to say if he'll get a close shave or just a trim. If my master's
> As good as I think, he should get a real fleecing! (266-9)

> Excellent! I'd take him over Thales the Wiseman, who was just an
> Amateur in comparison with my master here!
> Just look at how cleverly he plays the part of a slave! (274-6)

Tyndarus, meanwhile, shows himself to be most convincing as a master. He eloquently philosophizes about his new situation to Hegio, after Philocrates (as Tyndarus) has informed the *senex* of his family's status:

> Now that I've lost my country and liberty
> I can understand why he'd fear you more than me.
> An enemy assault has made him and me equals.
> I can remember when he didn't dare say a word against me; now he has
> The freedom to do as he wants. Fortune lifts and lowers us as she
>   pleases:
> I once was a free man—and she's brought me down from the top to the
>   bottom;
> I had grown accustomed to giving orders and now I must take them.
>   (300-6)

Similarly, in his words to the departing Philocrates, Tyndarus expertly plays the part of a master grateful for his loyal slave's service:

> Stress that I am fine, Tyndarus, and don't hesitate to talk yourself up:
> Mention how there has always been perfect harmony
> Between us, how I have never found fault with you or had to be harsh,
> How you have been a perfect slave to your master in times of
> Terrible troubles, never failing me in your thoughts or your deeds at
> Even our darkest moments. Tyndarus, once my father realizes how

> Well-disposed you've been to his son and to him,
> He will not hesitate to grant you your freedom—gratis. (401-8)

Following Philocrates' statement of reciprocal gratitude for his fair treatment (414-18), Hegio must exclaim:

> Such noble characters! They bring me to tears!
> It's obvious how much they care for each other—and for a slave
> To so lovingly lavish such praise on his master! (419-21)

To this point, Tyndarus is merely playing the role of humane master. But even after Hegio has uncovered the ruse, Tyndarus, in confessing his role in the deception, reveals idealism and high-minded sentiments conventionally associated with the freeborn of (esp.) the educated upper classes:

> **Tyndarus**
> I'm not afraid of dying, as long as it's not for an unjust cause.
> If he does not return and I die here, at least
> What I did will be remembered after my death,
> How I restored my master to his freedom, father, and fatherland
> After he had been captured and enslaved by the enemy,
> And how, to save his life, I choose to expose
> Myself to the ultimate danger.
> **Hegio**
> Then go ahead and reap the glory for your deed in Hades!
> **Tyndarus**
> He who dies courageously does not die entirely. (682-90)

Tyndarus' bravery in the face of an honorable death and his philosophical resignation to his fate continues as he is dragged off to the mines:

> Why ask for mercy when you won't grant it?
> The danger you put me in puts you in danger too.
> Once I'm dead, there's no evil in death to fear.
> It's only for a brief span of time I'll endure your punishments—
> Even if I live to a ripe old age. (739-43)

He then makes a final request (747-8) to meet with Philocrates if the latter returns that is met only with more anger from Hegio.

Captivi thus has thoroughly confounded its audience's predominant beliefs regarding the conventional behavior of masters and slaves, and suggested that good or bad character cannot be so directly correlated with free or servile status as the supporting ideology of slavery presumes. "Nobility," by implication, is not necessarily inborn, but is also a role that can be assumed or played. The notion that slavery is a condition of chance is emphasized throughout the play (302-8, 310-15, 543-4): as the prologist puts it in homely terms, "We are the gods' volleyballs" (22). In such a world of happenstance and the shifting social roles that result, the categories of free and slave do not allow for such sharp ideological division as is commonly assumed.

One possible consequence of recognizing the arbitrariness of rank and status is to follow the Golden Rule ("treat others as you would like to be treated"), or ethics of reciprocity, a near-universal concept in human society that long before Plautus had been articulated in Greek philosophy. Tyndarus and Philocrates, whose treatment of each other best illustrates this principle, give voice, directly or indirectly, to the Golden Rule on multiple occasions, e.g.:

Tyndarus to Philocrates as they launch the scheme:

> Let's hope you remember that when you have what you want!
> The vast majority of human beings are virtuous
> > When they want something; once they
> > Have it, they're through with virtue
> > > And turn into lying degenerates!
> So you can see how I want you to treat me. (231-6)

Tyndarus to Hegio:

> I once was just as free as your son.
> His freedom and mine were both taken away by an enemy attack;
> He is now a slave in my country, just as I am in your house.
> Surely a god is watching and listening to what we do, and will see
> That his treatment there matches your treatment of me here.
> Treat me well and he'll treat your son well—and vice-versa. (310-15)

Tyndarus to Hegio, who has just discovered that he has been deceived:

> Well, I beg to differ with you: I say it was the right thing to do.
> Suppose one of your slaves did the same thing
> For your son: wouldn't you be very grateful?
> Wouldn't you want to free that slave?
> Wouldn't he be the most beloved slave in your house? (710-14)

Philocrates to Hegio after he returns with Philopolemus:

> What I want is for you to return the slave I left here as security
> Back to me. He has always treated me better than he treats himself,
> And I want to reward him for all the good he's done for me. (938-40)

The point about reciprocity is most poignantly made when Hegio, who, although he has been repeatedly advised to treat his captives as he would like his son to be treated by his captors, realizes the cruelty he has inflicted upon his own son in the mines:

> Oh, this is bittersweet for me if what you say is true:
> If he really is my son, I have done a terrible, terrible thing to him!
> How much more—or less—than what is right I've done!
> To have done what I did—it's torturing me. If only it could be undone!
> Look, here he comes, dressed in a way someone like him doesn't
>   deserve! (993-7)

In the light of these repeated calls for the ethics of reciprocity, the import of the prologist's remark, "What follows here is fact for us actors, even if it's fiction for all of you" (52), becomes clearer. For most, if not all, of the members of the acting troupe, slavery was an everyday reality, and the prologist seems to be making a genuine appeal for humane consideration to the audience, however indirectly. This of course is not the same thing as calling for the abolishment of slavery, as the ending of the play makes clear. There, the final, bitter line is delivered by Stalagmus, the inexplicably malignant and unrepentant slave who abducted Tyndarus as a boy. Hegio's reference (966) to Stalagmus's compliant behavior as a boy perhaps is meant to suggest that despite the good treatment he received as a member of the household then, Stalagmus nonetheless turned out to be Hegio's worst enemy. At any rate, the transfer of Tyndarus' chains to Stalagmus (1021) very visually indicates that the institution of slavery is to continue. The play, however, clearly makes the case for the humane treatment of slaves, both on the grounds that they too may be as "noble" as free persons and, more practically, that slave owners in the audience may someday find themselves or their kin enslaved. This is an important step toward acknowledgment of the natural equality of all human beings, and one that was bound to inspire reflection in at least some audience members after they left Plautus' theater.

PSEUDOLUS

Pseudolus is often characterized as Plautus' most self-consciously theatrical play, and his most impressive comedy altogether. Its plot is extremely common in Plautus and New Comedy in general: a penniless young man faces the loss of his lover, as her pimp is about to sell her, in this case to a soldier. Despite the stereotypical plot, a translator quickly recognizes that he has entered new linguistic territory that is even more verbally playful and exuberant than is usual in Plautus. That language itself has moved even further to the forefront is suggested by the opening scene, where Pseudolus meticulously analyzes a letter from Phoenicium, Calidorus' beloved.[20] Handed what amounts to a script por-

---

20   Cf. Slater (1985) 118-46.

tending the lovers' permanent separation, and faced with Calidorus' paratragic reactions (38-9, 90) to it, Pseudolus is all dry-eyed (75-7). He rejects the script as melodrama, and mocks both Calidorus and this type of drama when he pretends to see (35-6) the image of Phoenicium herself in the wax tablet on which the "woeful" (cf. the pun at 74) letter is written. With the first hint that he is to assume the role of playwright, Pseudolus promises Calidorus that he will rework this sorry script into something with a more familiar, happy ending:

> As for your big showery show of tears:
> You're just pouring water down the drain.
> Fear not, lover-boy, I won't desert you.
> I hope to find you some help of the silvery variety—
> By some honest means, or perhaps in my usual way.
> I have absolutely no idea where I'll get it,
> But I know that I will: my twitching eyebrow says so. (101-7)

A seasoned Plautine audience knows that Pseudolus will assume the comically heroic role of clever slave, or *servus callidus*. By the end of this opening scene Pseudolus not only boastfully assures success in "getting the girl," but also establishes his preference to do so with linguistic novelty:

Calidorus
May the gods forever bless you! But look:
Out of respect for family duty, could you fleece my mother too?
Pseudolus
You can rest insured about that.
Calidorus
"Rest insured" or "rest assured?"
Pseudolus
My way is so less cliché!
And so there's no confusion, everyone listen up:
I hereby decree, to all citizens assembled here, to the
Entire populace, to all my friends and all who know me:
Be wary of me today and, above all, DON'T TRUST ME! (121-8)

The arch-crafty Pseudolus announces that his is to be a novel, virtuoso comic performance, one in which he will even openly apprise both his enemies and the audience of his every move to secure Phoenicium. Plautus' audience knows he will succeed. The chief pleasure for them lies in how the scheme is to be pulled off. The critical acts of deception that result in Phoenicium's release take place in just two brief scenes (7, 13). The play instead overwhelmingly focuses on Pseudolus' starts and mis-starts toward conceiving a plan, his constant interaction with the audience about his scheme's (non-) progress, and the rehearsal for what turns out to be the successful play-within-the-play, i.e., Simia's imperson-ation of the soldier's assistant Harpax. *Pseudolus* proves to be a play about the making of a Plautine comedy.

Despite all of Pseudolus' opening bluster and verbal fireworks, it soon becomes apparent that he has no plan whatsoever. For the first half of the play (Scenes 1-6), Pseudolus barely advances his scheme. He is present onstage, how-ever, throughout these scenes, and works hard to establish himself as the play's controlling force. First Pseudolus spoils Ballio's arresting and verbally brilliant comic debut (Scene 2) through his commentary on it as an eavesdropper (cf. 194, 202-7). Any further hope of Ballio's to establish rapport with the audience is de-stroyed in the scene following, in which the pimp's absurdly greedy and callous character is highlighted in his exchange with Pseudolus and Calidorus. Ballio and Calidorus exit and Pseudolus delivers his first monologue (Scene 4), where he confides to the audience that he has no plan and reflects on his predicament:

> Where to start weaving your web of deceit,
> Or how to bring that design to completion?
> But just like a poet takes up his tablet and though
> He looks for what doesn't exist at all, he still finds it, and
> Makes complete fiction seem like the truth.
> That's it! I'll become a poet and find
> The twenty minae which are nowhere! (399-405)

The absence of a plan only enhances his status as the Plautine trickster who can just as easily adapt and improvise in the face of shifting circumstances as he can plot and rehearse an elaborate scheme. Pseudolus here explicitly stakes his claim to being the play's controlling force, i.e., the playwright-within-the-play in search of a plot to find the needed sum of money to purchase Phoenicium. A brief scene follows in which Pseudolus meets his elder master Simo, the third obstacle in his way (in addition to Ballio and the soldier), and Simo's liberal-thinking friend Callipho. Pseudolus openly informs Simo (507ff.) that he will trick him out of the money and acquire the girl from the pimp, which inspires Callipho to speak for the audience when he exclaims: "It's a pleasure to be a spectator at your games" (552).

Pseudolus again is left alone onstage and delivers a second monologue, this time from an actor's perspective, and again promising the audience novelty, if not a precise plan:

> I have a sneaking suspicion that you all suspect
> I've only promised to do these daring deeds
> In order to entertain you during this play,
> And there's little chance I'll do what I promised.
> I'll keep my word. To the best of my knowledge,
> I don't know exactly how I'll do it, but I do know

> That I will. Now, it's the duty of every actor to be original
> Enough to bring something original on stage:
> If he can't, let him step aside for someone who can. (562-70)

Pseudolus then exits, ostensibly to develop a scheme, and leaves the piper to entertain the audience. He then emerges alone again onstage, for a third monologue, actually a song (Scene 6). He now triumphantly claims to have formulated a plan in his head (575), and bombastically assumes the persona of an aristocratic Roman general (579-91), a favorite conceit of Plautus' clever slaves. But he reveals no details of the plan beyond its already revealed targets, i.e., Ballio and Simo. At this point, Harpax, the soldier's agent, arrives to close the deal with Ballio. Pseudolus, as if improvising on the spot, launches an altogether new assault (601-3) by pretending that he is Ballio's slave. Though Harpax is unwilling to hand over the remaining five minae required to purchase Phoenicium, he provides Pseudolus with a letter from the soldier, complete with the soldier's personal seal. This letter, unlike the first letter from Phoenicium, will serve as an essential prop in the new plot to be launched by Harpax's fortuitous arrival. Yet another monologue follows (Scene 8), in which Pseudolus assures the audience that this newly improvised plot will succeed. The stage is now virtually set for the long-awaited play-within-the-play to seize Phoenicium.

With Pseudolus' position as controlling playwright now firmly established, and the critical prop in his possession, he requires only an actor to play Harpax. He specifically asks Calidorus' friend Charinus for a slave rather than a free man (728):

> ... Someone unscrupulous,
> Clever, devious and smart, a quick study
> Who has the natural talent to finish what he's started. (724-6)

His request functions on two distinct metatheatrical levels. First, the audience knows he is seeking the *servus callidus* familiar from so many other Plautine comedies to carry out the impersonation of Harpax. But his specific request for a slave also reflects the fact that the Roman acting troupe is predominantly or wholly comprised of slaves. Pseudolus adds that he needs someone capable of improvising in adverse circumstances (745). He will costume this person appropriately (751-2) and provide him with detailed instructions (764), i.e., a script, along with rehearsal. No longer just playwright and rewriter of the script, Pseudolus here also assumes the role of director.

We next see Pseudolus putting Simia through his final paces (Scene 12) before meeting Ballio. Simia is everything Pseudolus desired and more. He is a very quick study, already in character (905-19), and as brash and impertinent as any clever Plautine slave:

> I hope to god that the soldier's man,
> Shows up exactly at the same time I do.
> You can be damn sure I'll be a better Harpax than he is! So stay calm!
> I'll work all the kinks out of this plan for you nicely.
> My tricks and lies will so terrify our visiting soldier
> That he himself will deny that he is who he is,
> And solemnly swear that I am him! (924-30)

Simia plays the part of Harpax to perfection, the deception of Ballio (Scene 13) proceeds seamlessly, and Phoenicium is taken from the pimp (Scene 15). In a brief intervening monologue, Pseudolus expresses his apprehension that he may have hired a trickster even more clever than himself:

> Never, ever have I seen a worse human being,
> A more deviously wicked fellow than this Simia!
> He so awfully damn good he scares me!
> What if, just when things are going well,
> He turns his wily weapons against me
> As soon as he gets the chance? (1017-22)

In positing a controlling theatrical figure potentially more competent than himself and so capable of launching yet another play-within-the-play, Pseudolus here highlights some of the essential features of Plautine comedy: self-conscious theatricality, relentless play with convention, and the seemingly infinite expandability of duplicity in a duplicitous world.

Another way Pseudolus exerts control over the action of the play (and the audience's reception of it) are his metatheatrical references to the play's pacing. He twice rebuffs Calidorus' requests for further clarification about the scheme in just such terms:

> ... You'll know in good time. I don't want
> To have to repeat myself: plays are long enough as it is (387-8)

> ... Need I remind you this play is being performed for the spectators?
> They saw exactly what happened. I'll bring *you* up to speed later.
>   (720-1)

So too, in his third monologue, he abruptly cuts off his speech on Fortune's role: "Enough philosophizing! I digress and delay our plot" (687). Much of the appeal of Roman comedy lies in its swift and continuous action.

Other characters in *Pseudolus* often self-reflexively refer to themselves as conventional comic characters, and so remind the audience that they are watching a comedy mostly about play-making. The ridiculously lovesick young Calidorus speaks for all such characters of New Comedy when, in response to Pseudolus' call to control his emotions, he quips: "What's the fun of being in love

if you can't be a fool?" (239). Similar is Ballio's agreement with Pseudolus' asser-
tion that he is unlikely to give sound moral advice: "Now that's simply not in the
Pimp's Code of Ethics" (289). Ballio later placidly accepts the abuse heaped upon
him by Calidorus and Pseudolus (357ff.) in terms of comic convention:

> **Simo**
> But did you meet him [i.e., Pseudolus]?
> **Ballio**
>   Yes, I met both of them together.
> **Simo**
> Well, what did he say? What did he tell you?
> **Ballio**
> Typical theatrical blather, the usual abuse heaped on
> Pimps in the comedies. Kid's stuff, really—
> How I'm a nasty scumbag, a liar, etc. (1079-83)

Simia, in response to Pseudolus' characterization of him as clever and cunning,
and so likely to flee like a runaway slave, replies with the conventional glibness
of the Plautine *servus callidus*: "That would be perfectly in line with my line of
work" (914).

Pseudolus is Plautus' greatest comic superhero, a champion of both language and the crafting of plays, which in Plautine theater is tantamount to ruling
absolutely over the world of the play—as we saw was also the case for Cleostrata
in *Casina*. For a clever slave to seize control of the theatrical world is not of
course a subversive call for slaves to do the same in the world outside the theater;
Pseudolus is no more (or less) a abolitionist drama than *Captivi*. But as is true
for all the plays translated here, there is more at work than the state-sanctioned
"letting off of steam" in the context of festival. *Pseudolus*, by constantly laying
bare the conventions that make up a Plautine play, demonstrates how easily a
theatrical world and its social fabric, however implausible these may be, can
both be constructed and taken apart. The example of Pseudolus himself shows
that convention, like language itself, is not fixed, but malleable, and can always
be (re-)applied in novel ways. Since all the world's a stage, this suggests that
social roles and conventions are not so fixed as might be readily assumed in a
rigid social hierarchy such as that of ancient Rome. Theater can ease an audience
out of its comfort zone by radically challenging society's assumptions about status, gender, and power, even if it does not ultimately change these. Perhaps the
Roman authorities who for so long resisted theater on some level perceived this
deep and abiding challenge to conventionality inherent in the theater.

Translator's Note

My desire to translate Plautus initially grew out of my dissatisfaction with the translations I had used in Latin literature in translation courses. These seemed either ineptly stilted or too far removed from Plautus' Latin and his culture. A primary challenge of translating Plautus, or any ancient author, is to strike a satisfactory balance between accuracy and liveliness. This applies not just to linguistic style and idiom, but also to cultural beliefs, values, assumptions, ideologies, etc. So far as language is concerned, I have tried to navigate between the Scylla and Charybdis of slavish literalism on the one side, and the temptation to over-indulge in contemporary slang and other imminently doomed, ephemeral references on the other. It seems impossible to capture the rich vitality of Plautus' festival of words—the puns, assonance and alliteration, for example—without creating something that sounds very odd, if not altogether mad, to our ears. But I have nonetheless tried to preserve something of Plautus' extraordinarily playful style, as also his sometimes bizarre imagery and conceits (most of which were meant to sound bizarre to their original audience as well), while at the same time producing, I hope, smooth prose dialogue. In a similar attempt not to obliterate or over-familiarize the distant and strange culture behind the Latin text, I have preserved much of its foreignness by not modernizing the names of the characters and by mostly leaving in references to Roman (and Greek) places, deities, institutions, etc. These are explained in the notes at the bottom of the page, which assume a readership with no prior experience of Plautus or ancient literature and culture.

As a reflection of my wish to stay as close as possible to Plautus, I have mostly translated line by line. The majority of Plautus is written in spoken (i.e., iambic) and chanted or recitative (i.e., chiefly trochaic) verse based on the quantity of syllables or, more precisely, the relative time it took to pronounce them (i.e., "long" vs. "short"). These early Latin verse forms were relatively free and allowed for many (metrical) licenses, so that it is difficult for English ears to follow the rhythm of Latin verse without artificially imposing stress accents at regular intervals—which by translating Plautus into prose I have not done. The rest of Plautus is in sung meters, about which we know virtually nothing. Sung sections are so marked at the beginnings of scenes in the translations and the lines are arranged so as to (mostly) follow how they appear in modern Latin editions.

The plays are not here divided into acts and scenes, as this was not done until the Renaissance. There likewise are no stage directions in the manuscripts in which Plautus is preserved, and I have added these sparingly only where it seemed necessary in order to avoid possible confusion. The Latin texts themselves overwhelmingly explain what is taking place onstage.

I have most closely translated the Latin text of Lindsay (Oxford 1910), and also frequently followed that of Leo (Berlin 1895-6). For the individual plays, I have made extensive use of the following texts and commentaries: for *Casina*, MacCary and Willcock (Cambridge 1976); *Amphitryon*, Christenson (Cambridge 2000), *Captivi*, Lindsay (Oxford 1900); *Pseudolus*, Willcock (London 1987).

It is my hope that these translations will be of use to students and teachers in literature in translation courses, as well as to the general reader. While they are not primarily designed to serve as scripts for performance, it is also my hope that they could be adapted for use on the stage with relative ease.

Suggestions for Further Reading

NEW COMEDY

Arnott, W.G. 1975. *Menander, Plautus, and Terence*. Oxford.
Goldberg, S.M. 1980. *The Making of Menander's Comedy*. Berkeley.
Hunter, R.L. 1985. *The New Comedy of Greece and Rome*. Cambridge.
Wiles, D. 1991. *The Masks of Menander: Sign and Meaning in Greek and Roman Performance*. Cambridge.
Zagagi, N. 1994. *The Comedy of Menander*. London.

PLAUTUS AND ROMAN COMEDY

Anderson, W.S. 1993. *Barbarian Play: Plautus' Roman Comedy*. Toronto.
Beacham, R.C. 1992. *The Roman Theatre and its Audience*. Cambridge, MA. [includes a chapter on performing *Casina*]
Beare, W. 1964. *The Roman Stage*. 3rd edn. London.
Bieber, M. 1961. *The History of the Greek and Roman Theatre*. 2nd edn. Princeton.
Duckworth, G.E. 1952. *The Nature of Roman Comedy*. Princeton.
Fraenkel, E. 2007. *Plautine Elements in Plautus*, trs. T. Drevikovsky and F. Muecke. Oxford.
Gratwick, A.S. 1982. "Drama." In *The Cambridge History of Classical Literature II: Latin Literature*, ed. E.J. Kenney and W.V. Clausen, pp. 77-137. Cambridge.
Konstan, D. 1983. *Roman Comedy*. Ithaca, N.Y. [includes a chapter on *Captivi*]
Marshall, C.W. 2006. *The Stagecraft and Performance of Roman Comedy*. Cambridge.
McCarthy, K. 2000. *Slaves, Masters, and the Art of Authority in Plautine Comedy*. Princeton. [includes chapters on *Casina* and *Captivi*]
Moore, T.J. 1998. *The Theater of Plautus: Playing to the Audience*. Austin, TX. [includes chapters on *Amphitryon, Captivi, Casina*, and *Pseudolus*]
Segal, E. 1987. *Roman Laughter*. 2nd edn. Oxford. [includes an essay on *Amphitryon*]
Slater, N.W. 1985. *Plautus in Performance: the Theatre of the Mind*. Princeton. [includes a chapter on *Pseudolus*]

CASINA

Connors, C. 1997. "Scents and Sensibility in Plautus' *Casina*." *Classical Quarterly* 47 (1997): 305-9.
Gold, B. 1998. "Vested Interests in Plautus' *Casina*: Cross-Dressing in Roman Comedy." *Helios* 25: 17-29.
MacCary, W.T. 1975. "Patterns of Myth, Ritual, and Comedy in Plautus' *Casina*." *Texas Studies in Literature and Language* 15: 881-9.

MacCary, W.T. and Willcock, M.M. 1976. *Plautus: Casina*. Cambridge.
O'Bryhim, S. 1989. "The Originality of Plautus' *Casina.*" *American Journal of Philology* 110: 81-103.

AMPHITRYON

Christenson, D. 2000. *Plautus: Amphitruo*. Cambridge.
——. 2001. "Grotesque Realism in Plautus' *Amphitruo.*" *Classical Journal* 96: 243-60
Fantham, E. 1973. "Towards a Dramatic Reconstruction of the Fourth Act of Plautus' *Amphitruo.*" *Philologus*: 197-214.
Slater, N.W. 1990. "*Amphitruo, Bacchae* and Metatheatre." *Lexis* 6: 101-25.
Stewart, Z. 1958. "The *Amphitruo* of Plautus and Euripides' *Bacchae.*" *Transactions and Proceedings of the American Philological Association* 89: 348-73.

CAPTIVI

Franko, G.F. 1995. "Fides, Aetolia, and Plautus' *Captivi.*" *Transactions and Proceedings of the American Philological Association* 125: 155-76.
Leach, E.W. 1969. "Ergasilus and the Ironies of the *Captivi.*" *Classica et Mediaevalia* 30: 263-96.
Lindsay, W.M. repr. 1981. *Plautus: Captivi*. Bristol.
Lowe, J.C.B. 1991. "Prisoners, Guards, and Chains in Plautus, *Captivi.*" *American Journal of Philology* 112: 29-44.

PSEUDOLUS

Barsby, J. 1995. "Plautus' *Pseudolus* as Improvisatory Drama." In *Plautus und die Tradition des Stegreifspiels*, ed. L. Benz, E. Stärk, and G. Vogt-Spira, pp. 55-70. Tübingen.
Sharrock, A.R. 1996. "The Art of Deceit: *Pseudolus* and the Art of Reading." *Classical Quarterly* 46: 152-74.
Willcock, M.M. 1987. *Plautus: Pseudolus*. London.
Wright, J. 1975. "The Transformations of Pseudolus." *Transactions and Proceedings of the American Philological Association* 105: 403-16.

RELATED TOPICS

Bakhtin, M. 1984. *Rabelais and his World*, trs. H. Iswolsky. Bloomington, IN.
Bradley, K.R. 1994. *Slavery and Society at Rome*. Cambridge.
Bristol, M.D. 1985. *Carnival and Theater: Plebeian Culture and the Structure of Authority in Renaissance England*. New York and London.
Chalmers, W.R. 1965. "Plautus and his Audience." In *Roman Drama*, ed. T.A. Dorey and D.R. Dudley, pp. 21-50. London.
Edwards, C. 1993. *The Politics of Immorality in Ancient Rome*. Cambridge.
Gowers, E. 1993. *The Loaded Table: Representations of Food in Roman Literature*. Oxford.
Gratwick, A.S. 1973. "Titus Maccius Plautus." *Classical Quarterly* 23: 78-84.
Gruen, E.S. 1990. *Studies in Greek Culture and Roman Policy*. Leiden.
——. 1992. *Culture and National Identity in Republican Rome*. Ithaca, N.Y.
Harris, W.V. 1979. *War and Imperialism in Republican Rome*. Oxford.

Moore, T.J. 1994. "Seats and Social Status in the Plautine Theater." *Classical Journal* 90: 113-23.

Nelson, T.G.A. 1990. *Comedy.* Oxford.

Treggiari, S. 1991. *Roman Marriage.* Oxford.

Wright, J. 1974. *Dancing in Chains: The Stylistic Unity of the Comoedia Palliata.* Rome.

Casina

Characters With Speaking Parts

OLYMPIO, *slave of Lysidamus and foreman of his farm in the country*
CHALINUS, *slave of Lysidamus and sidekick of Lysidamus' son Euthynicus*
CLEOSTRATA, *wife of Lysidamus*
PARDALISCA, *Cleostrata's personal slave ("maidservant")*
MYRRHINA, *wife of Alcesimus and friend of Cleostrata*
LYSIDAMUS, *head of the household*
ALCESIMUS, *neighbor and friend of Lysidamus*
CITRIO, *a cook hired to prepare the "wedding" feast*

SCENE

Athens: the action takes place in front of the houses of Lysidamus and Alcesimus.

PROLOGUE[1]

Welcome, spectators! What a wonderful audience!
I know you respect Honesty,[2] just as she respects you.
So if you agree, show me you're fair-minded
By giving me a round of applause right now!

---

1   The Roman comic playwrights introduced the use of an impersonal prologist (perhaps the head of the acting troupe) to ancient comedy. Characters or gods (e.g., *Amphitryon*) also deliver prologues in Plautus, though not all Plautine plays have formal prologues.

2   *Fides*, one of many abstractions personified and worshipped in Roman religion. She had a prominent temple on the Capitoline Hill in Rome.

People who enjoy a vintage wine are smart,   5
And so are connoisseurs of ancient plays.
And since you appreciate aged words and workmanship,
You should also really like aged plays.
And aren't the new plays being produced today
Even more debased than the new coinage?[3]   10
Now there's a rumor making the rounds
That you're dying to see a play by Plautus.
So we present one of his vintage comedies:[4]
The oldsters among you loved this show,
But the youngsters here don't know it.   15
And we'll see that that changes.
The play was a hit the instant it hit the theater,
Back when our best playwrights flourished.
They may all be gone for good, but
Their plays live on and give us much pleasure.   20
So all of you please listen to my appeal,
And give our company your closest attention!
Got debts? Cast your worries aside,
There's no need to fear bill collectors today![5]
It's festival time! Forget about the bankers—   25
There's nothing but peace and quiet all throughout the forum!
Quite a racket those banks! No payments from you now,
And no payments *to you* after the festival!
Now listen up and try to be receptive:
It's time to learn the name of this play: 30
In Greek this comedy's called *Klerumenoi*,[6]
In Latin *Sortientes*. Diphilus[7] is the
Greek author. Plautus—he of the barking name[8]—

---

3   Debasement of coinage was a perennial problem in Republican Rome and so this reference does not help date the play.

4   Lines 5-22 were apparently composed for a revival of the play sometime after Plautus' death.

5   Plays were performed during Roman festivals, when commercial and legal business was normally suspended: see Introduction, pp. 5-6.

6   "The Lot-Drawers" in Greek (= *Sortientes* in Latin). The Greek play took its name from the scene (i.e., Scene 6 in Plautus) in which lots were drawn for the right to marry Casina (if that was her name in the Greek source play).

7   Popular Greek New Comedy playwright (cf. Introduction, pp. 3-5), born c. 360-350 BCE, who provided the source play for several surviving Roman comedies.

8   The Latin adjective *plautus*, "flat," was used to describe the floppy ears of a dog. For another interpretation of Plautus' name, see Introduction, pp. 1-2.

Got hold of it and reworked it all over again.[9]
An old man lives here. He's married and has a son   35
Who lives with him in this same house.
The old guy has a slave,[10] laid up sick now,
Or laid up in bed to be more precise.
At the very crack of dawn sixteen years ago
That same slave spotted a woman   40
Abandoning a baby girl. He went right up to her
And asked if he could have the baby.
His plea succeeded. He took it straight home,
And begged his mistress to raise the baby.
His mistress agreed and gave it all her care,   45
Just as if it were her very own daughter.
After the girl reached the age that
Attracts men's attention, the old man here
Fell desperately for her and so did his son.
Now each is lining up his troops against the other's, though   50
Neither father nor son knows the other's plans exactly.
The father's enlisted his farm's foreman to seek
The girl's hand in marriage. Once that's done,
The old man hopes to spend a night away from home with her
Without his wife knowing. Meanwhile the son has   55
Enlisted his trusty sidekick[11] to marry the girl. That way he can
Keep the girl he's so in love with close to home.
The old man's wife has gotten wind of his new love-interest,
And so she's taken up her son's cause.
Now after the old man found out that his son   60
Was in love, and seeing an obstacle to his plan,
He had the young man sent abroad.
But the mother, clever lady that she is, has become her son's ally.
In case you're wondering, the son won't return today.
Not in this comedy. That just wasn't Plautus' plan: 65
He brought down a bridge on the young man's way home.[12]
Now I'm sure some of you are saying to yourselves,

---

9   I.e., *Casina* is a creative adaptation of its Greek source play, not a close literal translation.

10 The slave never appears in Plautus's play, as he probably did in Diphilus', presumably in a scene in which the true identity of the exposed child was revealed.

11 The Latin word is *armiger* ("armour-bearer," "squire"). As the *armiger* Chalinus is also the son's slave, there is no English equivalent.

12 I.e., Plautus has removed the son who appeared in Diphilus' play from his adaptation.

"What the ...? How can it be? A slave wedding?"[13]
Since when do slaves propose or get married?
It's unheard of, and doesn't happen anywhere in the world!"   70
Ah, but it does in Greece[14] and in Carthage,[15]
And in Apulia[16] right here in our own backyard!
There the weddings of slaves tend to be
Bigger affairs than those of free folks.
Don't believe me? I'll bet anyone a bottle   75
Of sweet wine it's true—as long as the judge is a
Greek, Carthaginian, or an Apulian.[17]
Well, how about it? No takers? I guess no one needs a drink!
Now back to that abandoned girl,
The one the slaves are so eager to marry: 80
Turns out she's a freeborn virgin:
Yes, the daughter of an Athenian! So they'll be no
Fooling around with her in this comedy.
But trust me, as soon as the play's over,
I'm sure whoever counts out the cash to her   85
Can have his honeymoon[18]—no ceremony necessary!
That's the gist of it. Take care, good luck and continue
To win victories through your valor, as always!"[19]

---

13   Roman slaves were legal non-entities and so could not marry, though they did in fact often
      live together as husband and wife by a practice known as *contubernium* (lit., "the sharing of a
      hut"). Cf. Introduction, p. 21.

14   Informal connubial arrangements among slaves similar to those made in Rome (see n. 13
      above) seem to have occurred in Greece, though it is unlikely that such "marriages" were ever
      legally sanctioned.

15   Carthage was Rome's hated North African rival in the Punic Wars ongoing during much of
      Plautus' lifetime. Not enough evidence survives to determine whether or not slave marriages
      were legally binding in Carthage (or Apulia). Note the prologist's Roman (and prejudiced)
      point of view toward foreigners here.

16   Apulia (modern Puglia) is a region of southeastern Italy that was heavily influenced by
      Greeks and Greek culture from an early date.

17   Romans stereotypically viewed Carthaginians and Greeks as dishonest and untrustworthy, as
      also, apparently, the Greek-influenced Apulians. The joke here assumes that any judge from
      these places would be easily corruptible.

18   An allusion to the fact that Roman actors were mostly slaves in real life and so likely to
      prostitute themselves. The fact that they were also male perhaps lends a homoerotic twist to
      the jest as well.

19   Plautus's prologues usually end with a flattering valediction such as this to the audience,
      whose goodwill is being sought on behalf of the play and the troupe. Cf. *Captivi* 67-8 and
      Introduction, pp. 7-8.

SCENE 1

*Olympio emerges from the house of Lysidamus, followed
closely by Chalinus.*

Olympio[20]

I'm not allowed to take care of my own business,
All by myself, without your permission?   90
Damn it, why are you following me?

Chalinus

                         Oh, I'll

Follow you, all right—like a shadow!
And you can go to hell for all I care—
I'll be right there on your heels! Take that as your cue
As to whether or not you and all your tricks can steal away   95
Casina to be the wife of your dreams without my knowing about it.

Olympio

Mind your own business!

Chalinus

                      Have you no shame?

Just what is a worthless Rube like you creeping around in the city for?

Olympio

Whatever I feel like.

Chalinus

                   Shouldn't you be doing your duty out there on the farm?

Why stick your nose around here in city business   100
When you've got plenty to do out there?
You're only here to steal my bride! So go back to the farm!
There's more than enough *doodie* for you to deal with there!

Chalinus

I know exactly what my duty is,
And someone very capable is tending the farm.   105
And once I get what I came to town for—
Marrying that girl you're so hot for, your co-slave
(Ah Casina,[21] sweet, dear little Casina!),

---

20   The country slave's name calls to mind both Olympia, the chief religious site of Zeus (=
     Jupiter) in Greece, and Mt. Olympus, the mythical home of the gods. Plautus, not his Greek
     source plays, is probably responsible for such comically incongruous (Greek) names: see
     Introduction, p. 5.

21   Her name is related to *casia*, the Greek word for "cinnamon" that was taken over into Latin.
     Casina, who never appears in the play, remains a tantalizing and unattainable object of desire
     to the males in the play.

And escort her home to the country
And into my bed—then I'll do my duty!   110

Chalinus

You're going to marry her? Like hell you are!
Over my dead body! She won't be yours!

Olympio

She's *my* booty. You might as well kill yourself!

Chalinus

So she's *your* booty, you pile of crap?

Olympio

You'll see.

Chalinus

      Screw you!

Olympio

            I swear   115
I'll torture you to death at my wedding!

Chalinus

Just what do you have in mind?

Olympio

               Hmmm … what do I have in mind?
For starters, you can carry the wedding torch for my bride.
Then it's back to being your worthless self.
Next, once you're back on the farm,   120
It's business as usual—one pitcher, one path,
One well, one bucket, and eight vats.
These will always be full, or you'll have a back-full of bruises.
Lugging all that water will have you so bent over and tanned
We could make jock straps for horses out of you!   125
And then, when you get a hankering for a bite to eat,
You can feast yourself on cattle fodder, or eat
Dirt like a worm. I'll sure as hell see to it that you're
As famished as Famine[22] itself out there in the sticks!
And once you're exhausted and empty,   130
I'll see you get just the sleep you deserve.

Chalinus

How's that?

Olympio

      Tightly tied to my bedroom window,

---

22 Plautus often comically plays on Roman religion's tendency to personify abstractions: cf. n. 2
    above.

You'll be tied up in fits as you watch me kiss her,
And she says, "Olympio, my Olympio, love of my life,
Sweetie pie, honeykins, my one and only joy,   135
Let me kiss those little eyes of yours. Please, please,
My darling, let me love you up! You're my personal festival,
My little love-bird, my lovey-dovey, my cuddly-bunny!"
As you have to listen to her tell me all this, dirtbag,
You'll wriggle about like a mouse trapped in a wall!   140
And don't even think about talking back to me—
I'm going inside. I've had enough of your blather.

Chalinus

                                                I'm right behind you.
You can be damn sure nothing you do will get past me!

SCENE 2

Cleostrata and Pardalisca emerge from Lysidamus' house.

(SONG)

Cleostrata[23]

           Lock up the pantry and bring me the keys!
I'm going next door here to my neighbor's.   145
Come get me there if my husband wants me.

Pardalisca

           The old geezer's already demanded his lunch.

Cleostrata

        Shh!
Go off now! He'll get no lunch from me
And there'll be no cooking today!   150
I know he's against my son and me,
      And out to satisfy his lust,
        That disgrace to the human race!
I'll torture him with hunger, torture him with thirst,
Not to mention tough talk and tougher treatment. Loverboy!   155
Oh, I'll have him choking on my last bitter word!
I'll see he leads just the life he deserves—
      In hell's waiting room!
        That chaser of disgrace!
        That septic tank full of scum!   160

---

23   Her name means "renowned in the army," and is probably meant to recall the heroine of
     Aristophanes's *Lysistrata*, a similarly resourceful woman who in that play organizes a sex-
     strike to bring an end to the war between the Spartans and Athenians.

I'm off to complain to my neighbor.
Wait, her door's opening. Look, she's coming out here.
   Maybe this isn't the best time for me to visit.

SCENE 3

Myrrhina exits Alcesimus' house, addressing her slaves.

(*SONG*)

Myrrhina

   Follow me next door here, girls.
   Hey there, anybody listening?   165
       I'll be over there,
       If my husband or anyone else wants me.
   When I'm working all alone at home, I get so tired.   168-9
   Didn't I tell you to bring my knitting?[24]

Cleostrata

                    Hello, Myrrhina!   170-1

Myrrhina

   Oh, Hello! Why the stern look?   172-3

Cleostrata

   Oh you know how it is for any woman in a bad marriage: 174-5
More than enough trouble both inside and outside the house.   176-7
   I was just coming to see you.

Myrrhina

               And I was doing the same!
   Whatever could be bothering you so much?
   Whenever you're upset, I'm upset.   180-1

Cleostrata

   Oh yes, I know. You're my favorite neighbor,
   Always wanting what's best for me.

Myrrhina

       And I'm fond of you, too. Now,
   Please tell me what's the matter.   185

Cleostrata

   I am treated in the worst possible way in my own home!

Myrrhina

   Oh my, what is it? Tell me again, please—
   I really don't understand what's wrong!

---

24   Myrrhina pointedly is engaged in wool-working, the most traditional female activity in the
    ancient world.

Cleostrata

My husband treats me in the worst way,
And there's no way for me to exercise my rights! 190

Myrrhina

Strange if true. It's the men who usually
Are demanding more rights from their wives!

Cleostrata

Why, he wants my maid against my wishes!
She's the one I raised at my own expense.
    He says he wants her for his foreman, 195
But I know he's hot for her himself!

Myrrhina

                         Oh don't
Say that!

Cleostrata

         No, it's okay. We're alone.

Myrrhina

    So we are. But how can she be yours?
A good wife's not supposed to have private property
Without her husband's knowledge. If she does, it's damaged goods— 200
Stolen from her husband or earned in the sack!
In my opinion all you have is your husband's.[25]

Cleostrata

You're going up against your best friend in this?

Myrrhina

                     Shh!
Don't be silly! Now listen:
    Don't fight against your husband. 205
Let him lech and do whatever he wants, as long as he provides for you
    at home. 206-7

Cleostrata

Are you insane? Now you're acting against your own best interests.

Myrrhina

                     No, silly! 208-9
The one thing you never want your husband to say is—

---

25   Myrrhina here refers to a very old and conservative form of Roman marriage (*cum manu*) in which a father's absolute power over his daughter is transferred to her husband. Under this arrangement, a wife's property also became her husband's: see Introduction, p. 11. Alcmena in *Amphitryon* (cf. 928 and n. 51 there), by contrast, apparently remains in her father's power and retains control of her own property in marriage.

Cleostrata

    —What?

Myrrhina

       "Out of the house, woman!"[26] 210-12

Cleostrata

 Shh! Quiet now!

Myrrhina

    What is it?

Cleostrata

     Look!

Myrrhina

      Who's that?

Cleostrata

         It's my husband,

 Coming this way! Please go back into your house!

Myrrhina

        Okay, I'm off!

Cleostrata

 Let's talk some more later when we have a chance.   215

 Yes, Goodbye for now!

Myrrhina

    Goodbye!

SCENE 4

Lysidamus returns from the forum.

(Song through 251)

Lysidamus

 I do believe there's nothing brighter, nothing mightier than love!

 What could possibly have more taste and more grace?

 I really wonder why cooks who love their spices

 Leave out the very finest of them all.   220

 Just a dash of love and a dish is a winner;

 Minus the love there's no flavor, no savor!

 Love can turn bile to honey, and an old grump into a graceful gentleman.

 This I know directly from my own experience: since I fell for Casina,

 I'm aglow, and I know I'm the spitting image of Spiffiness herself![27] 225

 I keep the perfumers busy, sampling the finest scents

---

26 A formula of divorce, which was primarily a speech-act in ancient Rome.

27 Cf. n. 22 above.

To please her (which I do!). But my wife is a plague as long as she lives.
Look at her standing there so sour! Time to sweet talk the old bag.
How goes it my dearest and only delight?

Cleostrata

Get lost! And don't you dare touch me!

Lysidamus

My dear Juno, [28] there's no reason to be so sour with your Jove![29]   230
Where are you going?

Cleostrata

Let go of me!

Lysidamus

Wait!

Cleostrata

I'll do no such thing!

Lysidamus

Then I'll follow you!

Cleostrata

Are you crazy?

Lysidamus

Yes, crazy for you!

Cleostrata

Keep it to yourself—I don't want it!

Lysidamus

How can you resist me?

Cleostrata

Oh, You're killing me!

Lysidamus (*attempting not to be heard*)

I only wish!

Cleostrata

That I can believe!

Lysidamus

Look at me, sweetie.

Cleostrata

Oh I'm your sweetie now?   235
Do I smell cologne?

---

28   Juno (= Greek Hera) is the goddess of marriage and wife of Jupiter, who in myth tries either
     to frustrate her husband's many trysts or to punish his lovers and their offspring.

29   Jupiter (= Greek Zeus), the most powerful of the Olympian gods, in origin the Indo-European
     sky/weather-god.

Lysidamus (*aside*)

Caught red-handed! I'm toast! Better wipe my head off with my cloak!

Damn that perfumer who sold me this stuff!

Cleostrata

You worthless old coot! I can barely keep from telling you what you need
to hear:

An old slug like you, walking around town reeking of cologne—at your
age![30]　　　　　　　　　　　　　　　　　　　　　　　　　　　　240

Lysidamus

I was just helping a friend buy some cologne.

Cleostrata

　　　　　　　　　　　　　　　　　　He doesn't even hesitate to lie!

Have you no shame?

Lysidamus

　　　　　　　　　　　　I've got as much as you want me to.

Cleostrata

　　　　　　　　　　　　　　　　　Which whorehouse were you in?

Lysidamus

Me? In a whorehouse?

Cleostrata

　　　　　　　　　　　　I know more than you think.

Lysidamus

　　　　　　　　　　　　　　　You do? Just what do you know?

Cleostrata

That of all the worthless old slugs in the world none's more worthless than
you!

Where were you? Which whorehouse? Where were you drinking?　　　245

You're stinking drunk! And look at your cloak—all wrinkled!

Lysidamus

　　　　　　　　　　　　　　　　　　　　　The gods can blast

Us both to hell if I drank so much as a single drop of wine today!

Cleostrata

Oh go ahead and do whatever you like—drink, eat, waste your money!

Lysidamus

That's enough, wife! Get a hold of yourself! You're making my　　　249-50
ears ring!

　　　Save yourself a little something to nag about for tomorrow.

Now how about controlling your temper and doing what

30　When a man is wearing scented hair-oil in Roman comedy, this is a clear indication that
　　he has been engaging in, or intends to engage in, extramarital sexual activity, usually in
　　connection with banqueting where prostitutes would be present.

Your husband wants for once instead of always fighting him?
Cleostrata

                                        Such as?

Lysidamus

                                    Glad you asked.
Now about that maid Casina—she should marry our foreman.
He's a fine slave, and can provide her well with wood, warm water, food, 255
Clothing, and a nice place to raise their children.
Much better him than that worthless sidekick of my son
Who doesn't have a penny in the bank!
Cleostrata
I'm quite shocked that a man your age doesn't know how to act!
Lysidamus
What do you mean?
Cleostrata

                    It's hardly decent and proper of you   260
To be so concerned with the maid—that's my job!
Lysidamus
How in the hell could you possibly give her to that no-good Chalinus?
Cleostrata

                                    Because
We both should support our only son.
Lysidamus

                      So he's an only son—
That makes him no more my only son than I'm his only father.
He should be giving in to my wishes—not vice-versa!   265
Cleostrata
You're just asking for trouble, mister! Something stinks here!
Lysidamus (*aside*)

                            She's picked up my scent!
Me?
Cleostrata
      Yes, you! Why the stuttering? Why so hot and bothered all of a sudden?
Lysidamus
I just think she deserves an honorable slave, not a worthless one.
Cleostrata
What if I talk Olympio into giving her up to Chalinus
As a favor to me?
Lysidamus

                But what if I talk Chalinus into giving her to   270
Olympio? I think I can pull that off.

Cleostrata

Fair enough. Shall I call Chalinus out here for you?
You can ask him, I'll ask the foreman.

Lysidamus

Yes, absolutely!

Cleostrata

He'll be here in a second. Now we'll find out who can be more persuasive.

Lysidamus

At last I can say what I want to: may the gods damn that woman!   275
Poor, poor me! Here I'm being tortured by love and she makes it her business
To fight with me! She must have gotten wind of my plan—
And so that's why she's so set on joining Chalinus' camp.
I wish all the gods and goddesses would blast him!

SCENE 5

Chalinus enters from Lysidamus' house.

Chalinus

Your wife says you
Wanted to see me.

Lysidamus

I certainly do.

Chalinus

Fire away!   280

Lysidamus

First of all, show some respect when you talk to me:
It's stupid to scowl at your betters!
Now, I've long considered you a decent and honest fellow.

Chalinus

Great.
So then why don't you free me?

Lysidamus

I'd like to.   284-5
But what'd I *really* want is your wanting to do something for me.

Chalinus

Let me know what you want.

Lysidamus

Listen very carefully:
I promised the foreman Casina's hand in marriage.

Chalinus

But your wife and son promised her to me!

Lysidamus

Right.

But would you rather be a free bachelor   290
Or an enslaved husband—and the same goes for your children?
It's your choice. Take your pick.

Chalinus

If I'm free, I have to support myself. Now you do.
My mind's made up about Casina: she's mine and mine alone!

Lysidamus

Then go inside and call my wife out here this instant!   295
And bring back a water urn and some lots.

Chalinus

All righty.

Lysidamus

I'll dodge that bullet one way or another!
If you can't be persuaded, there's always the lots.
That's how I'll get my vengeance on you and your supporters.

Chalinus

Except that
The winning lot will be mine.

Lysidamus

The only thing you'll win is a whipping.   300

Chalinus

Try any scheme you want. She's marrying me.

Lysidamus

Out of my sight now!

Chalinus

Can't bear the sight of me? I'll survive.

Lysidamus

Am I a poor bastard or what? Could things get any worse?
Now I'm worried my wife's talked Olympio
Out of marrying Casina. If she has, you're looking at one ex-old man!   305
If she hasn't, at least there's a shred of hope for me in the lots.
But if things don't shake out for me, my sword will be my bed—
And I'll have to lie down on it. Oh goody! Here comes Olympio.

SCENE 6

Olympio comes out of Lysidamus' house, shouting back at
Cleostrata.

Olympio
> Lady, you might just as soon toss me in an oven
> And broil me into burned biscotti   310
> As get me to do you what you want!

Lysidamus
> Saved! Judging from this there's still hope!

Olympio
> Lady, you can threaten me all you want about my freedom:
> Even if you and your son don't want it,
> No matter how much the two of you oppose it,   315
> I can become free for just about nothing![31]

Lysidamus
> What's wrong Olympio? Who're you arguing with?

Olympio
> Same woman you always are.

Lysidamus
>   That would be my wife.

Olympio
> Your wife? You're more like a hunter and his dog—
> Spending night and day with that bitch!   320

Lysidamus
> So what's she up to? What's she saying to you?

Chalinus
>   She's begging
> And pleading with me not to marry Casina.

Lysidamus
>   Yes, and?

Olympio
> I said I wouldn't even let Jupiter have her,
> If he begged me.

Lysidamus
>   The gods will bless you!

Chalinus
> She's boiling all right, and ready to blow!   325

---

31 I.e., if he helps Lysidamus carry out his plan. Roman slaves could save up money to purchase
 · their freedom from their masters. Cf. Introduction, p. 21.

Lysidamus

Yes, I'd like to see her split right down the middle!

Chalinus

If you were any kind of man that would be your job.

But really, this love-affair of yours is getting to be a pain.

Your wife hates me, your son hates me,

The whole damn household hates me!

Lysidamus

Oh so what?   330

As long as good old Jupiter here is on your side

You shouldn't give a rat's ass for those lesser gods.

Olympio

Oh, nonsense! As if you weren't aware

How suddenly those human Jupiters can die off!

Tell me this, old Jupiter: when you die   335

And the lesser gods inherit your kingdom,

Who will there be to save my back, head, and legs?

Lysidamus

You'll be much better off than you can ever imagine

If we win and I get Casina in bed!

Chalinus

That's utterly impossible, I'm afraid! What with the way   340

Your wife's dead set against me marrying her!

Lysidamus

Here's my plan:

I toss the lots into the urn and draw one for

You and Chalinus. Hmm … but I see how it is:

We'll have to draw our swords and battle it out.

Chalinus

And what if the drawing turns out the other way?   345

Lysidamus

Bite your tongue! I trust in the gods, all hope lies with them!

Chalinus

Well I wouldn't bet the farm on that.

It may be that all mortals trust in the gods

But I've sure seen a lot of the faithful get fooled by them!

Lysidamus

Shh! Quiet a minute!

Olympio

Why?

Lysidamus

Chalinus is coming.   350

Out with the urn and the lots—
Time to close ranks and battle it out!

SCENE 7

Cleostrata and Chalinus, who has the urn and lots, emerge
from Lysidamus' house.

Cleostrata
Chalinus, What does my husband want me to do?
Chalinus
To go outside the city gate and climb up on your pyre.[32]
Cleostrata
Oh I'm pretty sure about that.
Chalinus
       Oh I think you can take the "pretty" off of that! 355
Lysidamus (*to Olympio*)
I've got more experts around here than I thought—this one's a regular
  soothsayer!
Why don't we raise the battle standards and charge?
Follow me! And just what are you two up to?
Chalinus
          I've got everything you ordered:
Wife, lots, urn, and yours truly.
Olympio
       And one of yours truly is truly one too many!
Chalinus
Damn straight about that: I'm the spur in your side,   360
And I'll rip your heart out! You're already sweating, you human punching
  bag!
Lysidamus
Shut up, Chalinus!
Chalinus
    Grab him!
Olympio
      No *him*—he actually likes that sort of thing.
Lysidamus
Put the urn here and give me the lots! Attention, everyone.
I did think, my dear wife, that you'd let Casina

---

32 Roman funerals, cremations, and burials had to performed outside the city.

Marry me—and I do think so now too. 365

Cleostrata

Casina marry you?

Lysidamus

Yes, me—oops, I didn't mean that!
I meant "me" when I said "him," wanting her all for myself as I do …
Oh damn! I got it all wrong!

Cleostrata

You certainly do, both your words and your behavior!

Lysidamus

"Him"—wait, no "me" … at least I'm back on the right track now.

Cleostrata

You seldom are.

Lysidamus

That can happen when you really want something. 370
But Olympio and I, recognizing your right in this, ask you—

Cleostrata

Yes?

Lysidamus

I'll tell you, honey pie. Regarding Casina—could you do
Our foreman a favor?

Cleostrata

I won't, and wouldn't even consider it!

Lysidamus

Well then I'll draw lots for both sides.

Cleostrata

Who's stopping you?

Lysidamus

In my judgement that would be the fairest and best thing. 375
If it goes our way, we'll celebrate afterwards.
If not, we'll keep a level head. Take a lot—
See what's written on it.

Olympio

One.

Chalinus

Not fair! You gave it to him first.

Lysidamus

Take this one, please.

Chalinus

Give me it! Wait, I just thought of something:
Let's see if there's another lot underwater.

Lysidamus

                              Scumbag!   380

Think I'm like you?

Cleostrata

                  Now calm down—there isn't one in there.

Chalinus

I pray the gods will give me—

Olympio

                     A pile of trouble!

Judging by your piety, that's what I expect is coming your way.

But wait a minute. That lot of yours there isn't made of wood, is it?

Chalinus

Why's that matter?

Olympio

                 Because I'm afraid it'll float on top of the water.   385

Lysidamus

Bravo! But be careful. Now throw them both in here.

Wife, stir up the lots.

Olympio

              Don't trust your wife!

Lysidamus

                      Calm down!

Olympio

Damn it, she'll jinx us if she gets her hands on them!

Lysidamus

                          Quiet!

Olympio

I am quiet. Dear gods, I pray you'll—

Chalinus

                 Bring a yoke and chain—

Olympio

That the lot falls out for me—

Chalinus

              And hang him by his feet!   390

Olympio

And that you blow your eyes right out your nose!

Chalinus

What are you worried about? There's a noose all ready for you.

Olympio

You are so dead!

Lysidamus

         Now both of you pay attention!

Olympio

I'm quiet.

Lysidamus

Now then Cleostrata,

So you won't have any suspicions about me cheating,
I'm letting you draw the lots.

Olympio

You're killing me!

Chalinus

No loss there.   395

Cleostrata

Very well then.

Chalinus

Dear gods—I pray your lot's escaped from the urn.

Olympio

Just because you're a runaway slave doesn't make everyone else one too!
And I hope yours is dissolved, just like
The clay lots of Hercules' descendants.[33]

Chalinus

Soon you'll be so warmed up from whipping that you'll dissolve!   400

Lysidamus

Olympio, pay attention now!

Olympio

I would if this man of letters[34] would let me!

Lysidamus

May all the good luck be on my side!

Olympio

Yes, and mine, too!

Chalinus

No, on my side!

Olympio

No, no, mine!

Chalinus

No, mine!

Cleostrata

My man will win—and your life will be miserable.

---

33 The descendants of Hercules (= Greek Herakles) drew lots to divide up regions of the
    Peloponnese among themselves. One of them secured Messenia by arranging for his rival's
    lot to be made of (dissolvable) sun-dried rather than kiln-fired clay.

34 Olympio refers to letters branded on Chalinus as a mark of slavery.

Lysidamus
Punch him in the face, Olympio. Well? How about it?
Olympio
Punch or slap?
Lysidamus
              Your call.
Olympio
                        Take THAT!   405
Cleostrata
Why'd you hit him?
Olympio
                   By order of Jupiter.
Cleostrata (*to Chalinus*)
Hit him right back in the jaw!
Olympio
                              Jupiter, he's pounding me to pieces!
Lysidamus
Why'd you hit this fellow?
Chalinus
                          By order of Juno.
Lysidamus
Not much we can do, if my wife exercises her power.
Cleostrata
Chalinus has every right to speak as much as Olympio does.
Olympio
                                                   Why'd   410
He have to ruin my prayers?
Lysidamus
                           Watch out for more trouble, Chalinus!
Chalinus
Oh, *now* you tell me—after I've been pounded to a pulp!
Lysidamus
                                        Come on now, wife,
Draw the lots! You two pay close attention. I'm so afraid, I've lost my
     bearings!
My heart's palpitating, dancing, pounding and
Absolutely thumping its way right out of my chest!
Cleostrata
                                   I've got a lot.
Lysidamus
                                   Pull it out!   415

Chalinus

Am I done for now?

Olympio

Let's see! It's mine!

Chalinus

Oh, this is pure hell!

Cleostrata

You lose, Chalinus.

Lysidamus

The gods were with us, Olympio!

Yahoo!

Olympio

All thanks to my piety, and that of my distinguished ancestors![35]

Lysidamus

Go inside, wife, and prepare for the wedding!

Cleostrata

As you wish.

Lysidamus

You know it's quite a trip from here to the country villa.

Cleostrata

Yes.   420

Lysidamus

Hard as it is for you, go inside and see that everything is done right.

Cleostrata

Okay.

Lysidamus

Let's both go in too, to move things along faster.

Olympio

I'm not stopping you.

Lysidamus

I don't want to say anything else in his presence.

---

35 Blustery language in the mouth of a slave, who by Roman law was denied parents, let alone distinguished ancestry. Cf. Introduction, p. 21.

SCENE 8

Chalinus is left alone onstage.

Chalinus

    It'd be a waste of energy to hang myself—

    A waste of energy and rope, that is!   425

    I'd just make my enemies happy.

    And what's the point when I'm already as good as dead already?

    The lot did me in and now the foreman's marrying Casina.

    What really bothers me is not his winning

    So much as all the old man's efforts   430

    To have her married to him rather than me!

    That old geezer was so jumpy and nervous,

    And the way he celebrated when the foreman won!

    Ah, the door's opening. I'll sneak over there.

    Well now, my dear old chums are coming out.   435

    I'll just set up a little ambush over here.

SCENE 9

*Olympio and Lysidamus return from inside and Chalinus
eavesdrops.*

Olympio

    Just let him come to the farm! I'll send the guy back to town

    Tied to a cart like a charcoal-hauler!

Lysidamus

    Just as it should be.

Olympio

                 I'll see it's all taken care of.

Lysidamus

    If Chalinus was home, I'd send him with you   440

    Out shopping for food as a way of piling up some

    Additional misery on our defeated foe!

Chalinus (*aside*)

    I'll make like a crab and creep back along the wall,

    To secretly eavesdrop on their conversation.

    One of them tortures me, the other disgusts me!   445

    Look at that low-life all dressed up in white!

    That punching bag! I'll put my own death on hold

    And push him on down to hell ahead of me!

Olympio

Now haven't I served you well, sir? Thanks to me
You've got what you're so hot for! 450
She'll be yours today, and your wife will be none the wiser.

Lysidamus

Shh!
And as the gods are my witness, I can barely keep my lips off you!
I could kiss you so hard, my dear!

Chalinus (*aside*)

What? "Kiss you so hard?" Huh? "My dear?"
I do believe he wants to plow a furrow right into his foreman! 455

Olympio

You do like me a little, don't you?

Lysidamus

Oh, more than I love myself.
Can I hug you?

Chalinus (*aside*)

Huh? Hug him?

Olympio

Okay.

Lysidamus

Holding you is like sipping sweet honey.

Olympio

Uggh! Off my back there, stud!

Chalinus (*aside*)

Oh, so *that's* how he got to be foreman! 460
You know, one night a while back I was escorting the old geezer home
And he tried to make me his butler—by way of my back door!

Olympio

Haven't I been obedient and an absolute delight to you today?

Lysidamus

I'll be better to you than I am to myself for the rest of my life!

Chalinus (*aside*)

Damn! These two will be wrestling together in no time! 465
The old guy has always liked the ones with beards!

Lysidamus

Oh the kisses I'll rain down on Casina today,
The delightfulness, the joy—and my wife won't know a thing!

Chalinus (*aside*)

Ah hah!
Now I'm back in the game!
So *he's* madly in love with Casina. Got ya! 470

Lysidamus
Oh, how I'm itching to hold and kiss her right now!
Olympio
Let her get married first. Damn! What's your rush?
Lysidamus
                                        I'm in love.
Olympio
I don't think that it can be pulled off today.
Lysidamus
                                Oh yes it can—
If you're planning to become a free man tomorrow.
Chalinus (*aside*)
Now they really have my attention!   475
Here's a chance to kill two birds with one stone.
Lysidamus
A place is ready at my friend's house next door.
He knows all about my little affair,
And said he'd provide just the place for it.
Olympio
What about his wife? Where'll she be?
Lysidamus
                                That's all neatly arranged.   480
My wife will call her over for the wedding,
To be with her, help her out, and spend the night.
I told her to do that and she said she would.
So my neighbor will be out of the house and his wife will be sleeping here.
You'll take your wife off to the farm—the "farm" being right next door
   here—   485
So Casina and I can enjoy our wedding night!
Then, tomorrow before dawn you take her to the real farm.
Clever, huh?
Olympio
            Pure genius!
Chalinus (*aside*)
                        Go ahead and plot away,
You'll live to regret your clever scheme!
Lysidamus
Know what you can do now?
Olympio
                        Tell me.
Lysidamus
                        Take this money,   490

And run off and buy some food, but not everyday stuff:
Only the finest delicacies, since she's so delicate herself!

Olympio

Okay.

Lysidamus

Cute little cuttlefish, calamari, and limpets
The finest fish you can find.

Chalinus (*aside*)

Or the fishiest fish, smart-guy!

Lysidamus

And sole.

Chalinus (*aside*)

Just the sole? Please buy a whole shoe 495
To smash your face in with, you worthless old man!

Olympio

Want any catfish?

Lysidamus

No, I've got more than enough of that already at home—
That catty wife of mine who never shuts up!

Olympio

Once I get to the fish market I'll decide
What looks best.

Lysidamus

Fine—now get out of here! 500
Don't worry about the price, and buy plenty!
Now I've got to meet my neighbor over here
To see he does his part for our cause.

Olympio

Can I go now?

Lysidamus

Yes.

Chalinus

Bribe me with my freedom three times over,
And you couldn't stop me from destroying those two today! 505
I'm going to tell my mistress every last detail.
I've caught my enemies red-handed!
If my mistress now is willing to play her part,
The game is ours, and those two will eat my dust!
Luck is on our side! The losers will soon be winners. 510
I'm going inside to add a little different
Spice to what that cook's got simmering.
What he thinks is ready won't be served,
And as for what I'm serving up—he's not ready for it!

SCENE 10

Lysidamus and Alcesimus emerge from Alcesimus' house.

Lysidamus

Now, Alcesimus, we'll see whether you're friend or foe.   515
Now's the time for the ultimate test!
And don't bother lecturing me about my love-life:
"With your grey hair!" "The age difference!"
To say nothing of "A married man!"

Alcesimus

I've never seen a man more disgustingly in love!   520

Lysidamus

Make sure the house is empty.

Alcesimus

                 Yes, Damn it, I told you I'd send
All the male slaves and every last maid over to your house!

Lysidamus

                         You smart, smart man!
But see that they follow the blackbird's song:
"With food and provisions, press on"[36]—as if they were off to the front!

Alcesimus

I won't forget.

Lysidamus

             Great! No degree, but you're smarter than a professor!   525
I'm off to the forum—take care. I'll be right back.

Alcesimus

                         Enjoy the walk.

Lysidamus

Oh, and teach your house the alphabet.

Alcesimus

                 The alphabet?

Lysidamus

                         Yes, especially "M" and "T"!

Alcesimus

Oh, you are so, so witty!

Lysidamus

And why bother being in love if you can't be suave and sophisticated?

---

36   A reference to a Roman army's march to the Etruscan town of Sutrium in the early 4th century
     BCE that had passed into the proverbial, grandiosely applied by Lysidamus to the stream of
     slaves flowing from Alcesimus's house to his own. The role of the blackbird is not clear.

Now don't make me have to come looking for you!

Alcesimus

I'll stay right at home. 530

SCENE 11

Cleostrata comes out of Lysidamus' house
and meets Alcesimus.

Cleostrata

So THIS is why my husband was so insistent that
I run out and invite my neighbor over here!
So he could free up a place for him to enjoy a taste of Casina!
That's why I won't be inviting her! There'll be no such
Opportunity for those impotent old goats! 535
But look who's coming—that pillar of the community, that sentinel of
the senate,
None other than my neighbor, the procurer of my husband's love nest!
He's hardly worth the salt he's made of!

Alcesimus

Odd my wife hasn't been invited next door yet.
She's all dressed up and has been waiting a long time for an invitation. 540
Oh, but look—here it comes! Hello, Cleostrata!

Cleostrata

Hello to you, Alcesimus!
Where's your wife?

Alcesimus

She's inside, waiting for an invitation from you.
Your husband asked me to send her over to help out there.
Should I call her?

Cleostrata

Oh no, not if she's busy.

Alcesimus

She's not.

Cleostrata

Never mind. I don't want to bother her. I'll see her later. 545

Alcesimus

Aren't you preparing for a wedding over there?

Cleostrata

Yes, I'm in charge of it.

Alcesimus

Don't you need help?

Cleostrata

There's plenty of that at home. I'll come see
Her after the wedding. Goodbye—and give her my best.

Alcesimus

What do I do now? Haven't I really disgraced myself now
Because of that utterly worthless and toothless old goat?   550
He dragged me into this and made me promise my wife's services
As if she were a maid! That disgrace of a human being, promising his wife
Would invite her over! And now she says she doesn't need her!
I wouldn't be surprised if the neighbor lady got wind of this.
On the other hand, when I think about it,   555
She'd have made a federal case out of it if she had.
I'll go in and put that old barge of mine back in mothballs.

Cleostrata

Now he's completely confused! The way these old fools fuss about!
If only that worthless and decrepit husband of mine would come
And take a dose of the same medicine as his friend!   560
What I'd really like is to set the two of them off against each other.
Oh, here he comes. What a distinguished look he has! As if he were
    respectable!

SCENE 12

Lysidamus returns from the forum.

Lysidamus (*to the audience*)

The way I see it, what could be more stupid
Than for a man in love to go to the forum
The very day he has his lover ready and waiting?   565
That's exactly how stupid I was, wasting the day
In court helping some damn relative of mine!
And I'm damn pleased to say he lost his case—
That should teach him to drag me into court on a day like today!
To my way of thinking, if you need a lawyer,   570
You'd better ask him first to see
If he's got his wits about him.
And if he says no, just send the witless fellow home!
But look, there's the wife out front. Oh no!
She'd pretty much have to be deaf not to have heard all this.   575

Cleostrata (*aside*)

Oh I heard—and you'll be plenty sorry I did!

Lysidamus

I'll go over to her. How are you, my heart's delight?

Cleostrata

I was just waiting for you.

Lysidamus

Everything all ready now?

Did you bring our neighbor over here

To help you?

Cleostrata

I invited her like you told me to,   580

But your best buddy over there

Had some kind of blow-up with his wife

And refused to send her over to me.

Lysidamus

That's your fault! You should have used some charm!

Cleostrata

Charm is what whores use on other women's husbands,   585

My dear, and is hardly a proper wife's duty!

You can go get her yourself! There are things to do inside

That need my attention, my dearest.

Lysidamus

Get to them then.

Cleostrata

All right.

He's in for a terrible fright, no doubt about it!

I'll see that pervert is utterly miserable today!   590

SCENE 13

Alcesimus emerges from his house.

Alcesimus

Let's see if the old stud is back home from the forum!

The nerve of that loon to make a fool of my wife and me!

Well there he is in front of his house. Hey, I was just coming to see you.

Lysidamus

And I to see you! You're utterly worthless! What do you have to say for
yourself?

What did I TELL you, what did I BEG you to do?

Alcesimus

What's your problem?   595

Lysidamus

Thanks for clearing out your house for me!
And thanks for bringing your wife to our place!
And thanks to you, I'm screwed—and so is my chance with Casina!

Alcesimus

Go screw yourself! Why, you told me your wife
Would invite my wife over to your house.   600

Lysidamus

Yes, she says she invited her, but you said
She couldn't come.

Alcesimus

      Is that so? She told me
Herself that she didn't need her help!

Lysidamus

Is that so? She just told me herself to invite her.

Alcesimus

Is that so? Ask me if I care.

Lysidamus

      Is that so? Oh, you're killing me!

Alcesimus

           Is that so? Good!   605
I'll just hang around for a while. I want to—

Lysidamus

Is that so?

Alcesimus

    —Cause you some trouble!

Lysidamus

        Is that so? I'll return the favor!
But you'll never get the last "Is that so?" in today!

Alcesimus

Is that so? May the gods damn you once and for all!

Lysidamus

Well, are you going to send your wife to my place or not?   610

Alcesimus

You can escort her to hell yourself—the whole bunch of
Them, your wife and your girlfriend included!
Get lost and let me take care of this! I'll tell my wife
To come over to your wife through the garden.

Lysidamus

Now there's a true friend!   615
What in the world could have jinxed my affair?

What could I have done to offend Venus[37] and
Cause a lover like me so many delays?
Hey!
What's all that noise coming from our house? 620

SCENE 14

Pardalisca rushes frantically out of Lysidamus' house.

(*SONG*)

Pardalisca[38]

    I dead, I'm gone, I'm totally dead!
    My heart's in shock, my poor limbs are trembling!
    Where can I find help, shelter, and safety?
    I have no idea even where to look.
    Such strange events I've seen inside— 625
    Boldness, brazenness never seen before!
    Beware, Cleostrata, I beg you flee from her,
    Lest her raging anger destroy you for good!
    She's out of her mind! Snatch the sword away!

Lysidamus

    What's scared her to death and made her run outside like this? 630
    Pardalisca!

Pardalisca

        Alas for me! What sound taketh up residence in my ears?[39]

Lysidamus

    Look back here at me.

Pardalisca

        Oh, master mine—

Lysidamus

        What's wrong?

Pardalisca

        I'm done for!

Lysidamus

    Done for?

Pardalisca

    Yes, and so are you!

---

37   Goddess of love/sex (= Greek Aphrodite).

38   Pardalisca's song here parodies similar entrances by distraught female characters in tragedy.
    Cf. the entrance of Bromia at *Amphitryon* 1053ff.

39   A parody of tragic language.

Lysidamus

What, me? How?

Pardalisca

Alas for you!

Lysidamus

Correction: that should be "alas for *you*."

Pardalisca

Please hold me before I fall!

Lysidamus

Whatever it is, tell me right now!

Pardalisca

Please hold my body,   635-6

And fan me with your cloak!

Lysidamus

Now this's got me nervous!   637-8

Unless she's just been sniffing Bacchus'[40] bouquet (the undiluted variety).

639-40

Pardalisca

Touch my face, hold me ...

Lysidamus

Go to hell!

And take your face, body, and warm breath with you!

If you don't tell me right now what's going on,

I'll take this stick and smash your brains out, you snake!

Bitch! Yanking my chain all this time ...   645

Pardalisca

Oh, my Master!

Lysidamus

Yes, my slave?

Pardalisca

You are too cruel!

Lysidamus

You have no idea!   646-7

Out with it, whatever's going on! Keep it short!

What was all the commotion in there?

Pardalisca

Just listen and I'll tell you.

---

40   Bacchus (= Greek Dionysus) is the god of wine. Ancient wine had a high alcohol content, and
     it was considered uncivilized to drink it without first adding water. The Roman *paterfamilias*
     took great pains to prevent women under his power from consuming alcohol.

It was horrible, absolutely horrible what just happened in our house!   650
Your maid started to behave in a manner
Hardly becoming a young lady raised in Athens!

Lysidamus

What'd she do?

Pardalisca

      Fear's grip has silenced my tongue.

Lysidamus

Any possible way just to tell me what's up?

Pardalisca

          Yes.
Your maid, the one you want the foreman to marry,   655
Inside now she—

Lysidamus

    She did what in there?

Pardalisca

She's chosen the worst possible role model,
She's threatening her husband, his life ...

Lysidamus

Huh?

Pardalisca

Ahhh!

Lysidamus

  What, what?

Pardalisca

     Yes, his life, she means to take his life!
And the sword ...

Lysidamus

    Huh?

Pardalisca

    The sword ...

Lysidamus

       What about the sword?   660

Pardalisca

It's in her hands.

Lysidamus

   Oh no, what for?

Pardalisca

She's on the attack all about the house.
No one can get near her, everybody's cowering
Under chests and beds in all the commotion.

Lysidamus

    That's it. I'm as good as dead!   665

    What illness has taken her so suddenly?

Pardalisca

    Insanity.

Lysidamus

        Who's more screwed than I am?

Pardalisca

    If you only knew what's she's saying

Lysidamus

    I've got to know! What'd she say?

Pardalisca

                Just listen!

    She swore by every god and goddess   670

    To murder the man beside her in bed tonight!

Lysidamus

    Murder ME?

Pardalisca

    Why, none of this has anything to do with you!

Lysidamus

                    Damn!

Pardalisca

    You've no business with her, right?

Lysidamus

            I meant to say "my foreman."   673-4

Pardalisca (*aside*)

    Now he he's really slipped into it!   675

Lysidamus

    There's no threat against me, is there?

Pardalisca

              Her anger's

    Aimed at you more than anyone else.

Lysidamus

           Why?

Pardalisca

             Because she

    Believes you're the one marrying her to Olympio.

    She says neither you nor her husband will last til' daylight.   678-80

    I was sent here to tell you

    To be on guard against her!

Lysidamus

        Oh my, I'm dead now!

Pardalisca (*aside*)

As well you should be!   682-3

Lysidamus (*aside*)

There has there ever been an old lover as
Unlucky as I am!

Pardalisca (*aside*)

I'm just playing with him for the fun of it!   685
Everything I told him happened was pure fiction!
My mistress and the woman next door are running the show,
And I'm here to have some fun with him!

Lysidamus

Hey, Pardalisca!

Pardalisca

Yes?

Lysidamus

There's something—

Pardalisca

What?

Lysidamus

—I want to ask you.

Pardalisca

You're holding me up!

Lysidamus

And you're bringing me down!   690
Now does Casina still have a sword?

Pardalisca

Not exactly—she has two of them!

Lysidamus

Why two?

Pardalisca

One to kill you right away,
And the other's for the foreman.

Lysidamus

Who among the living is as dead as I am!
The best thing for me to do is to put on some body armor!   695
What about my wife? Didn't she walk up to her and take them away?

Pardalisca

Nobody dares to get near her.

Lysidamus

How's about using a little persuasion?

Pardalisca

She has,

But Casina says there's no way in the world she's putting them down
Until she's assured she isn't marrying the foreman.

Lysidamus

Oh she'll marry him today, precisely because she doesn't want to!   700
There's no reason I won't finish what I started,
     And have her me marry me—
     I mean marry the foreman!

Pardalisca

                              You keep slipping up about that.

Lysidamus

It's fear: fear has my tongue all tied up!
But please tell my wife I'm begging   705
Her to beg Casina to put down the sword so I can come back into the house!

Pardalisca

                                          I'll tell her.

Lysidamus

Not just tell her—beg her.

Pardalisca

                      Yes, I'll beg her too.

Lysidamus

                             And in your usual winning way.
Now listen up: if you pull this off, I see a new pair of shoes in your future, a
gold ring for your finger and a whole lot of other good things.   708-12

Pardalisca

                    You've got my attention.

Lysidamus

                    See to it that you succeed!

Pardalisca

                    I'm off right now,   715
If you're done with me.

Lysidamus

                    Get along and do as I say.
Hey, it's my partner-in-crime, back from shopping at long last!
And he's leading a parade!

SCENE 15

*Olympio returns from the forum with Citrio,
his assistants and provisions.*

(*Song*)

Olympio

Hey, sticky-fingers, keep those prickers in line!

Citrio

Why do you call them prickers?   720

Olympio

Because they grab on to everything they touch. Try to take it back and they rip you to pieces! Wherever they're hired, they break their bosses' banks wide open!   721-2

Citrio

Come on!

Olympio

My master! I'll make myself all high and mighty[41] and go meet him!

Lysidamus

Greetings, my good man.

Olympio

I have to agree with you on that.

Lysidamus

What's up?

Olympio

You're horny. I'm hungry and thirsty.   724-5

Lysidamus

Quite a fancy entrance you made there!

Olympio

Ah, indeed, on this day ...

Lysidamus

Now wait a minute, however great you think you are—

Olympio

Pee-yew! The stench that comes out of your mouth![42]

Lysidamus

What's the matter?

---

41 Olympio literally says "in a patrician manner," another clear example of Romanization: see Introduction, pp. 2-3.

42 The old man's foul breath starkly contrasts with the sweet and aromatic scent associated with the young Casina (cf. n. 21 above). Cf. also the reference to a stinking goat in the epilogue (1018).

Olympio

That.

Lysidamus

Stand still.

Olympio

You are such a nuisance!

Lysidamus

I can be a greater nuisance to you,
And I will if you don't stand still.

Olympio

Great Zeus![43]   730

Keep away from me, unless
You want me to puke right now!

Lysidamus

Wait.

Olympio

What now? Who *is* this man?

Lysidamus

Your master.

Olympio

What master?

Lysidamus

The one whose slave you are.

Olympio

Me, a slave?

Lysidamus

Yes, mine.

Olympio

I'm not a free man then?   735

Think, think again—

Lysidamus

Now just stand still!

Olympio

Stop it!

Lysidamus

Okay, I'm *your* slave.

---

43   Cf. n. 29 above. Lysidamus and Olympio here intersperse broken Greek phrases with their
Latin. This apparently was commonly done in colloquial Latin, but there is also playful irony
here in that Athenian characters are made to pepper their Latin with what should be their
native Greek.

Olympio

                 Excellent!

Lysidamus

                        At your service, my dearest Olympio,

My father, my protector ...

Olympio

                    There, now

You're making sense.

Lysidamus

           Yes, I'm all yours.   740

Olympio

What good to me is a slave as worthless as you?

Lysidamus

Come on, when do I get my refreshments?

Olympio

When dinner is cooked!

Lysidamus

Then inside with this crew!

Olympio

Inside now, hurry along, in, in, in with you.   745

I'll be in soon myself. Let's make it a scrumptious feast,

All elegant, and spiffy. I've got no stomach for barbarian[44] gruel![45]   746-7

Still there?

Lysidamus

                You go. I'm staying here.

Olympio

                      What's holding you back?   749-50

Lysidamus

She says Casina has a sword in there and

She plans to kill us both with it!

Olympio

Whatever! Let her have it.

What nonsense! I know those women,

And they're bad apples.   754a

---

44   From the Greek perspective of Plautine plays, "barbarian" or "foreign" (*barbaricus*) by
      convention humorously refers to Romans and Italians.

45   The type of food mentioned is a kind of spinach, exemplary of simple fare. The joke turns
      on both Roman belief in a Greek feeling of cultural superiority (here measured in cuisine),
      and the Romans' own much exaggerated idealization of themselves as simple, practical, and
      frugal in comparison with Greeks. Cf. Hegio's insistence on simple fare in contrast with
      Ergasilus' extravagant culinary ambitions in Scene 2 of *Captivi*.

Come inside the house with me now.

Lysidamus

                            Well, I smell trouble!   755

You go first and check out what's happening in there

Olympio

I value my life just as much as you do yours.

Come along!

Lysidamus

            Okay, if you insist, in it is for both of us.

SCENE 16

Pardalisca reports what is going on inside Lysidamus' house.

Pardalisca

By the gods, I doubt there's ever been a festival at
Olympia or Nemea[46] as fun as the farce   760
Being performed inside at the expense of
Our old master and our foreman Olympio!
They're sprinting all about the house.
The old man is crashing about the kitchen, stirring up the cooks:
"How about today? If you're going to serve it, serve it now!   765
Hurry up! Dinner should already be done."
Meanwhile, the foreman is walking around with a garland,
Decked out in white and sparkling clean.
The two ladies are in the bedroom dressing the son's sidekick
In costume, to give his hand in marriage to our foreman!   770
And everything is so cleverly concealed, as if they didn't know
Exactly how this plot will end! And the cooks are playing their part
Just as smoothly, tipping over pots, dousing out the fire at the ladies'
Direction—all so the old man doesn't get his dinner! The ladies
Want to drive the old man out of the house without that dinner,   775
So they can stuff their stomachs all by themselves.
Those women are a pair of gourmandesses:
They could down a whole boatload of food!
Hey, the door's opening!

---

46   Olympia was the site of athletic contests, i.e. the ancient Olympics, which were part of the
      great festival of Zeus (= Jupiter) there (cf. n. 20 above). Nemea, on the northeast Peloponnese,
      was another of the four major panhellenic religious and athletic festivals, also held in Zeus'
      honor.

SCENE 17

Lysidamus exits his house and meets Pardalisca outside.

Lysidamus (*to Cleostrata inside*)
 I'll get dinner at the farm, my dear, but it makes sense   780
 For you two to dine here once dinner is ready.
 I'll escort the newlyweds to the farm.
 There are a lot of shady characters out there,
 And I don't want any of them grabbing her. Have a nice time.
 Now do send the two of them out right away,   785
 As we must get there before dark. I'll be back tomorrow.
 And tomorrow, my dear, I'll hold a feast here.
Pardalisca (*aside*)
 All's according to plan: the ladies are driving the old man
 Out of the house without dinner!
Lysidamus
        What are you doing here?
Pardalisca
 I'm on a mission for my mistress.
Lysidamus
       Seriously?
Pardalisca
         Seriously.   790
Lysidamus
 You're watching out for something, aren't you?
Pardalisca
        No, not a thing.
Lysidamus
         Move it, damn you!
 Here you are dawdling while everyone else is bustling about inside!
Pardalisca
          I'm going in.
Lysidamus
 Yes, please do, you queen of all the bitches!
 Finally gone? Now I can say what I want.
 By god, a horny man may be hungry, but it's not food he wants!   795
 Hey, look, here comes the foreman with garland and torch:
 My comrade, my colleague, my co-husband!

SCENE 18

Olympio steps out of Lysidamus' house.

Olympio

Come now, flute-player! When they bring the new bride out here,
Fill this whole street with the sweet sound of my wedding song,
                    Hymen, O Hymen, O Hymenaeus![47]   800

Lysidamus

How goes it, my savior?

Olympio

                    I'm really starved and there's no salvation in that!

Lysidamus

And I'm madly in love!

Olympio

                    And I really don't care at all. Love! You're full of it!
My guts have been grumbling from emptiness all day!

Lysidamus

Now just what is keeping those slowpokes in there so long?
It's intentional: the more I hurry them, the less progress I make!   805

Olympio

How's about I strike up the wedding song again? That'll bring them out.

Lysidamus

Okay, and I'll accompany you, seeing as we're co-bridegrooms!

Lysidamus & Olympio

Hymen, O Hymen, O Hymenaeus!

Lysidamus

Poor, poor miserable me! I may rip my gut open singing that
Wedding song before I get a chance to rip open what I really want.   810

Olympio

By god, if you were a stallion, there'd be no way to tame you!

Lysidamus

How's that?

Olympio

                    You're way too hard to handle.

Lysidamus

                                        But you've never even tried to.

Olympio

Uggh! May the gods forbid! Wait, the door's creaking. They're coming out.

---

47   A Greek wedding refrain. Hymen or Hymenaeus came to be thought of as a personified god
      of weddings.

Lysidamus

Oh, so the gods really are on my side!

SCENE 19

The "wedding" party (Chalinus, Pardalisca, Olympio,
Lysidamus, Cleostrata) moves out onstage.

(SONG)
Pardalisca

He-Casina has given off a stench from far away!
Gently lift your feet above the threshold, my new bride;   815
Safely start this journey,
And tread upon your husband always!
May all power preside in you to crush and defeat him,   819-20
Your voice, your command perched high to beat him!   821-2
His job is to fill your closets, yours to empty his pockets!
Strive to deceive him, both night and day!⁴⁸

Olympio

The slightest slip-up and she'll be sorry!   825

Lysidamus

Shut up!

Olympio

No!

Lysidamus

What's your problem?

Olympio

A nasty woman's giving nasty advice!

Lysidamus

You'll destroy everything I've worked for!
Can't you see that's what they want?

Pardalisca

Come now, Olympio,
Take her from us, as you want to.   830

Olympio

Give her to me right now, if you're ever going to give her to me.

Lysidamus

Inside with you then!

---

48   Pardalisca parodies wedding ritual here by turning the Roman ideal of a wife's subservience
and obedience to her husband on its head.

Cleostrata

                        Please be gentle with this gentle virgin.

Olympio
   Yeah, sure.
   Goodbye.

Lysidamus

              Go, go on now.

Cleostrata

                        Goodbye, then.

Lysidamus
   Is my wife gone yet?

Olympio

                  No need to worry—she's inside.

Lysidamus

                                             Woohoo!   835
   A free man at last now!
   My little sweetheart, my honey-bun, my sweet breath of fresh-air.

Olympio

                                                        Hey,
   You're cruisin' for a bruisin'!
   She's mine!

Lysidamus

              Yes, but I get the first pickings.

Olympio
   Hold this torch.

Lysidamus

              No, I prefer to hold her.   840
   Mighty Venus, what a gift you granted me when
   You granted me to hold her!

Olympio

                        Oh,
   Your sweet little body, so soft,
   My teeny-weeny wifey-poo. Ow! What the …

Lysidamus

              What's the matter?

Olympio

                        She just stomped on my foot   845
   Like an elephant!

Lysidamus

                  Quiet now!
   Her breasts are softer than a cloud.

Olympio

What a pretty little nipple—Ouch!

Lysidamus

What's the matter?

Olympio

She smacked me in the chest. And it was a battering ram, not an elbow!

Lysidamus

Why are you so rough when you touch her?   850
Try making love to her, not war, just like me.
Ouch!

Olympio

What's the matter?

Lysidamus

Damn, she's strong!
She almost knocked me out.

Olympio

Now that you mention knocking her up …

Lysidamus

Why don't we just go in then.

Olympio

Come along, my pretty little pretty!

SCENE 20

Myrrhina, Pardalisca, and Cleostrata
come out of Lysidamus' house.

Myrrhina

Such fine and fitting entertainment inside!   855
We're out here on the street now to watch the wedding festival.
My goodness, I've never laughed so much in my life
And doubt I'll ever laugh like that again!

Pardalisca

I so want to know what the new He-bride is doing with his new husband!

Myrrhina

No playwright has ever devised a better   860
Plot than this clever production of ours!

Cleostrata

Oh, to see the old man come out with his brains beaten in!
Surely he's earned the title "world's most worthless old man:"
Not even his pimp of a neighbor

Can challenge him for that. 865

* * * *

* * * *

Take up a position here, Pardalisca,
To mock whichever man comes out.

Pardalisca

It'll be my pleasure, as always!

Cleostrata

Watch them from here and tell us everything they do in there! 870-1
Right behind me now, dear.

Myrrhina

Right, so then you can speak
Out as brashly as you want.

Cleostrata

Quiet!
The door creaked.

SCENE 21

*Olympio rushes out of Lysidamus' house
and joins the women onstage.*

(SONG)
Olympio

I've got nowhere to run, nowhere to hide, and nowhere to hide
my shame! 875
This disgraceful marriage of ours! My master and I have really
done it
This time! I don't know if I'm more ashamed or more afraid,
But I do know the two of us are laughingstocks! This idiocy is all new to me,
I'm
Ashamed to admit I've never been so shamed before this. Listen up and I'll
go over
What happened to me, the whole mess I made inside, complete farce that it
was! 880
But it's well worth your trouble to listen to. I led my new bride inside and
took her straight
To the backroom. It was as dark in there as if we'd fallen down a well.
The old man was off somewhere, so I say to her "lie down!"
I get her situated, prop her up, talk real sweet to her,
(Wanting so badly to beat the old man to the first fruits). 885
I started slow since I was constantly on guard for him.
I ask her for a little kiss, and a little foreplay.

But she pushed my hand away
And didn't even let me kiss her!
Now I start to hurry things up, as I'm really hot for a piece of Casina!   890-1
I decide that's *my* duty, not the old man's, and so I bolt the door to keep him
    from taking me by surprise.   892-3

Cleostrata
Come on, go up to him now.

Pardalisca
             Now where's that new bride of yours?

Olympio
Damn, I'm dead! She knows everything!

Pardalisca
                  Then you'd better come clean   895
With all the details.
          What's going on in there? What's Casina doing?
So is she obeying your every wish?

Olympio
              I'm too ashamed to say.

Pardalisca
                   Come on, the details,
   just as you started.   897-8

Olympio
      No, no, I'm so ashamed!

Pardalisca
               Suck it up!   899-900
Tell me what happened after you got into bed.

Olympio
It's disgraceful!

Pardalisca
      It'll be a good lesson for everyone here to hear.

Olympio
It's all so …

Pardalisca
    Stop stalling. Continue.

Olympio
           When I reach down there …

Pardalisca
Yes?

Olympio
  Uggh!   904-5

Pardalisca
Yes?

Olympio

    Horrible!

Pardalisca

What was it?

Olympio

    It was huge …

I was afraid she had a sword. I started to look for it,

And as I'm groping around for the sword, I get hold of a handle.

But I realized it was no sword—the shaft would have been colder.   910

Pardalisca

Keep going!

Olympio

    I can't, I'm ashamed.

Pardalisca

        It wasn't a radish now, was it?

Olympio

            No.

Pardalisca

            How about a cucumber?

Olympio

No, it definitely wasn't any kind of vegetable at all!

Whatever is was, it'd never suffered any kind of crop damage.

    All I can say is, it was full-grown …

Pardalisca

Then what happened? Details!

Olympio

        Then I say to her, "please, Casina,   915-6

My little wifey-poo, please don't reject your husband like this.   917-8

    It's so unfair to treat me this way,

    After all I did to get you."   920

She says not a word and wraps her clothes tightly around that thing

Only you women have. When I see that pass is blocked,

I request to come in by another route. I want to turn her over

With my arms. Still not a peep out of her.

I start to move up for a …   925

And then she …

Myrrhina

What a charming story!

Olympio

… for a kiss and …

A bristly beard pricks my lips!

I jumped right up on my knees, and she bashes my chest with both of

    her feet!   930

I fall headfirst from the bed, she jumps down and starts pounding my face!
So without saying a word I got up and ran, all the worse for the wear,
And thinking I'd let the old man have a taste of that same medicine.

Pardalisca

Fantastic!

But where's your little cloak?

Olympio

I left it inside there.

Pardalisca

Well now, is that enough trickery for the two of you?

Olympio

Yeah,   935

We deserved it. Hey, the doors creaked. She better not still be after me!

SCENE 22

Lysidamus runs out of his house.

(Song)
Lysidamus

Oh, the disgrace! I'm burning with shame,
I've got no idea what to do in this mess,
Nor how I can look my wife in the face—
I'm so dead!   940
All my disgrace is out in the open, all of poor me
Is totally dead!
My wife has me by the throat, caught red-handed,
No possible way to clear myself.
Poor, poor cloak-less me,   945
Thanks to my not-so-secret nuptials!
The way I see it,
It's best to face my wife,
To go inside the house
And offer her my hide for punishment!   950
Anyone of you care to fill in for me there?
There's no hope for my shoulders inside of that house.   952-3
Apart from playing the bad slave and hitting the road,
I'm fresh out of ideas.   955
Think that's all nonsense?
Truth of it is, I'll be beaten:
I may deserve it but that doesn't mean I like it!
I think I'll just take off this way—

Chalinus

    Hey, stop right there, lover!   960

Lysidamus

    I'm dead! Someone's calling me. Better pretend I didn't hear—   961-2

SCENE 23

Chalinus joins the group onstage.

Chalinus

    Just where do you think you're going, my Greek-loving friend?

    If you're planning to mount me, now's the time!

    Please come back to bed. Oh, you are so dead!   965

    I have a little extra-judicial justice for you: this stick of mine is a stickler
       for punishment.

Lysidamus (*aside*)

    Yes, I am dead! This guy and his club are aiming to rip the skin right off
       my back!

    That's a one-way street to an ass-cracking! I'd better go this way

Cleostrata

    A very good day to you, lover.

Lysidamus (*aside*)

                  Oh no, my wife!

    Stuck right between a rock and a hard place,[49] and nowhere to run!   970

    Wolves on the left, dogs on the right! And the wolf has a club!

    Damn! I'd better reverse the proverb,

    And go this way along the path of the bitch!

Myrrhina

    What are you up to, bigamist?

Cleostrata

               What happened to you, dear husband?

    What have you done with your stick? And where is your cloak?   975

Myrrhina

    I do believe he lost them while he was boffing Casina!

Lysidamus

    I'm so dead.

Chalinus

          Aren't we going to bed? I'm Casina.

Lysidamus

                  Go to hell!

---

49   The Latin proverb here is "between the sacrificial victim and the knife."

Chalinus

    I thought you loved me?

Cleostrata

               Now answer me: what happened to your cloak?

Lysidamus

    I swear, my dear, some Bacchants[50]—

Cleostrata

                   Bacchants?

Lysidamus

                         Yes dear, right, Bacchants—

Myrrhina

                                  Lies,

And he knows it! There most certainly aren't any Bacchic rites now![51]

Lysidamus

                         Right, I forgot.   980

    Still, the Bacchants…

Cleostrata

               What about the Bacchants?

Lysidamus

                      Well if that's impossible—

Cleostrata

    My, my, you're terrified.

Lysidamus

           Me afraid? Nonsense!

Cleostrata

                   You're terribly pale!   982

Lines 983-990 are almost entirely obliterated; Lysidamus presumably continues to ineptly defend himself.

Olympio

    It's *his* shamefulness that made a miserable joke out of me!   991

Lysidamus

    Shut up!

---

50   Female worshippers of Bacchus (Dionysus). See further n. 51 below.

51   The Roman senate outlawed the worship of Bacchus in 186 BCE. The reference to their emergency resolution here dates the play to sometime shortly after this event, i.e., at a very late stage of Plautus's career. See further Introduction, pp. 13-14.

Olympio

I most certainly will not! You begged
And begged me to marry Casina,
All because of your lust!

Lysidamus

I did that?

Olympio

NO, it was Hector of Troy![52]   994-5

Lysidamus

Yeah? Well, he would have banged you up. Did I really do what you say?

Cleostrata

Do you even have to ask?

Lysidamus

If I did those things, I did wrong.

Cleostrata

Go back into the house. I'll be there soon to refresh your memory.

Lysidamus

Not necessary: I'll take your word for it.
But, my dear, do forgive your husband. And ask her to, Myrrhina.   1000
If ever in the future I lust after Casina, or just start to lust after her,
Or if from now on I do anything of this sort, you have the right
To hang me up and give me a good whipping, my dear.

Myrrhina

I think you should forgive him, Cleostrata.

Cleostrata

All right, I will.
But the only reason I'm going to forgive him   1005
Is that this play is long and I don't want to make it any longer.

Lysidamus

You're not mad?

Cleostrata

No.

Lysidamus

I can trust you on that?

Cleostrata

Yes you can.

Lysidamus

Does anyone in the world have a more sensible wife than mine?

---

52   Trojan hero killed by Achilles in the *Iliad*. Olympio is stressing the absurdity of Lysidamus'
claim of innocence.

Cleostrata

All right, give him his stick and cloak back.

Chalinus

Here, they're all yours.

But, damn it, this new bride's been terribly wronged!   1010
I married two men, and neither did me his husbandly duty!

EPILOGUE[53]

Spectators, here's what will happen inside:
It'll be discovered that this Casina is the neighbor's daughter
And she'll marry our young master, Euthynicus.[54]
Now the right thing for you to do is to give us the thundering applause   1015
We so richly deserve. Those who do will win the whore of their dreams
(and the wife will be none the wiser).[55] Those who don't applaud as loudly as
     possible,
Will take a he-goat bathed in sewer-water[56] to bed instead!

---

53   It is unclear who delivers the epilogue—Chalinus, who last spoke, or the leader of the troupe
      (cf. n. 1 above)?

54   The process of revealing Casina's true identity probably constituted an entire (recognition)
      scene in Diphilus that is suppressed by Plautus. Cf. n. 10 above.

55   Though the play has adopted a surprisingly feminist perspective, the epilogist's joke here
      signals a return to more conventional gender relations between husbands and wives. Cf.
      Introduction, pp. 10-14.

56   Cf. the foul odor associated with Lysidamus at 727.

Amphitryon

Characters with Speaking Parts

MERCURY, *Olympian god and son of Jupiter*
SOSIA, *slave of Amphitryon*
JUPITER (JOVE), *chief Olympian god and Alcmena's lover*
ALCMENA, *wife of Amphitryon*
AMPHITRYON, *Theban general and head of the household*
BLEPHARO, *captain of Amphitryon's ship*
BROMIA, *Alcmena's personal slave ("maidservant")*

SCENE

Thebes: in front of Amphitryon's house, which has two storeys and may look like a palace.

PROLOGUE

Mercury[1]

Inasmuch as you want me to aid and assist you
With all your buying and selling,
Whenever you're hustling and bustling,
And inasmuch as you want the affairs
Of all your family and friends to succeed   5
(At Rome or away from home),

---

1 Mercury (= Greek Hermes) was a god of boundaries, who for the Romans oversaw commerce, travel and the transfer of messages, including those from gods to mortals.

And inasmuch as you want me to shower you and yours
With good news both for now and for ever,
And favorable messages for all your affairs,
(You all know the other gods have   10
Made me prince of profits and reports),[2]
And inasmuch as you want me to lavish my labors
On lining your pockets with endless lucre—
Accordingly I say, accordingly and forthwith
I request that you keep quiet for the sake of this play   15
And act as just and fair critics today![3]
Now then, why I'm here and who sent me:
I'll tell you that and tell you my name.
I'm Mercury and Jupiter[4] is why I came.
Yes, I'm here as Jupiter's ambassador.   20
His power is so great he figured you'd do
Whatever he told you—we all know how much
You fear and revere him, seeing he's Jove—
But he decided to have me win you over
With winning words, not threats.   25
The fact of the matter is, the Jove who sent me
Fears a flogging as much as you or yours truly.[5]
Small wonder he's afraid for his hide,
Since his father's no god, his mother's no goddess!
And I'm also afraid for my back side—   30
Through guilt by association with dear old dad.
That being so, I come in peace to help piece this together:
It's a just and simple matter I seek,
As I plead out of justice to people just like you.

---

2   The audience probably now realizes Mercury's identity. He does not reveal his name until
     19, though some may have already guessed it from the clues given in his preceding lines. He
     appears in the costume and mask of a comic slave, in imitation of his double Sosia, but the
     traveler's hat (see 143) he wears belongs to the god's iconography, and so provided a visual
     clue as to his identity as well.

3   In delivering this legalistic prologue, Mercury cleverly plays on his divine identity. Roman
     religion was contractual, with the worshipper's attitude toward a god being summarized by
     the formula *do ut des*, "I give (offerings) so that you may give (to me)." Mercury—really here
     as the promoter of the acting troupe and play—in lines 1-16 restates the religious formula
     from a god's perspective: "If you give the play a fair hearing, I'll continue to support you."

4   Jupiter (= Jove and Greek Zeus) was the most powerful of the Olympian gods.

5   Actors in Roman were usually slaves (see Introduction, p. 6) and so could be beaten for a bad
     performance. Mercury here playfully and metatheatrically (see Introduction, pp. 8-10) steps
     out of character to identify himself and Jupiter as slave-actors in real life.

It's just wrong to seek justice from the unjust,   35
And it's just plain silly to expect anything but injustice from those
Who know little of justice and even less of how to justify it.
Confused? Now everyone pay close attention to what I have to say!
Our wishes should be *your* wishes.
You and the state owe father and me: 40
Need I mention—as those other gods in the tragedies,[6]
Neptune,[7] Virtue,[8] Victory, Mars,[9] Bellona,
Who constantly remind you of every little thing they've done for you—
All the good deeds my father has accomplished for you,
My father, ruler of the gods, master of the universe?   45
No, it's not my father's style to parade his good deeds
Before the good people he's done them for!
No, he's grateful for your gratitude, and
Thinks you get exactly what you deserve.
Now first listen up to what I've come to ask,   50
And then I'll reveal the plot of this tragedy—
Did I say tragedy? Are you frowning at that word tragedy?
Okay, I'll change it, seeing as I'm a god:
I'll make this same play a comedy instead of a tragedy,
Without changing any of the lines.   55
Comedy or not? What do you want?
Silly me! As if I didn't know what you wanted!
I can read your minds exactly, seeing as I'm a god!
I'll just mix it up: let's call it "tragicomedy."[10]
It's not right to call it straight comedy   60
When you've got important people and gods onstage.
And so, seeing there's a slave's part,
Let's call it, as I just said, a tragicomedy.
Now here's the special favor Jupiter wants me to ask you:
Police officers are to be placed among you all,   65
In every row of the theater,

---

6   Mercury refers to patriotic appeals made by divine prologists of Roman tragedies, no
     examples of which survive among the fragments of early Roman tragedy.

7   Neptune (= Greek Poseidon), god of horses and the sea, was an Italic god of water in origin.

8   An example, as also Victory (= Greek Nike), of Roman religion's penchant for personifying
     and deifying abstractions. There were temples and shrines of both *Virtus* and *Victoria*.

9   Chief Roman god of war (= Greek Ares). Bellona similarly was a Roman goddess of war who
     had a temple on the Campus Martius, where formal declarations of war were made.

10   Plautus coins the word *tragicomoedia* here to describe a mythical burlesque (see Introduction,
     p. 15), not to indicate that the play will combine tragedy with comedy.

And if they catch any plants out there,[11]
They are to impound their togas on the spot!
Likewise, if anyone has campaigned for any actor or artisan,
Either by letter, in person, or intermediary,   70
Or if it turns out that the aediles[12]
Award the palm unfairly, Jove declares
The very same law to apply as applies
To those who bribe their way to high office.
He firmly believes you prevail by merit,   75
Not by bribery, and not by trickery:
The same holds for the great man *and* the actor!
You all should succeed by merit, not through lobbyists,
And merit is always earned by honest acts—
As long as the judges in question are fair.   80
Now here's another favor Jupiter requested:
Police officers are to be assigned to the actors,
And if anyone has planted someone out there for himself
Or hired others to boo a fellow actor,
His costume's to be trashed and he's to be thrashed!   85
Now I don't want you wondering (stop it now!)
Why Jove has taken a sudden interest in acting:
Yes, he'll be appearing in person in this comedy.
You're not surprised, are you?
As if it were unusual for Jove to act in a play!   90
Why, just last year he came onstage[13]
When the actors called to him for help.

                              * * * *

In this play, right here today, I say,
Jove will perform, and so will I!   95
Now pay attention while I lay out this comedy's plot.
Over here is Thebes. Amphitryon lives right there.
He was born an Argive from an Argive father.

---

11   Judging from Mercury's extended legal parody here, there was a competition for best actor at
     the Roman festivals and the audience had a say in the judging, but we do not know any of the
     details.

12   Roman magistrates (see Introduction, pp. 5-6) whose duties included sponsorship and
     administration of the festivals.

13   Jupiter presumably appeared in a Roman tragedy as a *deus ex machina*, i.e., as "the god from
     a machine" who magically appears to resolve conflicts and tie up loose ends at the end of a
     play. Jupiter in fact will play this role in *Amphitryon* (1131-43).

He's married to Alcmena, Electryon's daughter. [14]
Amphitryon's currently commanding an army   100
Since the Thebans and Teleboans[15] are at war.
Before he went away on campaign
He got his wife Alcmena pregnant.
Now you all know how my father is,
How uncontrollable he is in these matters, and   105
How he gets carried away when something catches his eye!
He's hooked up with Alcmena without her husband knowing:
In other words, he's "borrowed" her body for his private use.
They've shared a bed and now she's pregnant by him too.
Got it straight about Alcmena?   110
She's pregnant by both her husband and by mighty Jove![16]
My father's cuddled up in bed with her right now,
And so the night's been lengthened for him[17]
To have his way some more with the woman he's so hot for.
What's more, he's disguised as Amphitryon.   115
Now don't be wondering at this get-up of mine,
And my coming out here in a slave's costume.
It's only natural I wear something novel
When we're presenting an old and hackneyed story fresh.
So my father Jove's right there inside now,   120
And he's made himself into the spitting image of Amphitryon,
And every slave who sees him thinks it's his master.
He's quite the magician when he wants to be!
I've taken on the appearance of Sosia,
The slave who went off on campaign with Amphitryon.   125
In his get-up, I'll slave it for my love-struck father,

---

14   In the oldest surviving version of the Greek myth, Amphitryon, a native of Argos on the
     Peloponnese in Greece, kills Alcmena's father Electryon in a dispute over oxen and then
     marries Alcmena. The couple flees to Thebes, where Alcmena refuses to consummate the
     marriage until Amphitryon avenges the death of her brothers at the hand of the Teleboans
     (and Taphians). Zeus subsequently visited Alcmena and impregnated her on the very night
     Amphitryon returned from his campaign against the Teleboans.

15   The Teleboae inhabited islands off the cost of Acarnania on the western Greek mainland, and
     were believed to have colonized the island of Capri.

16   She will give birth to the great hero and eventual Olympian god Hercules (Jupiter's son)
     and Iphicles (Amphitryon's mortal son). The male actor playing Alcmena apparently wore
     a costume reflecting her advanced pregnancy with the twins, as Alcmena's condition and
     appearance are frequently the butt of jokes: see Introduction, pp. 15-16.

17   The folktale motif behind the lengthened night is that the conception of a hero as powerful as
     Hercules (= Greek Herakles) requires prolonged sexual intercourse.

That way avoiding questions about who I am
As I hustle and bustle about the house here.
Now, being a slave just like the others,
No one will ask who I am or what I'm up to.   130
So father's inside, indulging his desire,
All wrapped around the woman he wants so badly!
He's telling Alcmena all that happened in the war.
She thinks he's her husband, not the lech he really is!
My father's in there right now chatting her up,   135
Telling her how he blew the enemy troops away
And all about the awards he won. By the way,
We've absconded with those very awards:
What my father wants, my father gets.
Okay, so today Amphitryon comes home from the war,   140
Along with the slave I'm impersonating.
And so you can tell us all apart,
I'll keep these feathers on my hat,[18]
And my father will have a tassel on his
(Amphitryon won't have one on his hat).   145
These items will be invisible to the entire household,
But all of you will see them clear as day.
But wait! There's Amphitryon's slave Sosia.
Coming right from the harbor with a lantern in hand.
My job's to drive him away.   150
Now pay close attention! It'll be well worth your while
To watch Jove and Mercury running the show here!

SCENE 1

Sosia enters from the harbor, carrying a lantern
to signify it is nighttime.

(*SONG through 262*)
Sosia

Who can match my daring and my determination, I who boldly walk alone
In the dead of night, when all the young thugs are out and about?
But what could I do if the cops tossed me in a cell?   155
Sealed up like a bottle of wine, I'd be uncorked tomorrow—for a beating!
No chance to plead my case, no chance of master's help,

---

18   The hat here (*petasus*) is a broad-brimmed hat worn by travelers, and so in the play it is worn
     by Mercury, Sosia, Amphitryon, and Jupiter.

Everyone assuming I just plain deserved it.
Eight big, strong guys would beat on me like an anvil!

*   *   *   *   160

    This is a fine public welcome for a traveler from abroad!
It's all because of master's unreasonableness that I'm here,
      Roused out of bed at the harbor
        Completely against my will!
He couldn't have sent me to do this in the morning?   165
      Slaving it for a rich man is rough enough.
      What makes it worse is
Night and day it never stops,
Always something to do, something to say, no chance to rest.
But your rich master doesn't lift a finger   170
Except to point you to a job that suits his fancy.
Not a thought about fairness, no second thought about the work.
He doesn't even consider whether the command is fair or not!
There's just a whole lot of injustice in being a slave,
An endless burden to bear and bear …   175

Mercury (*aside*)
    I'm the one who should be griping!
    Just today I was free
    And now my father's enslaved me![19]
    But this uppity slave's the one complaining.

Sosia
I really am an uppity slave![20] And a human punching bag too!   180
Did I even think to thank the gods for my safe arrival?
No, I really deserve a whipping,
Or to have somebody rearrange my face—
That would be my just desert.

Mercury
How strange—a human who knows exactly what he deserves!   185

Sosia
What I never expected, what nobody dreamed of has happened!
We made it back, safe and sound!

---

19   Mercury's jest would have special resonance for an audience in Rome, where the
      paterfamilias (see Introduction, pp. 20-21) could lawfully sell his children into slavery.

20   Sosia unrealistically picks up on Mercury's designation of him as an "uppity slave" (Latin
      verna, which refers to a slave born in the master's house and so of a higher status than slaves
      purchased on the market: see Introduction, p. 21), which as an aside he is not supposed to
      hear. Strict realism is generally not a goal of Plautine theater (see Introduction, p. 5).

The war's over, our victorious army is coming home,
The enemy's totally slaughtered![21]
The enemy stronghold that spelled bitter death for Thebes   190
Is crushed and defeated by our soldiers' courage and strength,
All under the brave command of my master Amphitryon!
He's lavished loot, land, and glory on his men,
And secured King Creon's[22] throne at Thebes.
The reason he sent me home from the harbor   195
Was to tell his wife how his leadership has saved the state.
I should practice what I'll tell her when I get there:
If I mix in a lie or two, well—that's just my usual way.
Actually, the moment they started to fight, I started from sight!
But I'll pretend I was there and tell her what I heard.   200
Now to put together just the right pack of lies,
I think I'll rehearse here first. Here goes:
When we got there, as soon as we touched the shore,
Amphitryon selects some men, real *crème de la crème*!
He makes them legates and has them tell the Teloboans the following: 205
"If you willingly and peacefully hand over plunder and plunderers,
If you restore all you have taken away, Amphitryon will immediately
Return home, together with all the Argives, and peace will be yours;
But if you do not intend to return what he demands,
He will overcome you with all his might and manpower."   210
After they conveyed this message word for word, the Teleboans,
Fully confident in their own courage and strength
Scoffed at our legates with disdain,
And said they were fully capable of defending themselves,
And ordered our army out of their land.[23]   215
This report received, Amphitryon
Marshals his troops immediately. The enemy
Does the same, decked out in shining armor.
    A full force is arrayed on each side,
    Men at their stations, ranks all in order,   220
    Our own legions adroitly drawn up,

---

21   What follows is a brilliant parody of tragic messenger speeches, which in tragedy relate
      events that would be difficult to stage. Sosia's speech is thoroughly Romanized (see
      Introduction, p. 2), both in its poetic style and its ideology of war.

22   Creon ("Ruler" in Greek) is a generic name for a king in Greek myth and tragedy.

23   The mythic situation is recast in terms of Roman imperialist ideology, specifically the
      concept of *bellum iustum* or "just war," according to which war was only to be undertaken
      from a defensive posture in response to foreign aggression and arrogance.

Face to face with those of the enemy.
Then the two generals meet in the middle,
And hold a conference between the ranks.
They agree that whoever loses the battle   225
Must surrender homes, fields, hearths, and themselves.
That decided, the trumpets sound on each side.
The earth rumbles, shouts are raised from both sides.
Both generals pray to Jove,
Both rally their troops to valor.   230
Every warrior then gives forth all he's got,
Swords clash, spears shatter, the whole sky
    Resounds with groans of men, their furious panting
    Forms a fog, men fall in a flurry of wounds![24]
Finally, our prayers are answered, we begin to win!   235
We press all the harder as the enemy drops in droves!
    Our fierce warriors prevail perforce!
Not a single man flees or is afraid,
Not a one gives his ground once it's gained!
They leave this life before leaving their post: 240
Even in death they all keep their ranks.
My master Amphitryon surveys the scene
And sends in the cavalry from the right.
Swiftly they follow his order
    And swoop in with a screaming assault,   245
Trampling and tearing apart the enemy troops,
    A justified slaughter![25]

Mercury (*aside*)

Not an ounce of fiction to this point!
I was right there (so was my father) throughout the battle.

Sosia

The enemy plunges into flight, we take courage: 250
The backs of the fleeing Teleboans bristle with spears!
Amphitryon slaughters King Pterelas by his own hand.[26]
    The battle raged on from dawn to dusk

---

24   Sosia here echoes the language of early Roman epic poetry.

25   According to the ideology of "just war" (cf. n. 23 above), defeat of the enemy was taken as
    proof that the gods were on the Romans' side and that the cause for undertaking war had
    indeed been just.

26   The highest award, the *spolia opima*, a Roman general could receive was earned when he
    killed the enemy commander in single combat. Roman tradition maintained that the award
    was bestowed only three times, the first instance being that of the mythical founder Romulus.

(I remember exactly because I missed lunch),
And only the blackness of night could put it to rest.   255
The next day their leaders came to our camp crying,
With olive branches in hand they plea for mercy,
Surrendering themselves, their city, their children,
All things sacred and other, to the will of us Thebans.
Next Amphitryon was awarded a golden bowl for his valor,   260
One their king used to get drunk with. That's what I'll say.
So off I go to carry out master's orders.

Mercury (*aside*)
Ah yes, on his way here! I'll greet him all right,
Though he won't enter the house tonight!
Now that we look the same, he's easy game: 265
I've taken his appearance, taken his look,
Time to take his way of doing things too.
I've got to be crafty, clever, utterly cunning—
That way I'll drive him away by his own devices.
But wait—he's looking up at the sky. Now what's he up to?   270

Sosia
Damn straight! If there's anything I know for sure,
It's that Night has passed out drunk tonight!
The Big Bear hasn't budged a bit,
The Moon hasn't moved since she rose,
Orion, Pleiades, Evening Star—all dead still: 275
No movement, no sign of night giving way to day!

Mercury (*aside*)
Keep it up, Night, indulge my father's desires:
Fine work in fine fashion for the finest god, and a fine investment of effort!

Sosia
I've never seen a longer night than this one,
Except maybe that one I spent being whipped and strung up.   280
But this one seems even longer.
I'm sure the Sun's asleep and totally tanked.
I wouldn't be surprised if he hoisted a few too many at dinner!

Mercury (*aside*)
Is that so, punching bag? You think the gods are like you?
I'll give you just the welcome you deserve, scumbag!   285
Do please come over here and face your fate.

Sosia

Where are those horny dudes who hate an empty bed?[27]

What a perfect night for a romp with a high-priced whore!

Mercury (*aside*)

My father's got that right—lying in bed

With his ladyfriend Alcmena, indulging his every desire!   290

Sosia

Time to tell Alcmena master's news …

Hey, who's that guy standing by the house—at this time of night? I don't
    like this!

Mercury (*aside*)

Have you ever seen such a coward?

Sosia (*aside*)

                           It seems that

This guy may want to tear me and my cloak to pieces!

Mercury (*aside*)

He's so scared! Time to have some fun with him.

Sosia

                     I've had it—my teeth are t-t-tingling!   295

I'm sure he's going to greet me with his fists.

Maybe he's merciful? Nice of master to make me stay up—

And just as nice of him and his fists to put me to sleep!

I'm so dead! My god, he's big and strong!

Mercury (*aside*)

I'll speak out aloud so he can hear every word.   300

That way I'll really, really scare him!

All right, fists! It's been a long time since you had your fill.

Seems an eternity since you knocked those four guys out cold.

Sosia (*aside*)

                        I've a strong suspicion

My name's about to be changed from Sosia to Quintus:[28]   305

He said he's already clocked four guys

Looks like my number is next.

Mercury

                There now, just right!

---

27   A direct appeal to the males in the audience, as the opening formula *ubi sunt* … ("Where are
     the …") shows.

28   *Quintus* is a common Roman first name (*praenomen*) and is spelled the same as the word
     meaning "fifth."

Sosia (*aside*)
Oh, oh, he's all girded up for battle.
Mercury
                                        No way he avoids a whipping.
Sosia (*aside*)
Who?
Mercury
         Whoever comes this way gets a knuckle sandwich.
Sosia (*aside*)
No thanks, I'm full and I don't normally eat this time of night.   310
Better to save *that* for somebody hungry.
Mercury
Pretty good punch I pack here.
Sosia (*aside*)
                                   Oh no, now he's packing punches!
Mercury
What about a nice long treatment to put his lights out?
Sosia (*aside*)
                                        You'd be doing me a favor,
Since I haven't slept in three nights.
Mercury (*shadow boxing*)
                              Wrong!
Now who taught you fists to hit like that?   315
Just a slight graze and your victim should get a complete makeover!
Sosia (*aside*)
Oh, no, that's one face job I don't need.
Mercury
Properly, the face should be filleted, like a fish.
Sosia (*aside*)
Now he wants to fillet me like an eel!
Damn this people-filleter! I'm dead if he sees me!   320
Mercury
I smell a run of bad luck for somebody.
Sosia (*aside*)
                                   Oh, oh I smell?
Mercury
And it's right here, though it used to be far, far away.
Sosia (*aside*)
This guy's a wizard!
Mercury
                         My fists are raging to go.

Sosia (*aside*)
How about having them rage against the wall, not me?
Mercury
A voice wings its way toward my ears.[29]
Sosia (*aside*)
                                                        Just my luck!   325
My voice and its damn wings! I should have clipped those off!
Mercury
This fool is in a load of trouble.
Sosia (*aside*)
Load? I don't have a load of anything.
Mercury
                                        What he really needs is a load of my fists.
Sosia (*aside*)
Goodness, I'm tired out from the voyage here,
And a bit seasick! Please don't unload on me!   330
Mercury
Somebody's speaking here.
Sosia (*aside*)
                                        Pfew, he doesn't see me!
He says "Somebody's" talking. I'm Sosia—a nobody!
Mercury
A sound doth strike my ears from the right, methinks.
Sosia (*aside*)
I'm about to take a fall for this striking voice of mine!
Mercury (*aside*)
Excellent! Coming right my way.
Sosia (*aside*)
                                        I'm so scared,   335
I couldn't even tell you where in the hell I am now!
And I'm so petrified, I can't even move my limbs!
That does it: Sosia and his message are both goners!
But I've got to face him like a man,
At least try to seem tough, to make him a little less rough.   340
Mercury
Who approacheth with Vulcan in a lantern?[30]

---

29   Mercury (as also at 333) uses mock-tragic language here.

30   Mercury parodies the language of tragic and epic poetry. Vulcan (= Greek Hephaestus) is a
        god of fire, for which he stands here (by metonymy).

Sosia

What's it to you, O mighty face-filleter?

Mercury

Are you a slave or a freeman?

Sosia

Whichever I want.

Mercury

That so?

Sosia

Certainly is so.

Mercury

You're so dead!

Sosia

You lie.

Mercury

You'll soon see I'm telling the truth.

Sosia

Is that necessary?   345

Mercury

Where you going? What's your business? Who owns you?

Sosia

I'm coming here. I'm my master's slave. Happy?

Mercury

I'll wipe that smile off your face, smartass.

Sosia

No need for that,

It's already wiped neat and clean.

Mercury

Still at it!

What's your business here?

Sosia

The question is, what's *yours* here?   350

Mercury

King Creon always sets guards here at night.

Sosia

Glad to hear they watched the place while we were away.
But you can leave now. Tell the king we're all back.

Mercury

I don't know whose family you're in, but you'd best leave
Unless you want to be welcomed in an un-familial way!   355

Sosia

I live right here, I'm one of their slaves.

Mercury

Know what?

If you stay, I'll see that you rise up in the world.

Sosia

How so?

Mercury

Thanks to my trusty club, you'll be raised aloft—on a stretcher.

Sosia

But I really am a slave of the family here.

Mercury

Still here? How soon would you like your beating? 360

Sosia

Expect to keep me away, when I just got back from abroad?

Mercury

This is your house?

Sosia

Yes.

Mercury

Who's your master?

Sosia

Amphitryon, commander of the Theban army.

He's married to Alcmena.

Mercury

What? What's your name?

Sosia

The Thebans call me Sosia. My sire was Davus.[31] 365

Mercury

Now you've really sewn up your fate, with this

Patchwork of lies, you mountain of mendacity!

Sosia

The only thing sewn up here is this patched tunic I came with.

Mercury

Lying again! You got here with your feet, not your tunic.

Sosia

Yes, of course.

---

31 A bombastic claim, as Roman slaves could claim no ancestry (see Introduction, p. 21). Davus is a common name for slaves in Greek comedy; Plautus may be metatheatrically referring to the fact that the slave in his Greek source play for *Amphitryon* was named Davus (see Introduction, p. 5).

Mercury

So of course you'll be lashed for lying!   370

Sosia

Hardly the course I prefer!

Mercury

But the one I of course do.

This course of course is set, as you'll see in due course.

Sosia

I beg your mercy!

Mercury

Still dare to say you're Sosia,

When that's me?

Sosia

I'm toast!

Mercury

Not as toasty as you'll soon be.

Who owns you?

Sosia

You. Your fists have pretty much closed the deal.   375

Help, please Thebans!

Mercury

Crying now, scum?

Say what you're here for!

Sosia

To be your personal punching bag.

Mercury

Who owns you?

Sosia

Amphitryon. I'm Sosia.

Mercury

Want another one

For lying? I'm Sosia, not you!

Sosia

Well, I wish it were so—I'd be doing the beating!   380

Mercury

Mumbling away now?

Sosia

I'll shut up.

Mercury

Who owns you?

Sosia

Your call.

Mercury
Okay, so what's your name?
Sosia
Your call again.
Mercury
You said you were Amphitryon's slave Sosia.
Sosia
My mistake.
I meant to say I'm Amphitryon's associate.
Mercury
See, I knew I was the only Sosia round here.   385
Your mistake.
Sosia
There's no mistaking those fists of yours.
Mercury
I'm the Sosia you kept claiming you were.
Sosia
Is it possible to have a word with you, maybe without the fists?
Mercury
We can have a truce, if you want to say something.
Sosia
I'll only speak with a peace treaty: your fists are so scary!   390
Mercury
You're safe now to say what you want.
Sosia
Do I have your word?
Mercury
Yes.
Sosia
What if you trick me?
Mercury
Then may Sosia suffer Mercury's wrath!
Sosia
Listen up now that I can speak freely:
I'm Amphitryon's slave Sosia.
Mercury
Not that again?
Sosia
We had a treaty. I'm telling the truth!
Mercury
Take *that*!   395

Sosia

Do whatever you like, since you've got more firepower in your fists.

But whatever you decide, I'm sticking to my story, damn it!

Mercury

Try to make me not be Sosia to your last dying day. It won't happen.

Sosia

And you sure as hell won't make me have another master:

Apart from me there's no other slave Sosia in this house!   400

Mercury

This guy's crazy.

Sosia

              That's the pot calling the kettle black!

Damn it, how could I not be Amphitryon's slave Sosia,

The same one who went away with him to the war?

Item: did I not I arrive by ship tonight from the Port of Persia?[32]

Item: did my master not send me here to carry out his orders?   405

Item: do I not now stand before the house, lantern in hand?

Item: am I not speaking here wide-awake, and didn't I just get beaten?

Oh it happened all right—my poor aching jaw's proof of that!

What am I waiting for? Why don't I walk right into our house?

Mercury

Your house?

Sosia

           Yes, absolutely.

Mercury

                It's all a lie,   410

Every word you've said. *I'm* Amphitryon's slave Sosia.

Tonight we set out from the Port of Persia,

We had stormed the town King Pteralas ruled,

We overcame the Teleboan legions by our might,

And Amphitryon slaughtered King Pterelas with his own hands.   415

Sosia

I can hardly believe my ears when he says all this!

He's got it down perfectly, just as it happened!

Tell me, though: what prize did Amphitryon win from the Teleboans?

Mercury

The golden bowl King Pterelas used to get drunk with.

---

32   Perhaps the name of a harbor on the Gulf of Euboea used by Thebans, or simply a geographical blunder on Plautus' part.

Sosia

That's it! And where's the cup now?

Mercury

In a chest,   420

Sealed with Amphitryon's very own seal.

Sosia

Which is?

Mercury

The Sun, rising in his chariot. Thought you'd trick me, scumbag?

Sosia

That's enough for me! I've got to get a new name!

I don't know how he saw all that, but I've got an idea to catch him:

He can't possibly know what I did in the tent by myself—   425

No chance of that since no one else was ever there.

If you really are Sosia, what were you doing in the tent

At the height of the battle? Tell me that and you win.

Mercury

I had a cask of wine and I poured out a jugful.

Sosia

He's on the right track.

Mercury

I emptied it out—pure as it came from its mother![33]   430

Sosia

Exactly right! I drank the entire jug of uncut wine!

Wouldn't surprise me if this guy was hiding at the bottom of it!

Mercury

So, have I convinced you you're not Sosia?

Sosia

Are you saying I'm not?

Mercury

Yes, since *I'm* Sosia.

Sosia

By Jupiter, I swear I am, and that's no lie!   435

Mercury

Well I swear by Mercury that Jove doesn't believe you.

He'd believe me more than you even if I don't swear under oath.

---

33   The image of the grapevine as the mother of the wine is an ancient commonplace. In Greco-Roman antiquity, it generally was considered uncivilized to drink wine (which typically was high in alcohol content) without first diluting it with water.

Sosia

 Who am I then if I'm not Sosia? Answer me that.

Mercury

 You can be Sosia when I don't want to be any more;

 But as it is, I'm Sosia and you're nobody—leave or you're dead!   440

Sosia

 Damn! Now that I look at the two of us closely

 (And I've often seen myself in the mirror), he's my spitting image!

 Same hat, same clothes—he's as like me as I am!

 Legs, feet, height, haircut, eyes, nose and lips,

 Jaw, chin, beard, neck—all the same![34] What can I say?   445

 If his back's all scarred up,[35] he's got to be me!

 Yet when I think about it, I'm the same person I always was.

 I know my master. I know the house. My mind is sound.

 I'm not giving in, whatever he says! I'm knocking on the door.

Mercury

 Going somewhere?

Sosia

     Yeah, home.

Mercury

        You could mount Jove's chariot   450

 And you still couldn't escape what's coming to you!

Sosia

 Can't I just tell my mistress what my master told me to?

Mercury

 Tell *her* what you want—just stay away from our mistress here!

 Bother me anymore and you'll get a shellacking, and become a mere shell

  of a man!

Sosia

 I'm out of here. Immortal gods, I beg your mercy!   455

 Where did I die? How was I changed? How'd I lose my appearance?

 Or did I forget who I was and left the real me at that harbor?

 Why this guy's got my likeness, which used to be exclusively mine!

 What's happening to me now will never happen when I'm dead![36]

 I'm off to the port to tell master what's happened here,   460

---

34 See *Pseudolus* 1218-20 for a detailed description of the slave's costume.

35 I.e., from whippings. For the comic slave, such scars are a decisive mark of identity.

36 Sosia refers to Roman aristocratic funeral ritual, in which paid actors wore lifelike wax
  portrait masks of distinguished ancestors of the dead man's family.

Unless he claims not to know me either—and, by Jove,
If he does, I'll shave my head and slap on a freedman's cap![37]

SCENE 2

*Mercury remains on stage and directly
addresses the audience.*

Mercury

All's proceeding just according to plan today,
I've pushed that pesky pest away from the door,
To give my father a chance to languish in bed with his lover.   465
Now when this pest meets his master back at the port,
And tells him how his slave Sosia drove him away,
Amphitryon will assume he's lying,
And that he didn't come here as he was ordered.
I'll have the two of them and Amphitryon's entire household   470
Perplexed to the point of utter insanity!
All this so that my philandering father can have his fill
Of his girlfriend! Only then will everybody learn
What's happened. Ultimately, Jove will restore
Alcmena and her husband's longstanding harmony.   475
You see, Amphitryon will raise quite a commotion,
And accuse his wife of adultery. But eventually
My father will intervene and stop their quarrel.
Now there's something I neglected to say about Alcmena:
She's about to give birth to two sons—twins—today!   480

* * * *
* * * *

One is Amphitryon's son, the other Jove's:
So the younger boy has the greater father,
The older boy the lesser one. Got it?   485
My father, out of his considerable respect for Alcmena,
Has arranged for a double birth—
Like killing two birds with one stone.

* * * *
* * * *   490

Like I said, Amphitryon will learn about the
Whole affair. Of course, no one will place the blame

---

37   As a symbol of new life, manumitted slaves in Rome shaved their heads and wore the "cap of freedom" (*pilleus*) until their hair grew out again.

On Alcmena; it'd hardly be fair
For a god to let a mortal take all the heat
For his not-so-subtle indiscretions!   495
Time for me to hush up! The door's creaking.
Ah, it's the faux Amphitryon coming out
With Alcmena, his lovely wife on loan!

SCENE 3

Jupiter and Alcmena enter from Amphitryon's house.

Jupiter
Goodbye, Alcmena, take care for our shared concern, as you are.
And please take it easy: you see your time is close at hand.   500
I must leave you now; raise the child as ours once it's born.[38]

Alcmena
What's so pressing, my dear? Why do you have to go away from me
So suddenly?

Jupiter
      Be assured it's not boredom with you or being at home,
But when the commander's away, the troops will play,
And sooner or later something that shouldn't happen does.   505

Mercury (*aside*)
Quite the con-artist, a clear case of "like father, like son!"[39]
Just watch how smoothly and thickly he'll pour on the old charm.

Alcmena
Well, I'm finding out just how much you think of me!

Jupiter
Isn't it enough that I love you more than any woman in the world?

Mercury (*aside*)
Make no mistake about it, if the lady upstairs found out about your little
    affair   510
Down here, I'd guarantee you'd rather be Amphitryon than Jove.[40]

Alcmena
I'd prefer first-hand experience of that, not just talk.
You barely warmed a spot on the bed and now you're off!
You show up in the middle of the night and then take off. Is that right?

---

38   Jupiter uses a standard Roman formula here in instructing Alcmena not to expose the child.

39   Mercury/Hermes is also a god of trickery and tricksters (cf. n. 1 above).

40   Mercury refers to Jupiter's wife Juno (= Greek Hera), who tries to keep vigilant watch over
    her husband's many extramarital affairs.

Mercury (*aside*)

    I'll go speak to her and play the parasite[41] for my father.   515

    I do declare there's never been a man on earth

    Who loved his wife so deeply as he loves you.

Jupiter

    Scumbag, I know what you're up to! Get out of my sight!

    Since when is this your business, you whipping-post? One more peep

      out of you ...

    You do see this cane?

Alcmena

              No, don't!

Jupiter

                        Just one more peep out of you and ...   520

Mercury (*aside*)

    My first stab at parasititude was not much of a performance!

Jupiter

    Now as to what you're saying, my dear, don't be angry with me.

    I went AWOL to steal away a few moments with you,

    And so you'd be the first to know of my service to the state.

    I told you every last detail. I wouldn't have done all that   525

    If I didn't love you the most.

Mercury (*aside*)

              See, what'd I tell you? Stroking the poor dear!

Jupiter

    Now, to keep the troops in the dark about this, I've got to sneak off.

    I can't have them thinking I put wife over country.

Alcmena

    Going away just like that, with your wife all in tears?

Jupiter

                    Shh! Now, now,

    Your eyes will get red. I'll be back soon.

Alcmena

                 "Soon" is too long!   530

Jupiter

    It's not like I want to go and leave you—

Alcmena

              Oh, I can see that:

    In at midnight, out before morning!

---

41   One of the conventional duties of the comic parasite, or professional dinner guest (cf.
Ergasilus in *Captivi*), was to assist his benefactor in his love-affairs.

Jupiter

You've got to let me go.

It's high time for me to leave the city before daybreak.

First I have a present, though: take this bowl I won for my valor.

It's the one King Pterelas got drunk with before I killed him with my

    own hands.   535

It's yours, Alcmena.

Alcmena

Just like you to do this!

A great gift and a greater giver!

Mercury

Au contraire, a great gift and a great giftee!

Jupiter

At it again, dirtbag? Is there no way to get rid of you?

Alcmena

Please, Amphitryon, don't be angry with Sosia. For me?   540

Jupiter

All right, for you.

Mercury (*aside*)

What a beast love makes him into!

Jupiter

Is that all?

Alcmena

Just one thing: love me while I'm away, as sure as I love you here today.

Mercury

Let's go, Amphitryon. The sun's coming up now.

Jupiter

Go on ahead, Sosia

I'll be right behind you. Anything else?

Alcmena

Yes. Come back soon!

Jupiter

Okay,

I will, sooner than you imagine. Put a smile on your face.   545

Now, O Night, you who stayed for me, it's time to yield to Day,

And to bring your bright light for all mortals to see.

I'll make the Day coming shorter

By as much as you were longer to even things out.[42]

So let Night step aside for Day.[43] I'm off to catch Mercury.   550

---

42   In the Greek mythic tradition, the night of Herakles' conception was tripled (cf. n. 17 above).

43   In ancient (open-air) theater, sudden shifts of time and place can be conventionally signaled merely by words.

SCENE 4

*Amphitryon and Sosia enter, with slaves carrying
their baggage, from the harbor.*

(*Song*)

Amphitryon

Come on, move it!

Sosia

I am, I'm right on your heels!

Amphitryron

You're absolutely worthless!

Sosia

Why?

Amphitryon

Because you keep telling me what's completely impossible,
And what always was and always will be impossible!

Sosia

There you go again,
Never trusting any of your people at all!   555

Amphitryon

Huh? How's that? I swear, you scum, I'm going to slice
That sassy tongue of yours right out of your mouth!

Sosia

You own me,
So you can do whatever you like.
But the one thing you can't do is scare
Me into changing a single word of my story.   560

Amphitryon

Listen up, you bag of crap, do you have the audacity to claim to me
That you're at home when you're here with me?

Sosia

It's the truth!

Amphitryon

I see two punishments in store for you—mine today
And the gods' tomorrow!

Sosia

You're the boss. You own me.

Amphitryon

Dare to mock your master, you human punching bag?   565
Dare to claim the impossible, what no man's ever seen,
And cannot happen? The same person,
In two places, at the same time?

Sosia

That's my story and I'm sticking to it.

Amphitryon

I hope Jupiter blasts you!

Sosia

What have I done to you to deserve this, master?   570

Amphitryon

You degenerate! You have to ask what you've done?

Sosia

You'd have every right to call me names if I were lying,
But I'm not! It happened just as I said.

Amphitryon

This guy's drunk—he has to be!

Sosia

Yea, I only wish!

Amphitryon

Why wish for what's already true?   575

Sosia

I'm not.

Amphitryon

Tell me, you. Where'd you get the wine?

Sosia

I never had a drop.

Amphitryon

Just what sort of a person is this?   576

Sosia

I told you a hundred times
I'm at home, I tell you,   577
And I—Sosia—am right here with you. Are you deaf?
Is it clear enough? Got it,   578
Master?

Amphitryon

It's pointless! Get away from me!

Sosia

What's the matter?   580

Amphitryon

You must have the plague!

Sosia

Why do you say that?
I'm just fine, fit as fiddle!

Amphitryon

Oh, I'll see you get exactly

What you deserve today!
You'll find yourself feeling rather sick
Once I'm safely home. Now kindly follow me.   585a
How dare you mock your master! You and all your crazy talk!   585b
It's not enough for you to ignore your master's orders,
No, you've got to laugh right in his face—
Your claim of what's impossible, what's unprecedented, dogmeat!
Trust me, each of your lies will leave a mark on your back!

Sosia

Amphitryon, it's a very sad day for an honorable slave   590
Who tells his master the truth, and the truth does not prevail.[44]

Amphitryon

Damn it, think it through again! How can it possibly be
That you're both here and at home now? Answer me that!

Sosia

I swear I'm here and there! I don't care who thinks it strange.
It seems just as strange to me as it does to you.   595

Amphitryon

How so?

Sosia

I repeat: it's stranger to me than it is to you!
As the gods are my witness, at first I didn't believe it myself, I mean Sosia,
Until that Sosia, I mean myself, made me believe him.
He knew every last detail of what happened in the war,
And to top that off, he stole my appearance along with my name!   600
Two peas in a pod could not be more alike than he and I are!
Why, when you sent me home from the port a while back—

Amphitryon

What?

Sosia

I was standing in front of the house long before I arrived there!

Amphitryon

Damn it, what utter nonsense! Are you insane?

Sosia

No, as you can plainly see.

Amphitryon

Some sort of sorcerer has beguiled this poor fellow   605
After he left me!

---

44 The "good slave" speech is a Plautine commonplace, usually ironically undercut (as at
Pseudolus 1103-15, where Harpax is failing his master), whereas here Sosia is actually telling
the truth to his master. Cf. 958-61 and 991-4.

Sosia

Yeah, beguiled me with his fists!

Amphitryon

Who beat you up?

Sosia

I did, I mean the me who's at home now.

Amphitryon

Here now, just answer my questions, nothing more.
First of all tell me this: who's that Sosia?

Sosia

Your slave.

Amphitryon

I've got one more of you than I want as it is!   610
In my entire life I've never had a slave named Sosia except you.

Sosia

But I'm telling you, Amphitryon, I guarantee when you get home
You're going to meet a second slave named Sosia besides me,
Sired by Davus just like me, same face, same age as me.
What can I say? Your Sosia's got a twin there!   615

Amphitryon

Astounding! But did you get to see my wife?

Sosia

Fat chance of that! I wasn't even let into the house!

Amphitryon

Who stopped you?

Sosia

I already told you, that Sosia who beat me up.

Amphitryon

Which Sosia?

Sosia

Me, I swear! How many times do I have to tell you?

Amphitryon

What do you mean? Did you doze off a little while ago?

Sosia

NO!   620

Amphitryon

Hmm. Maybe you saw that other Sosia in a dream …

Sosia

I'm not in the habit of carrying out my master's orders asleep!
I was wide awake when I saw him, I'm wide awake talking to you now,
I was wide awake when he whacked me a while ago, and so was he!

Amphitryon

Who?

Sosia

Sosia, the other me. Please tell me you get it now!   625

Amphitryon

How the hell could anyone get it? Such complete nonsense!

Sosia

You'll know what I mean when you meet that other Sosia.

Amphitryon

Then follow me this way. I'll investigate this immediately.

* * * *

* * * *   630

* * * *

May the gods undo everything you say was done!

SCENE 5

Alcmena enters from the house;
Amphitryon and Sosia remain onstage and
perhaps pantomime their continuing journey home.

(*SONG through 653*)

Alcmena

How slight are the pleasures in our lives

Compared with all our pains! Thus it is ordained for mortals.

Thus the gods approve that sorrow walks at pleasure's side.   635

Why, no sooner do we enjoy some good than a mountain of misfortune
  rises up!

This I know from my own experience: I was given just the briefest
  pleasure,

The chance to see my dear husband

For one night only. Then he suddenly left, before the break of dawn.

So alone am I, while the only one I love is away.   640

Greater was my sorrow at his leaving than the pleasure I took from his
  coming.

            One thing only brings me joy: 641a

He's beaten the enemy host and come home in full glory!

            This is my solace.

        If he must leave me, let him always return home

A hero. I'll endure, yes I'll endure   645

His departure with a heart of steel, if only it's my reward

            To hear my husband hailed a champion!

               That would be enough for me.   647a

> Manhood is the finest prize,
> Manhood is the greatest thing alive on earth:
> Through it health, liberty, loved ones, life, and fatherland   650
> Are kept safe and sound.
> Manhood encompasses all, and all that is good
> Falls to the man with manhood.

Amphitryon

I'm absolutely sure my wife must be excited to see me,
Seeing that we're so in love! Especially now that   655
The war's succeeded, and the enemy that was thought to be unbeatable
Was defeated in the very first skirmish—all under my excellent leadership.
No doubt about it, she's dying to see me!

Sosia

And what about me? There's a lady awaiting my arrival too.

Alcmena

Why here's my husband!

Amphitryon

> Come along!

Alcmena

> What's he back for?   660

He had to hurry off just a little while ago. Maybe he's testing me,
To see how much I miss him after he's gone?
I'm not unhappy to see him though.

Sosia

Oh, oh. We'd better go back to the ship.

Amphitryon

> Why?

Sosia

Because no one's going to give us lunch here.   665

Amphitryon

What gives you that idea?

Sosia

> Because we're too late.

Amphitryon

Huh?

Sosia

> Alcmena's standing in front of the house looking quite stuffed.[45]

Alcmena

She was pregnant when I left.

---

45   The first of several jokes on Alcmena's advanced pregnancy turned by Sosia (cf. n. 16 above).

Sosia
> Oh, damn!

Amphitryon
> What's the matter with you?

Sosia
> > I'm back just in time to fetch the water—
> It's the ninth month, if we're counting right!   670

Amphitryon
> Settle down!

Sosia
> > Settle down? If I pick up that bucket,
> Never trust me again from this day forward,
> If I don't drain the life out of that well once I'm started!

Amphitryon
> Come along this way! Never mind, I'll put someone else on that job.

Alcmena
> I suppose I'm expected to go and greet him.   675

Amphitryon
> Amphitryon greets his lovely wife with joy,
> Whom he considers the single finest woman of all,
> Whose virtue all my fellow Thebans praise.
> Are you well? Glad to see me back?

Sosia (*aside*)
> > Hardly.
> About as warm a welcome as a stray dog would get.   680

Amphitryon
> And so pregnant, so pretty and plump! It's a joy to see!

Alcmena
> Why are you mocking me with this greeting?
> As if you hadn't just seen me a while ago
> And were just now arriving home from war,
> Greeting me as if you hadn't seen me for a long time!   685

Amphitryon
> Why I haven't seen you in ages—until now.

Alcmena
> Why do you deny it?

Amphitryon
> > Because I've learned to tell the truth!

Alcmena
> > And it's foolish
> To unlearn what you've learned. Or are you testing out
> My feelings? But why are you back so soon?

Help up by a bad omen? Did bad weather   690
Keep you from joining the troops like you just said you would?

Amphitryon

"Just said?" How recently was that?

Alcmena

You're testing me. A while back. Just now.

Amphitryon

How's what you say possible: "A while back. Just now?"

Alcmena

What do you think? I'm the one mocking you,
After you pretend you're coming home just now?   695

Amphitryon

This is crazy talk!

Sosia

Wait a little while
And maybe she'll sleep off this dream.

Amphitryon

What? She dreams wide-awake?

Alcmena

I most certainly am awake and what I'm telling you happened is no dream!
I saw both of you just a while ago before dawn.

Amphitryon

Where?

Alcmena

Right here in your own house.

Amphitryon

Never happened.

Sosia

Wait a minute.   700
What if the ship brought us here from the port in our sleep?

Amphitryon

You're not taking her side, are you?

Sosia

What do you expect?
You do understand that if you stand up to a raving Maenad,[46]
You get double the insanity, and double the punches.
Humor her, and maybe you'll get off with just one good belt.

---

46   A Maenad is a female worshipper of Bacchus (= Greek Dionysus), conventionally portrayed
     as being in a frenzied state of religious ecstasy when celebrating his rites.

Amphitryon

One thing's for sure,   705
She's getting a piece of my mind for not properly greeting me
Home today.

Sosia

You'll just stir up a hornet's nest.

Amphitryon

Quiet!
Alcmena, I have something to ask you.

Alcmena

Ask away.

Amphitryon

What's behind your behavior? Foolishness or arrogance?

Alcmena

What in the world makes you ask me that, my dear husband?   710

Amphitryon

Because up to now you've always welcomed me home warmly,
Just as virtuous wives are supposed to do.
But now I come home to find you've changed your ways.

Alcmena

Goodness me, I did too welcome you when you arrived yesterday!
And I asked how you were, my dear,   715
And I took your hand and greeted you with a kiss.

Sosia

You greeted him yesterday?

Alcmena

Yes, and you too, Sosia.

Sosia

Amphitryon, I'd hoped she'd give you a son,
But that's no boy that she's got in her.

Amphitryon

No, what is it?

Sosia

Insanity!

Alcmena

I'm perfectly sane and if the gods are with me I'll have a healthy son![47]   720
You'll have more than you can handle if he does his duty!
A curse on you for cursing me!

---

47   The cultural preference. Mercury has already told the audience (480) that she will bear twin
       sons.

Sosia (*aside*)

    A pregnant woman's always gorging or disgorging.

    She's either gnawing at something or something's gnawing at her.

Amphitryon

    You saw me here yesterday?

Alcmena

                     Yes, for the tenth time!   725

Amphitryon

    Maybe in your dreams.

Alcmena

               I was wide awake—and so were you!

Amphitryon

                                      Oh no!

Sosia

    What's the matter with you?

Amphitryon

               My wife's insane!

Sosia

                         Probably a touch of black bile.

    Nothing else drives people to madness so fast!

Amphitryon

    When, woman, did you first feel it coming over you?

Alcmena

    I swear I'm perfectly sane!

Amphitryon

                  Why, then, do you claim   730

    You saw me yesterday when we only put into port last night?

    I ate dinner there and I slept all night on board the ship.

    And I haven't set foot in this house since I went

    To war with the army against the Teleboans.

Alcmena

    No! You were fed *here* and then we went to bed.

Amphitryon

                          What's that now?   735

Alcmena

    The truth.

Amphitryon

         That last part isn't, I'll guarantee! I'm not sure about the rest.

Alcmena

    And you went off to the army at the crack of dawn.

Amphitryon

                      How can that be?

Sosia

That's just how she remembers it—from her dream.
But madam, after you awoke today, you should have offered
A salty cake to Jove of Prodigies,[48] and prayed to him with incense.   740

Alcmena

How dare you!

Sosia

                    Same to you—I mean, yes Mam'.

Alcmena

That's the second time he's been rude to me and gotten away with it!

Amphitryon

Quiet, you! But, tell me: I left you today at the crack of dawn?

Alcmena

How else could I know about the war except from you?

Amphitryon

You know about that too?

Alcmena

                            Yes, from you personally, how you seized the city 745
And how you killed King Pterelas yourself!

Amphitryon

I told you that?

Alcmena

                    Yes, and Sosia was standing here too.

Amphitryon

Did *you* hear me saying all this today?

Sosia

                                    How could I have heard that?

Amphitryon

Ask her.

Sosia

            As far as I know, it didn't happen in my presence!

Alcmena

Big surprise he's on your side.

Amphitryon

                        Sosia, look closely at me.   750

Sosia

I am.

---

48   I.e., she should make an offering to Jupiter in his capacity to ward off bad omens, such as those associated with bad dreams.

Amphitryon

    Now tell me the truth and don't be a yes man.

    Did you hear me say a word of what she says I did to her today?

Sosia

    Oh no! Are you crazy too? Asking me that when

    I'm seeing her now for the first time, same as you?

Amphitryon

    What of that, woman? Hear him?

Alcmena

                        Yes I do, and he's lying.   755

Amphitryon

    You don't believe him or *me*, your very own husband?

Alcmena

                                       No,

    I only believe myself—things happened just as I say.

Amphitryon

    You're saying I came here yesterday?

Alcmena

                      You're saying you didn't leave here today?

Amphitryon

    Absolutely! I'm coming home to you now for the first time!

Alcmena

    Will you also deny that you gave me a golden bowl   760

    Today that they awarded you on your campaign?

Amphitryon

    I did no such thing! But I meant to give you it

    And I still do. But how'd you hear about that?

Alcmena

    From you of course, and you gave me the bowl

    Personally.

Amphitryon

            Wait a minute, now! I'm completely baffled, Sosia!   765

    How could she know I'd been given the gold cup

    Unless you came earlier and told her everything?

Sosia

    I most certainly didn't! And I've only seen her together with you.

Amphitryon

    What sort of a person would—

Alcmena

                Want to see the cup?

Amphitryon

                      I do.

Alcmena

Fine. Thessala,[49] bring out the bowl   770
My husband gave me today.

Amphitryon

Sosia, over here!
This will be the most amazing thing to me of all,
If she's got the cup!

Sosia

You don't really believe that? It's right here in this chest
Sealed with your very own seal.

Amphitryon

Still sealed?

Sosia

See for yourself.

Amphitryon

Yes, it's unbroken.

Sosia

Don't you think you should call   775
An exorcist?

Amphitryon

I damn well better—
I'll be damned if she's not full of demons! What can I say?

Alcmena

Hah! See, there's the bowl.

Amphitryon

Give me it!

Alcmena

Go ahead and look.
Still denying what you've already done? I've got proof right here.
Isn't this the cup they gave you there?

Amphitryon

Jove Almighty,   780
I don't believe my eyes! The very cup! I'm done for, Sosia!

Sosia

Either this woman's the world's best witch
Or the cup's got to be in here!

Amphitryon

Come on, open the chest!

---

49   The region of Thessaly in northern Greece was considered to be a haven for magical
practices. The mute character's name here reflects the play's pervasive theme of magic.

Sosia

Why bother, it's sealed just as it should be, so everything's in order.
You've begotten another Amphitryon, I a second Sosia.   785
If the bowl now begets a bowl, we've all twinned together!

Amphitryon

That chest has got to come open.

Sosia

                                        Please check the seal first,
So you can't blame me afterwards.

Amphitryon

                                        Just open it.
Otherwise, her crazy talk will drive us to insanity!

Alcmena

Where else would I get this except from you?   790

Amphitryon

I intend to find that out.

Sosia

                        Jupiter, holy Jupiter!

Amphitryon

What is it?

Sosia

            There's no bowl here in the chest!

Amphitryon

                                        I don't believe my ears!

Sosia

It's the honest truth!

Amphitryon

                        There's torture in store for you if it isn't in there!

Alcmena

This one's right here.

Amphitryon

                        Who gave you that?

Alcmena

                                        The person asking me.

Sosia

Are you trying to trap me? You secretly took a shortcut here   795
From the ship, took the bowl out of here and
Gave it to her, and then resealed the chest.

Amphitryon

Not you too? Feeding her madness now?
You say we got here yesterday?

Alcmena

Yes, and as soon as you did
We greeted each other and I gave you a kiss. 800

Sosia

I don't like that opening about the kiss at all!

Amphitryon

Go on!

Alcmena

You took a bath.

Amphitryon

And after that?

Alcmena

You dined.

Sosia

Excellent,
Keep at her!

Amphitryon

Stop interrupting! Continue with the story.

Alcmena

Dinner was served. We ate together, side by side.

Amphitryon

On the same couch?

Alcmena

Yes, the same one.

Sosia

This dinner's not going to sit well! 805

Amphitryon

Let her state her case! What about after dinner?

Alcmena

You said you were sleepy. The table was cleared. We went off to bed together.

Amphitryon

Where'd you sleep?

Alcmena

In our room, in the same bed with you.

Amphitryon

I'm dead!

Sosia

What's the matter with you?

Amphitryon

She's killing me here.

Alcmena

What is it, dear?

Amphitryon
> Don't speak to me!

Sosia
> What's wrong?

Amphitryon
> I'm completely screwed!   810
While I was away from here she's committed adultery!

Alcmena
My goodness! I can't believe my husband would say such a thing!

Amphitryon
Your husband? You do me wrong and then you call me by the wrong name.

Sosia (*aside*)
He's no longer her man,[50] so he's a woman? Very messy business!

Alcmena
What did I ever do to deserve this?   815

Amphitryon
You have to ask after you publicly announced your crime?

Alcmena
How was it wrong for me to be with the man I'm married to?

Amphitryon
You were with me, huh? How indecent can a person be?
No shame, and too shameless even to pretend otherwise!

Alcmena
What you accuse me of disgraces my entire family!   820
You won't catch me in adultery!

Amphitryon
By the immortal gods, Sosia, you at least know me, don't you?

Sosia
I'm pretty sure I do.

Amphitryon
> And I ate dinner on board the ship yesterday?

Alcmena
I also have witnesses to back up my story.

Sosia
I'm at a loss to explain all this, unless maybe there's   825
Another Amphitryon who fills in when you're away,
And does all your duties for you here at home.
That second Sosia was shocking enough,
But this other Amphitryon's even more astounding!

---

50   The Latin word *vir* used here means both "man" and "husband."

Amphitryon

Surely some magician's cast a spell over this woman! 830

Alcmena

I swear by mightiest Jove and matronly Juno,
The goddess I fear and reverence above all:
The only mortal to wrap his body around mine is you,
And I've not committed adultery!

Amphitryon

I can only wish!

Alcmena

It's the honest truth. But, honestly, why bother? You won't believe me. 835

Amphitryon

A woman's words don't hold water!

Alcmena

They do if the woman is right, as I am.
I have every right to speak up and defend myself.

Amphitryon

You've said more than enough!

Alcmena

As an innocent women should!

Amphitryon

Innocent only in words!

Alcmena

My idea of a dowry differs from what people generally think:
I also brought you chastity, purity, and a modest passion, plus 840
Fear of the gods, love of parents, harmony at home,
And I'm a dutiful wife to you, a servant of all your needs, and a doer of
good deeds.

Sosia (*aside*)

My god, if all that's true, she's downright perfect!

Amphitryon

I'm so muddled I'm not sure who I am!

Sosia

You're Amphitryon, all right—don't cash in your chips yet. 845
It's other folks who are acting strange since we came home.

Amphitryon

Women, I *will* continue this investigation.

Alcmena

By all means, that's just fine by me.

Amphitryon

Really? Now tell me:
What if I bring your Uncle Naucrates here from the ship?

He went with me to war. If he denies   850
All you say, what should be done with you?
Can you think of any reason I shouldn't divorce you?

Alcmena

Not if I've done something wrong.

Amphitryon

                             Agreed. Sosia,
Take the slaves and baggage inside. I'll go to the ship and fetch Naucrates.

Sosia

Now that we're alone, in all honesty, tell me the truth: 855
Is there a second Sosia in there just like me?

Alcmena

Get away from me! You're as bad as your master!

Sosia

                           I'm out of here, if that's what you want.

Alcmena

Completely bizarre, the way my husband seems to enjoy
Falsely accusing me of something so horrible!
Maybe my uncle Naucrates can tell me what's happening.   860

SCENE 6

*Jupiter emerges from the house
and directly addresses the audience.*

Jupiter

I'm the Amphitryon with the slave Sosia
Who becomes Mercury when it's convenient.
I'm the one who lives in the highest storey
And turns into Jupiter whenever I want.
But as soon as I arrive here,   865
I change costume and become Amphitryon.
I'm really here now for your sake,
So this comedy can find some closure.
I'm also here for Alcmena. Poor thing,
Wrongly accused of adultery by Amphitryon!   870
Hardly fair for that guiltless creature
To take the rap for my little hoax.
Now I'm going to impersonate Amphitryon,
As I did earlier, and throw the whole household
Into even more confusion!   875
Eventually, everything will come to light, and
I'll help Alcmena in her time of need
By arranging for a painless double birth

Of both my son and her husband's.
Mercury's under orders to be at my side   880
The second I call him. Time to talk to her.

SCENE 7

Alcmena enters from the house, at first not noticing Jupiter.

Alcmena
I will not stay in that house! The nerve of my husband,
Accusing me of adultery and shameful acts,
Ranting about what never happened,
False accusations, things I'd never do!   885
He thinks I'll just stand there and take it!
No way! I will not endure these accusations!
Either he apologizes to me or I'm leaving him.
He'll also have to swear to me
He didn't mean the horrible things he said.   890

Jupiter (*aside*)
I'll have to do things her way
If she's to be my lover again.
Amphitryon's all in a bind because of my doings.
My little affair's caused him some trouble,
Innocent though he was. Now I'm the innocent one,   895
And must pay the price for his angry words.

Alcmena
Oh, there's the man who accuses me of adultery
And indecency!

Jupiter
           I'd like a word with you, dear.
Why do you turn away?

Alcmena
              It's not in my nature to look at you:
I hate the very sight of my enemies!   900

Jupiter
Come, now! Enemies?

Alcmena
            Yes, precisely that—
Unless you say that's a lie too!

Jupiter
You're far too angry—

Alcmena
           Could you keep your hands off me?
You know, if you had any sense or sensitivity,

You wouldn't have a word to say, either serious or in jest,   905
To a woman you consider unfaithful, and said so—
Unless you're an absolute ass!

Jupiter

If I did say so, that doesn't mean I meant it.
The reason I've come here is to apologize.
My heart has never been as pained as when   910
I heard you were angry with me.
Why did I say it then, you're wondering? I'll explain.
Be assured I didn't believe you were unfaithful.
It was all a test of your feelings,
To see how you react, and what you would do.   915
What I said a while back was all in good fun,
All just a joke. Go ahead and ask Sosia.

Alcmena

Why aren't you off to get my Uncle Naucrates?
Wasn't he supposed to come here and say
You hadn't already been here?

Jupiter

                              If something was said in jest   920
It makes no sense for you to take it seriously.

Alcmena

All I know is your joking broke my heart.

Jupiter

Please Alcmena, I beg you by your own right hand,
Pardon me. Forgive me—and don't stay mad.

Alcmena

My good character refutes your wild claims.   925
Since my life's been free of deceitfulness,
I prefer to steer clear of any mention of infidelity.
Goodbye. Keep your property, return mine.[51]
Will you be sending my attendants?

Jupiter

                              Are you crazy?

Alcmena

                                        If you don't send them,

---

51   Alcmena utters the Roman formula for divorce (a speech-act), which apparently could in
      some circumstances be initiated by women as well as men. That she has remained under her
      father's control during the marriage is suggested by the fact that she has her own property Cf.
      Casina 202 and n. 25 there.

I'll go by myself. Chastity[52] will accompany me. 930
Jupiter
    Wait! I'll swear whatever oath you want
    That I believe you are my faithful wife!
    If my oath is insincere, I call upon you, Almighty Jove,
    To vent your eternal rage against Amphitryon!
Alcmena
    No no, eternally bless him!
Jupiter
                  I'm pretty sure he will, 935
    Since the oath I swore to you was genuine.
    You're not angry with me any more, are you?
Alcmena
                      No.
Jupiter
                      Good.
    In our life things often turn out this way:
    Our pleasures are followed closely by our pains.
    Anger comes and goes, and harmony is re-established. 940
    But after the anger has flared out between two people
    And peace is restored between them,
    There's double the love there was before.
Alcmena
    You shouldn't have said those things in the first place,
    But you've apologized, and all is forgotten. 945
Jupiter
    Have the sacred vessels made ready for me:
    While I was off to war I vowed that once I got safely home
    I'd pay back the gods for all my success.
Alcmena
    I'll have it done.
Jupiter (*to slaves inside*)
              And tell Sosia to come out here.
    Have him go get Blepharo, the captain of my ship, 950
    And invite him to lunch with us today. (*aside*)
    Lunch he'll miss, but he'll get his fill of frustration
    When he sees Amphitryon hauled off and hog-tied!

---

52 *Pudicitia*, the personification of chastity and modesty, was worshipped by Roman women
(women married more than once were excluded from her cult).

Alcmena

    Strange how he talks to himself over there.

    Oh look, the door's opening—it's Sosia.   955

SCENE 8

Sosia joins Jupiter and Alcmena onstage.

Sosia

    Amphitryon, I'm here. Your every wish is my command.

Jupiter

    Oh Sosia, just in time.

Sosia

                   So you two have made up?

    I'm thrilled to see you two back together!

    It seems best for a slave who wants to be good

    To do as his master does, to take a face from his,   960

    And to be sad when he's sad, and glad when he's glad.

    Tell me though, are you two all made up?

Jupiter

    Stop joking—you know all was said in jest before.

Sosia

    You were joking? It seemed very serious to me.

Amphitryon

    I've cleared up the matter. We've made our peace.

Sosia

                          Excellent!   965

Jupiter

    I've got some divine business[53] to attend to inside.

Sosia

                           Right.

Jupiter

    Bring Blepharo here from the port for me,

    To have lunch here after the sacrifice.

Sosia

    I'll be back before you know it.

Jupiter

               Hurry back.

Alcmena

    Anything else, or should I go in and get things ready for the sacrifice?   970

---

53   Jupiter's words ostensibly refer to the sacrifice he is to make inside (983), but the Latin phrase
     may also refer to sexual intercourse (cf. 980-1).

Jupiter

Go on in, and get everything ready as soon as possible.

Alcmena

Come in whenever you like. I'll see there's no delay.

Jupiter

Well put—just as a good wife should. (*she exits*)
Both of them tricked, slave and mistress!
They think I'm Amphitryon. Big mistake!   975
You, the immortal Sosia, appear here right now
(I know you can hear me wherever you are)!
Drive away Amphitryon right when he arrives,
Using whatever you want from your bag of tricks.
I want him fooled while I fool around with   980
My lovely wife on loan. Now see everything's done
According to my precise wishes. Understand?
Do me this service while I do a sacrifice to myself.

SCENE 9

*Mercury enters, perhaps passing through the audience,
and directly addresses them.*

Mercury[54]

Out of the way, clear a path, step aside!
Step in my way and you're pushing your luck!   985
A god has just as much right to threaten
The people in his way as some lowly slave in a comedy!
He's there to say the ship's arrived safely, or the old man's on his way home.
I do the bidding of Jove, as I'm here to do now—
All the more reason for the right of way.   990
Father calls and I appear, obedient to his every command
The instant he utters it, as a good son should be to his father.[55]
When he's in love my role's simple: aid and abet, share in his joy.
Whatever father fancies strikes my fancy too!
As for his little affair here: he's smart, doing it right, indulging his passion 995
As every man should do—well, at least in moderation.
Now father wants Amphitryon befuddled, a
Performance to be done for an audience just like you.
I'll wear this garland and pretend I'm hammered.

---

54 Mercury here plays the stock comic role of the "running slave," who bombastically enters
    with news. Cf. Ergasilus's entrance at *Captivi* 778ff. and n. 43 there.

55 For the parody of the "good slave" speech, see n. 44 above. For the notion of a son being a
    slave to his father, see n. 19 above.

I'll climb up above, and from there it'll be easy   1000
To drive him away. I'll see he's sloshed yet sober!
And then his slave Sosia will have to take the rap
For all I'm about to do. What do I care?
My duty's to indulge all my father's desires.
There's Amphitryon, soon to be a laughingstock,   1005
If you'll kindly give us your attention.
I'm going in to alter my outfit a bit, so I look wasted.
Then it's up to the roof to torture Amphitryon.

SCENE 10

Amphitryon enters from the forum, after conducting
a futile search for Naucrates.

Amphitryon

Not a trace of Naucrates at the ship!
He wasn't at home, or in the city, and not a soul has seen him!   1010
I dragged myself down every street, to the gyms, perfume shops,
The marketplace, the wrestling school, the forum,
Then the doctors' offices, barbershops, and every last temple!
The man's nowhere to be found and I'm beat from searching!
I'm going inside to interrogate my wife some more.   1015
I've got to know just who's had his way with her.
I'd sooner die than let that investigation slide
But wait a minute—the doors are shut! O great,
Par for the course the way things are going here!
I'll just have to knock. Hey, open up here! Somebody let me in!   1020

SCENE 11

Mercury suddenly appears on the upper storey
of the stage house.

Mercury

Who's there?

Amphitryon

            I am.

Mercury

            Huh? "I am"?

Amphitryon

                        You've got that right!

Mercury

                                    Trying to break down the door?
I hope Jove and the rest of the gods blast you to hell!

Amphitryon
How's that?

Mercury
It's like this: I hope the rest of your life is one living hell!

Amphitryon
Sosia!

Mercury
Yeah, that's my name—don't wear it out!
So what do you want?

Amphitryon
You scum! You dare ask me that?   1025

Mercury
Sure do. You almost pounded the door off its hinges, fathead!
Do you think doors are supplied to us by the state?
What you staring at, stupid? What do you want, whoever you are?

Amphitryon
You have the audacity to ask that, you punching bag?
A bundle of elm rods will perish on your bloody back today!   1030

Mercury
You must have really been a squanderer in your youth—

Amphitryon
Huh?

Mercury
Judging by the way you're out begging for a fight as a geezer.[56]

Amphitryon
You'll live to dearly regret those words, you uppity slave!

Mercury
I'd like to honor you—

Amphitryon
What?

Mercury
I hereby solemnly award you with trouble!   1034

A substantial part of the play is lost here, probably parts
or the entirety of four scenes (as is suggested by the few
surviving fragments quoted by later authors). Mercury
continues to abuse Amphitryon and then goes back into the

---

56 Mercury's reference to Amphitryon's advanced age here, along with Bromia's later
    characterization of him as "an old man" (1072), show that both Amphitryon and Jupiter were
    costumed as a *senex*, or father of the family: see Introduction, pp. 16-18.

house. Alcmena comes out and joins Amphitryon, and, since
her last encounter with Jupiter left her believing that she had
reconciled with her husband, a confused exchange ensues, in
which Amphitryon reiterates the charge of adultery and his
contention that she is insane. Alcmena angrily exits and Sosia
shows up with Blepharo. Amphitryon does not understand
why Blepharo has been summoned, and Sosia must bear the
consequences for Mercury's abuse of his master from the roof.
Sosia exits and does not reappear in the play, presumably out
of fear of serious punishment by Amphitryon.

SCENE 14

When the text picks up again, Jupiter, who for
some reason has come out of the house,
Amphitryon and Blepharo are onstage.

Blepharo

Divide her up between the two of you! I'm out of here!
I've got stuff to do!   1035
Never in my life have I seen such utterly strange things![57]

Amphitryon

Blepharo, please! Stay and help me, don't go!

Blepharo

                                               Later!
Why should I stay and help if I don't know which one of you I'm supposed
to help?

Jupiter

Time for me to go inside. Alcmena's giving birth.

Amphitryon

                                          I'm all but dead!
Now what? All my friends and allies have deserted me!   1040
I swear, that joker's not getting away with this, whoever he is!
I'm going straight to the king and telling him what's happened.
Oh, I'll have my vengeance on that Thessalian[58] sorcerer today
Who's confused and confounded my entire household!
But where'd he go? I think he went inside to my wife.   1045
Whose life in all of Thebes is more wretched than mine? What should I do

---

57   Part of the humor here is that Blepharo, whose name in Greek means "eye," cannot believe
      what he sees.

58   For the associations of Thessaly with magic, see n. 49 above.

When no one in the world knows me, and I'm the butt of every joke?
Here's my plan: I'm breaking into the house and the first person I see,
Maid, slave, my wife, her lover, my father, my grandfather—
It makes no difference to me—is dead right there on the spot!   1050
No one can stop me, not Jove or all the gods united together!
Yes, my mind's all made up! I'm going right into the house—(*thunder and
lightning*)

SCENE 15

*Bromia enters from the house, at first
not noticing the collapsed Amphitryon.*

(*SONG through 1085*)

Bromia[59]

My life, my hopes, all lie buried deep within my heart!
No prospects or possibilities—I've lost them all!
Sea, land, and sky together hound me,   1055
And want to see me die! Poor, poor me—what can I do?
Such strange events inside the house! Poor, poor me!
I'm feeling sick! Water please! I'm through, I'm finished!
My head is aching, my hearing's shaky, and I can barely see!
No woman's worse off, nor could ever be!   1060
You won't believe what's happened! My mistress was in labor.
    She'd called the gods for help and ... crash, boom, bang! The thunder!
At that clap of thunder we fell straight to the floor, and someone
    In a mighty voice says: "Alcmena, fear not. Help is at hand:
    A sky-dweller sheds his grace on you and yours.   1065
Rise," he says, "you who have fallen in dread and fear."
I rose from where I had fallen, and it seemed the house was burning,
Blazing everywhere! Alcmena called out but fear froze me in my tracks.
But my fear for her prevailed, and so I ran to help her.
To my amazement she'd given birth to twins, two boys,   1070
Though none of us had seen how or when!
What's this over here? Who's this old man lying in front of the house?
    Zapped by Jove perhaps?
By Jupiter I think he has been! Looks like he's laid out for burial!
I'll take a look-see. Why it's Amphitryon, my master!   1075
Amphitryon!

---

59 Bromia delivers the play's second messenger's speech (cf. 186-261 and n. 21 above) to
    relate the miraculous events that have occurred in the house. Bromia's name reflects one of
    Bacchus's cult titles (*Bromius*), and so immediately characterizes her as a raving Maenad (cf.
    n. 46 above).

Amphitryon
> I'm dead.

Bromia
> Get up.

Amphitryon
> I'm a goner.

Bromia
> Here, take my hand.

Amphitryon
> Whose hand is that?

Bromia
Your slave Bromia's.

Amphitryon
> That blast of Jupiter still has me shaking.
I feel like I've just risen from the dead. But why are you out here?

Bromia
We were dumbstruck with the same fright as you, right there
In the house! Utterly amazing things! Poor, poor me,   1080
Amphitryon! I've just about lost my mind!

Amphitryon
> Tell me now:
Are you sure I'm your master Amphitryon?

Bromia
> Yes!

Amphitryon
> Look again!

Bromia
> It's you.

Amphitryon
This is the only sane person left in my houshold!

Bromia
No, we're all perfectly sane!

Amphitryon
> Except that my wife and all her shameful deeds
Are driving me insane.

Bromia
> I'll have you changing that tune, Amphitryon!   1085
You'll see, your wife's a faithful and honorable woman.
I've plenty of proof of that and it won't take me long to show you.
Article number one: Alcmena's given birth to twin boys.

Amphitryon
Really? Twins?

Bromia

        Twins.

Amphitryon

          The gods are in my corner!

Bromia

                    Let me go on.

You won't believe how much the gods favor you and your wife!   1090

Amphitryon

Go on!

Bromia

       Now as your wife's time approached today and

She went into labor, she, as any woman giving birth would do,

Prays to the immortal gods for help, and

Washes her hands and covers her head.[60] No sooner had she done that

Than there's a great peel of thunder! We thought the whole house

    was collapsing!   1095

Everything was glowing, as if it was made out of gold!

Amphitryon

Enough suspense! Get on with it.

So what happened next?

Bromia

           While all this is happening, not one of us

Heard a single groan or cry out of your wife—

The birth was utterly painless!

Amphitryon

           I'm glad enough for that,   1100

Regardless of what she's done to me!

Bromia

             Oh, put that out of your head and listen.

Next she had us wash the two boys. We started to,

But the one I was washing was so big and so strong!

Not one of us could wrap him in his swaddling clothes!

Amphitryon

Utterly amazing! If it's all true, I've a sneaking suspicion   1105

My wife had plenty of help from the gods up in heaven!

Bromia

This'll make you more amazed! Once he was in his cradle,

---

60   Alcmena prays like a Roman: whereas Greeks bared their heads during prayer to open
     themselves up to positive divine influences, Romans scrupulously covered theirs to shield
     themselves from bad omens.

Two enormous crested snakes[61] wind down to the catchment.
Then they lift their heads up high.

Amphitryon

Oh no!

Bromia

No need to fear! Then with their eyes they survey the scene.   1110
They spot the boys and make a beeline for the cradles.
Slowly, slowly, I backed away pulling the cradles,
Frightened for the boys, fearing for myself. The snakes
Came all the fiercer. The one boy eyeballs them
And leaps out of his cradle and goes straight at them!   1115
Quick as a flash he has hold of one snake in each hand!

Amphitryon

This is astounding and gives me the shivers!
Oh me, oh my! Your story makes my hair stand on end!
What next? Keep going!

Bromia

The boy strangles each of the snakes!
At that moment he calls your wife in a mighty voice!   1120

Amphitryon

Who? What's this man's name?

Bromia

Jupiter, almighty lord of men and gods!
He said he secretly slept with Alcmena, and shared her bed,
And that the boy who strangled the snakes was his son.
The other boy is yours.

Amphitryon

That's not the worst thing in the world,
Splitting up half of my good fortune with Jove![62]   1125
I'll go inside and prepare the ritual items at once!
I've got to sacrifice to Jupiter and earn his blessing.
First I'll summon Tiresias[63] the seer and explain
All that's happened, and see what he thinks we should do.
What's that? That was some thunder! Save us all, almighty gods!   1130

---

61   In the mythic tradition, the snakes are sent by the jealous Juno (cf. n. 40 above). The scene
       described here is depicted in a wall-painting from the House of the Vetii at Pompeii.

62   The image of "splitting" can have crude sexual connotations in Latin: cf. 1035 and *Casina*
       326-7.

63   Tiresias is the soothsayer par excellence of Theban myth.

SCENE 16

Jupiter appears to Amphitryon as deus ex machina,[64]
probably on the upper storey of the stage house.

Jupiter

Calm down, Amphitryon, I am here to help you and yours.
There is nothing to fear. Forget about prophets and seers.
I can reveal your future and show you your past
Far better than they can. I'm Jove after all.
First of all, I borrowed Alcmena's body,   1135
And made her pregnant with my son.
You also impregnated her before you
Went on campaign. She bore both boys together.
The one I sired will bring honor
To you through his glorious deeds.   1140
Restore your domestic harmony with
Alcmena. There is no reason to blame her.
I forced her. Now back to heaven for me.

SCENE 17

Amphitryon, left alone onstage.

Amphitryon

So be it. Please honor your pledge.
I'm off to see my wife—forget about Tiresias.   1145
And now how about some applause for mighty Jove?

---

64   Jupiter appears as *deus ex machina* (cf. n. 13 above), perhaps from the roof of the stage house,
     and presumably no longer costumed as Amphitryon's double.

Captivi ("The Prisoners")

Characters with Speaking Parts

ERGASILUS, *a parasite, i.e., a glutton and professional dinner-guest*
HEGIO, *head of the household*
GUARD, *slave of Hegio in charge of guarding Philocrates and Tyndarus*
PHILOCRATES, *a prisoner of war from Elis*
TYNDARUS, *slave of Philocrates*
ARISTOPHONTES, *a prisoner of war from Elis*
BOXER, *slave and enforcer of Hegio*
SLAVE BOY, *slave of Hegio*
PHILOPOLEMUS, *son of Hegio taken as a prisoner of war by the Eleans*
STALAGMUS, *runaway slave of Hegio*

SCENE

Aetolia: in front of the house of Hegio.

PROLOGUE[1]

See these two prisoners standing here?[2] They're not sitting
For the same reason those folks are standing up in back.

---

1   The Roman comic playwrights introduced the use of an impersonal prologist (perhaps the head of the acting troupe) to ancient comedy. Characters or gods (e.g., *Amphitryon*) also deliver prologues in Plautus, though not all Plautine plays have formal prologues.

2   The appearance of the two characters onstage during the prologue is unusual, and is probably intended to prevent confusion about their identities, which they swap during the play.

You all know I'm telling the truth about that! [3]
An old man named Hegio lives here—he's the father of this prisoner (*points to Tyndarus*),
Who also now happens to be his own father's slave.[4]   5
Now do kindly turn your attention to my prologue.
This old man had two sons. When one of them was just
Four years old, he was stolen by a slave, who then
High-tailed it out of here and sold the boy in Elis to the
Father of this captive. (*points to Philocrates*) Got it? Great!   10
What? The guy in back doesn't? Come on up, sir:
Rather than making me bust my lungs like a beggar,
You can either quietly take a seat or take a hike! Make more sense
Than having me explain everything again just for your sake?[5]
As for those of you fine citizens who pay taxes:[6]   15
I still owe you some information, so let me pay it back with interest.
Now as I said before, the fugitive slave stole the young boy—
In other words his master—and sold him to this guy's father.
The father then gave the boy to his own son to be his personal
Property and playmate, since the two were about the same age.   20
But now he's a slave to his own father, in his own home—and
Nobody knows it! We are the gods' volleyballs!
So now you know how he lost the one son.
Years later there was a war between the Aetolians[7] and Eleans,[8]
And the other son was taken prisoner, as happens in war, and   25

---

3   Seating in the Roman theater was hierarchical (front row seats were reserved for senators from 194 BCE on), and so those standing in back were probably slaves and free persons of low social status. The prologist here calls attention to the shared status of the captives on stage, the slave-actors playing them, and these low-ranking members of the audience.

4   The idea of a son serving his father as a slave emphasized here (cf. 49-50) would have special significance for an audience in Rome, where the power of the *paterfamilias* over his children was absolute. Cf. Introduction, pp. 20-21 and *Amphitryon* 178 and n. 19 there.

5   The scripted jest with the audience member is part of the process of drawing the audience into the world of the play (see Introduction, pp. 7-8), and should not be taken as evidence for rowdy conditions in the Roman theater.

6   The Latin literally says "those of you who are enrolled on the Censor's list," thus indicating the free, propertied classes of Rome. The list was used to determine voting rights, eligibility for the military, and tax obligations.

7   Aetolia is a region on the west-central mainland of Greece. The Aetolians had a history of conflict with the Romans, and at the time of the play may have been at war with them. They were finally defeated by the Romans in 189 BCE, and, as Rome's other enemies, were stereotyped as treacherous and unreliable.

8   Elis is on the Peloponnese near the site of Zeus' (= Jupiter's) chief religious site at Olympia.

He was sold to a doctor in Elis named Menarchus.
Hegio then started trying to corner the market in Elean POWs,
Hoping he could buy someone to exchange for his captured son.
He has no idea his other son is in his own house now.
Yesterday he heard that an Elean of the upper class,   30
A knight from a fine family, had been captured, and
Decided to spare no expense to save his son.
So, to expedite his son's return home, he bought
Both these prisoners of war at the public auction.
These two however have privately put together a plot   35
To have the master sent home in his slave's place.
And so they've exchanged both their clothes and names.
That one now goes by Philocrates, this one by Tyndarus.
So today each will impersonate the other.[9]
Tyndarus will masterfully pull off a scheme to   40
Free his master, and in the very same stroke
Rescue his brother, and restore him to his
Father and fatherland as a free man—though he doesn't even
Know he's doing that! Often we do more good when
We have no idea what we're doing than when we think we do!   45
So without knowing it, these two have
Devised and ingeniously improvised a plot,
A masterpiece of their own making, so that
This one will stay here as his father's slave,
Though he has no idea his master is also his own father.   50
When you think about it, we mortals are wretched fools!
What follows here is fact for us actors, even if it's fiction for all of you.
There's one more thing I'd like to say just a few words about:
It really is in your best interests to pay attention to this play, since
It's not the same-old-same-old you see in other comedies.[10]   55
They'll be no dirty lines not worth repeating;[11]
Here you'll see no greedy pimp, no nasty whore,
No bragging soldier;[12] and don't you worry
About that war between the Aetolians and Eleans.

---

9   Presumably this means that Philocrates is wearing the mask and costume of a slave and Tyndarus that of a (free) young man.

10   For the special pleading on behalf of the play here, see Introduction, p. 19.

11   There is in fact virtually no obscenity in Plautus.

12   The greedy pimp (e.g., Ballio in *Pseudolus*), the manipulative prostitute, and the braggart soldier are stock characters in New Comedy.

All the battles will take place offstage.   60
It'd be downright wrong for a comic
Troupe like ours to suddenly go tragic on you![13]
So if anyone is bent on a battle—take it to court!
If you meet your match there, I guarantee you'll find
Such a frightful fight that you'll never, ever,   65
Want to feast your eyes on war again!
I'm out of here. Best of luck to you all, you justest of judges
In peace, and stoutest of warriors in war![14]

SCENE 1

Ergasilus enters from the forum.

Ergasilus[15]

The young men have nicknamed me "the call-girl" because
I show up at parties even if I'm not invited.   70
Now some of you smart asses may think the nickname is
Silly, but I beg to differ. We all know men call out the names of their
Favorite whores when they're gambling at parties.
And isn't being called pretty much the same thing as being invited?
So you can see how this applies to us parasites: 75
Whether we're invited or called, you'll always find us at parties,
Gnawing like mice on other people's food—it's our calling!
When it's holiday time and men vacation in the country,
Our teeth also go out of business.
Like snails who in the summer heat retreat to   80
Their shells and live off their own slime,
We poor parasites are forced to fend for ourselves
At the height of the holiday season, since the
Feasts we normally crash are off at the beach.
We start looking like greyhounds until the holiday's over,   85
And then we become chow-hounds again,
Actually a restless and persistent pack of wolf-downs.

---

13 Cf. Mercury's remarks (*Amphitryon* 51ff.) about the relationship between comedy and tragedy
    in his prologue.

14 Plautus's prologues usually end with a flattering valediction such as this to the audience,
    whose goodwill is being sought on behalf of the play and the troupe. Cf. *Casina* 87-8 and
    Introduction, p. 7.

15 Ergasilus is a "parasite," a stock comic figure who lives off the hospitality of others. Plautine
    parasites are relentless and raucous in their endless pursuit of a free meal. The loud entrance
    of a comic stereotype who immediately explains why he is nicknamed "the call-girl" (Latin
    scortum or "whore") partly undermines what the prologist has just asserted about the play's
    "purity" (53-8).

If a person in my line of work isn't prepared to take a few beatings
Or pots raining down upon his head, in no time he'll find himself
Carrying luggage at the Gate of Three Arches.[16]   90
That may very well be the sort of fate I'm facing,
Since my patron and savior has fallen into enemy hands.
It just so happens the Aetolians and Eleans are at war;
Now this is Aetolia here, and off that way is Elis, where
Philopolemus was captured. He's the son of the old man, Hegio,   95
Who lives here in this house—and what a house of sorrow it is
For me! Every time I look at it I lick my chops—and just cry!
Now for his son's sake, Hegio has become a slave-dealer
(a shameful profession and not at all in keeping with his character),
And is buying up captured prisoners, to see if   100
He can find one to trade for his son.
There's nothing I want more than for him to succeed:
If his son's not recovered, I'll never recover.
You can't expect anything from young men nowadays, self-absorbed
As they are. But that young man is an old-fashioned gentleman;   105
I never brought a smile to his face without earning a reward.
And the father is no less a gentleman than his son.
I'll go see him now. Hey, the door's opening—Oh my, how often
I've slipped out of there ripped and gorged!

SCENE 2

Hegio enters from his house with a guard and his assistants;
the captives may have remained onstage since the prologue.

Hegio

Listen up, you: take the heavy chains off those   110
Two captives I bought at the auction yesterday
And put separate cuffs on each of them, so they're
Not joined at the hip. They can walk about
As they wish, inside or out of the house,
As long as they're watched very carefully.   115
A free captive is like a wild bird: give it
Just the slightest chance to fly and it flees,
And you'll never be able to catch it again.

---

16 The Porta Trigemina in Rome, where beggars congregated. Note the casual allusion to the
    topography of Rome, despite the play's nominally Greek setting in Aetolia. The reference
    dates the play to 193 BCE or later. For Romanization in Plautus, see Introduction, pp. 2-3.

Guard[17]

    I'm pretty sure we'd all prefer to be free men
    Rather than slaves.

Hegio

                 Doesn't seem like you do.[18]   120

Guard

    Seeing I've nothing to give you for that, maybe I should give you the slip?

Hegio

    Just try it, and you'll get something from me you'll never forget.

Guard

    Maybe I'll turn into that wild bird you were just talking about.

Hegio

    Go ahead—I'll shut you right up in a cage.
    Enough chatter. Go and carry out my orders.   125
    I'm off to my brother's house to check on my other
    Captives and to see if they caused any trouble last night.
    And then I'm coming straight home.

Ergasilus

    It does trouble me to see this poor old man turned
    Slave-warden because of his son's troubles.   130
    But I could even put up with his becoming an
    Executioner if that would bring his son home.

Hegio

    Who's that talking?

Ergasilus

              Someone who is miserably melting with grief—
    Wasting, aging, and evaporating away!
    I'm skin and bones, shriveling up on a diet of sadness.   135
    I get no pleasure out of dining at home, but
    The slightest bite while dining out is sheer delight.

Hegio

    Hello, Ergasilus.

Ergasilus

          May the gods bless you, Hegio!

Hegio

    Don't cry!

---

17   The character type here serves as a general enforcer for his master, usually by whipping or
    chaining. Only in this Plautine play, however, does the Guard have a significant speaking
    part.

18   Hegio suggests that the Guard has not been saving money to buy his freedom, as Roman
    slaves regularly did.

Ergasilus

> Don't cry? How can I not cry for
Such a fine young man?

Hegio

> I always felt   140
You were a good friend to my son—as he was to you.

Ergasilus

> We mortals never appreciate the good things
We have until we lose them! It was only after
Your son fell into the hands of the enemy that I
Realized how much he meant to me—and now I do miss him!   145

Hegio

> Seeing how hard a stranger like you is taking his misfortune,
How do you think I feel? I'm his father and he's my only son.

Ergasilus

> A stranger! Me? A stranger to him? O, Hegio,
Don't ever say that—and don't ever even think it!
Yes, he is your only son—but he's my one and only friend.   150

Hegio

> You consider your friend's misfortune to be your own. I appreciate that.
But cheer up!

Ergasilus

> But it's as if the whole Food Corps
Has been dismissed: that, alas, is what grieves me most.

Hegio

> Haven't you found anyone else to command that
Army you say has been decommissioned?   155

Ergasilus

> Can you believe it? That's the one commission no one's filled
Ever since our commander Philopolemus was captured!

Hegio

> It doesn't really surprise me that no one wants the job.
You require so many soldiers, and of so many flavors:
First of all, you need a battalion of bakers,   160
Specialists from bakeries all over the world,
Recruits from as far as Baguettistan[19] and Pieland!
You require other recruits from Thrusha and Colomba;
And as for mustering up seafood—you'll need an entire battalion of
   marines!

---

19   The comic Latin place-names Plautus creates here combine aspects of food and food
     production with the names of actual places.

Ergasilus

How often the most exquisite gifts are kept hidden: 165
Underneath those civvies lies the heart of a true Commander-in-chef!

Hegio

Cheer up now. I'm quite confident I'll have him
Back home within just a few days.
You see, I have a young Elean captive inside, who is
A member of the upper class and as rich as can be. 170
I should be able to exchange him for my son.

Ergasilus

Let's hope the gods and goddesses are all for that! You haven't been
Invited out to dinner, have you?

Hegio

                         Not to my knowledge.
But why do you ask?

Ergasilus

                        Because it's my birthday.
And I'd like to see you invited to dinner—at your own house. 175

Hegio

Clever. All right, but only if you'll be content with
Something simple.[20]

Ergasilus

                     Not too simple though—
Since that's the sort of fare I'm used to feasting on at home.
So make me an offer: unless someone comes along with a more
Tantalizing one for my associates and me, I'll auction 180
Myself off to you like an expansive estate, on my terms of course.

Hegio

You're much more like a bottomless pit.
If you're coming, be sure to be on time.

Ergasilus

                         Oh, I can come right now.

Hegio

You'll have to go hunting for hare yourself—right now you're looking at possum.
The fare at my home travels along a rough and rocky road. 185

---

20   The contrast here between the simple fare Hegio advocates and Ergasilus' extravagant culinary fantasies reflects exaggerated stereotypes of both Greek luxury and "good old-fashioned" Roman simplicity. Cf. *Casina* 747 and n. 45 there.

Ergasilus

You can't scare me off that easily, Hegio:

I'll come riding on teeth that are shod like a horse.

Hegio

My fare is quite harsh.

Ergasilus

How so? Do you serve harshmallows?

Hegio

My dinners are earthy.

Ergasilus

Pigs roll on the earth before they become hams.

Hegio

I'm talking about lots of vegetables.

Egasilus

Then you're more of an herbalist than a host! 190

Is that it?

Hegio

Come on time.

Ergasilus

I'm the last person you need to tell that.

Hegio

I'll go inside and do a little accounting,

To figure out just how much I've got in the bank.

Then it's off to my brother's, as I'd planned.

SCENE 3

The captives are left with the Guard and his assistants.

(*SONG through 241*)

Guard

Since this burden of yours is the gods' will, you should just   195

Calmly endure it: The load you bear will be lighter that way.

I'm guessing you were free men back home:

Now that slavery is your lot, the prudent course is obedience and

Lightening that lot by carefully carrying out your master's commands.

And remember: when your master does wrong, wrong becomes right.

Captives

Oh, no!   200

Guard

There's no point in whining and tears:

It helps to buck up when the chips are down.

Tyndarus

But we're ashamed to be in chains!

Guard

Yes, but wouldn't it
Be a crying shame for my master if he unchained you and
Let you loose, seeing that he paid good money for you?   205

Tyndarus

What's he afraid of? Even if he let us loose
We know exactly what our duty is.

Guard

You'd hit the road. I know what you're up to.

Tyndarus

We'd escape? To where?

Guard

Home.

Tyndarus

The idea that we'd act like
Fugitive slaves!

Guard

Hey, I wouldn't discourage you if you had the chance. 210

Tyndarus

Can we ask you for just one favor?

Guard

And what would that be?

Tyndarus

Giving us a chance
To talk with each other away from you and these guys.

Guard

Fine. Move aside, you (*to the other guards*).
I'll go over here—but keep it short.

Tyndarus

That's what I planned. Come on over here!

Guard

Leave them be!   215

Tyndarus

We're both very grateful to you for giving us
The opportunity to do what we want.

Philocrates

Come on a little farther off this way.
We don't want any witnesses, or our
Whole plan will be leaked out.   220
Plots are not properly plots
If they're not cleverly crafted;
Those that are revealed in advance are utter disasters!

Right now you're passing as my master and I as your slave;
Still, we need to keep a close watch, and play this thing out   225
    Sensibly, smartly, carefully, and cautiously—
    And without an audience! We've taken on quite a task,
    So no sleeping on the job!

Tyndarus
                             I won't let you down.

Philocrates
                                    I hope not.

Tyndarus
    Though I value my own life, you know I
    I value it less than I do yours.   230

Philocrates
  I know that.

Tyndarus
    Let's hope you remember that when you have what you want!
The vast majority of human beings are virtuous
    When they want something; once they
    Have it, they're through with virtue
        And turn into lying degenerates!   235
    So you can see how I want you to treat me.

                  * * * *

Philocrates
    Just so you know, I'd call you my father if I dared to:
    You are like a second father to me!

Tyndarus
  I know.

Philocrates
    And so I have to keep reminding you that   240
I'm not your master, but now I'm your slave. Most importantly of all:
Seeing that it now is the immortal gods' will that
I be your fellow slave and not your master, and that instead of
Exercising my right to order you about I now must beg and beseech you,
Please, out of respect for our shared danger and my father's kindness
    to you,   245
And for this slavery we now share thanks to the hazards of war,
Please respect me the same as when you were my slave.
Above all, remember who you were and who you are now!

Tyndarus
  Yes, I know that for now I am you and you am I.

Philocrates

Yes, and as long as
You keep that close to heart, there's hope for our scheme.   250

SCENE 4

Hegio comes out of his house.

Hegio

I'll be back inside soon, once I learn what I want from these men.
But where are they? I gave orders for them to be brought out of the house.

Philocrates

You've certainly taken care to keep us close to home,
What with all the chains and guards you've walled us in with.

Hegio

If you're looking not to be scammed, you must always be on the lookout;   255
You throw caution to the wind when you believe you've taken all precautions.
And don't I have every reason to keep a close watch on you, seeing that
I bought you at a very high price, and in cash?

Philocrates

We don't blame you for wanting to keep an eye on us—and if
The chance to escape arises, don't blame us for fleeing.   260

Hegio

My son is a prisoner in your country, exactly as you are here.

Philocrates

He's a captive?

Hegio

Yes.

Philocrates

So at least we aren't the only cowards.

Hegio

Come on over here. I want to ask you a few things in private.
And I don't want you to lie to me about any of them.

Philocrates

I'll tell the truth about what I know; the same goes for what I don't.   265

Tyndarus (*aside*)

The old man has entered the barbershop and is about to be clipped.
And not so much as a towel to keep his clothes clean!
Hard to tell if he'll get a close shave or just a trim. If my master's
As good as I think, he should get a real fleecing!

Hegio

So tell me: would you rather be a slave or a free man?   270

Philocrates

Whichever involves the most pleasure and the least pain.

Slavery has never been a lot of trouble for me,
And I was treated just like a son in the family.

Tyndarus

Excellent! I'd take him over Thales[21] the Wiseman, who was just an
Amateur in comparison with my master here! 275
Just look at how cleverly he's playing the part of a slave.

Hegio

So tell me about the family of Philocrates over there.

Philocrates

He's a member of the Rich[22] clan,
The single most powerful and influential family in Elis.

Hegio

Is he much respected there?

Philocrates

Very much so, and by the most influential citizens.

Hegio

If he's as important in Elis as you say then, 280
I take it that the family's quite rich.

Philocrates

Filthy rich.

Hegio

Is the father alive?

Philocrates

Was when we left.
Of course only Hades knows for sure if that's still true now.

Tyndarus (*aside*)

Fabulous! He's a liar and a philosopher!

Hegio

What's his name?

Philocrates

Unmatchedmountainofmoneyides.[23] 285

Hegio

A name he no doubt earned because of his wealth?

Philocrates

Heavens, no! Because of his greed and aggression.

---

21   6th century BCE Greek philosopher, geometer, and astronomer, and one of the Seven Sages of
the ancient world. His name became a proverbial way to describe genius (cf. the similar use
of "Einstein").

22   The name is Polyplusius, which means "extremely wealthy" in Greek.

23   *Thensaurochrysonicochrysides*, a ridiculous and probably Plautine coinage (cf. Introduction,
p. 5) which in Greek literally means "Son of gold, prevailing in treasures of gold."

Tyndarus (*aside*)

    His father's real name is Theodoromedes.

Hegio

    Oh? So his father's tight-fisted?

Philocrates

                        I'd say completely close-fisted.

    Let me give you an example: when he sacrifices to his Guiding Spirit,[24]   290

    He performs the necessary rites with the cheapest plates, because he's afraid

    His Guiding Spirit will steal them. How do you think he treats everyone else?

Hegio

    Follow me over there then, and I'll ask your master these same questions.

    Philocrates, your slave here has behaved like an honest man.

    Thanks to him, I know all about your family.   295

    It's to your advantage to be equally honest with me—

    Though I think I got everything I need from him.

Tyndarus

                          He was just doing his duty

    When he gave it to you straight—though I was trying

    To keep you in the dark about my wealth and family, Hegio.

    Now that I've lost my country and liberty   300

    I can understand why he'd fear you more than me.

    An enemy assault has made him and me equals.

    I can remember when he didn't dare say a word against me; now he has

    The freedom to do as he wants. Fortune[25] lifts and lowers us as she pleases:

    I once was a free man—and she's brought me down from the top to the

        bottom;   305

    I'd grown accustomed to giving orders and now I must take them.

    I can only hope to find a master just like I was,

    One from whom I can expect fair and gentle treatment.

    If you don't mind, Hegio, I'd like to offer you one piece of advice.

Hegio

    Go ahead.

Tyndarus

                  I once was just as free as your son.   310

    His freedom and mine were both taken away by an enemy attack.

---

24   Every Roman male was thought to have been born with a divine "Guiding Spirit" or "Second-Self" (*genius*) that dwelt within him throughout his life. The *genius* of the *paterfamilias* was worshipped by the entire household.

25   One of many abstractions that were personified in Roman religion (in contrast with Greek religion); there were temples dedicated to *Fortuna*, a goddess of "luck" in Rome and throughout Italy from an early date.

He is now a slave in my country, just as I am in your house.
Surely a god is watching and listening to what we do, and will see
That his treatment there matches your treatment of me here.
Treat me well and he'll treat your son well—and vice-versa. 315
My father misses me just as much as you miss your son.

Hegio

I know that. But do you admit that what he said was true?

Tyndarus

I admit that my father is extremely wealthy and that
I come from a distinguished family. But please, Hegio,
Don't get greedy because of my wealth. 320
Even though I'm an only son, my father might think it more honorable
For me to be your well-fed and well-clothed slave than
To live in shame like a beggar in my own country.

Hegio

Thanks to the gods and my family inheritance, I'm rich enough.
I'm not one to assume every chance for profit is advantageous. 325
And I know lust for filthy lucre has corrupted many men,
And there are even times when a loss beats a gain.
As for gold? I despise it: it often leads men astray.
Now look. Here's what I have in mind:
My son was captured in Elis and is now a slave there; 330
Get him back to me and I'll release the both of you. I won't
Ask for a penny more, but that's the only way you'll be freed.

Tyndarus

That's completely reasonable and fair. You are a very reasonable man.
But is your son publicly owned or is he someone's private slave?

Hegio

He's owned by Menarchus the doctor.

Tyndarus (*aside*)

Oh, he's one of my master's clients. 335
(*to Hegio*) This will be as easy as finding water in a rainstorm!

Hegio

So get him ransomed.

Tyndarus

I will. But I have one request, Hegio—

Hegio

Yes, whatever you want, as long as it doesn't hinder my plan.

Tyndarus

Here's my idea:
You needn't release me until your son's back here.
Please agree to release my slave on bail to my father, 340

So that your son can be ransomed for him.
Hegio

                           No, no, I'd rather send someone else there
Once there's a truce, to meet with your father
And carry out your instructions to the letter.
Tyndarus

There's no point in sending a stranger—you'd be wasting your time and effort.
Send him: he'll finish off this business right when he gets there.   345
There's no slave in the whole world more trustworthy,
No one more in tune with my father's thinking, and there's absolutely
No one my father would rather entrust his son to.
There's no reason to fear: the risk for this test of honor is all mine.
I trust his character: he'll treat me in kind for my kindness to him.   350
Hegio

I'll let him go on bail—and you'll be my security for that then?
Tyndarus

                                             Yes.

And I'd like to see this deal sealed as soon as possible.
Hegio

And if he doesn't return, you agree to pay me twenty minae[26]
For him?
Tyndarus

            Yes, absolutely.
Hegio

                          Release him then—and this one too.
Tyndarus

May the gods grant you everything you want!   355
Thank you for respecting me and unchaining me.
Ah, that's nice, not having a collar around my neck!
Hegio

Do an honorable man a favor and he'll do you one back.
Since you're sending him there, give him very precise instructions
On what to tell your father. I'll call him over here.
Tyndarus

                                Please do.   360
Hegio

Let's hope this turns out well for us all—my son, myself,
And you two. As your new master,

---

26   A Greek form of currency, equivalent to one hundred ancient drachmas. In the late Classical
       period, a skilled Athenian laborer made one drachma per day in wages.

I want you to faithfully obey your old one.
He's put up twenty minae as bail for you, so you
Can go off to his father and ransom back my son from him. 365
There's to be an exchange between his father
And me—an exchange of our sons, that is.
Philocrates
I'll do what's right by each of you.
Consider me to be a wheel at your service:
Turn me this way, turn me that way—I'm at your command. 370
Hegio
You are really serving your best interests
When you bear your slavery at it should be borne.
Follow me. Here's your man.
Tyndarus
Thanks
For giving me this opportunity to send
Him off to my parents with news about 375
How I'm doing here and the details of
What I need them to do for me there.
Now Tyndarus, this gentleman and I have agreed
To send you home to Elis on bail; if you don't
Return here, I have to pay him twenty minae. 380
Philocrates
That's just fine by me.
I'm sure your father is waiting for me or someone else
To bring him news about you.
Tyndarus
So listen up closely to
The message I want you to take back to my father.
Philocrates
Philocrates, you can count on me to do everything I can 385
To see that your best interests are served; I'll
Give it all my heart and soul, as I always have.
Tyndarus
Exactly as you should. Okay, listen up:
First, give my best to my parents and any other
Of my relatives and friends you see. 390
Tell them all that I'm well and I'm a slave to a
Perfect gentleman who treats me with complete respect.
Philocrates
You don't need to remind me of that.

Tyndarus
     Except for the guard, I'm living like a free man.
     And tell my father about the agreement he and I have   395
     Made about his son.
Philocrates
                              I've got it. Don't waste time reminding me.
Tyndarus
     And that he should ransom him and send him here in exchange for us both.
Philocrates
     Yes, I've got it.
Hegio
                         And as quickly as possible, for both our sakes.
Philocrates
     He wants to see his son just as much as you do yours.
Hegio
     Yes, all fathers love their sons.
Philocrates
                              Anything else I should tell your father?   400
Tyndarus
     Stress that I'm fine, Tyndarus, and don't hesitate to talk yourself up:
     Mention how there has always been perfect harmony
     Between us, how I have never found fault with you or had to be harsh,
     How you have been a perfect slave to your master in times of
     Terrible trouble, never failing me in your thoughts or your deeds at   405
     Even our darkest moments. Tyndarus, once my father realizes how
     Well-disposed you've been to his son and to him,
     He won't hesitate to grant you your freedom—gratis.
     And when I return there, I'll see that he does exactly that.
     I have a chance to see my parents again only   410
     Because of your hard work, our friendship, and your courage.
     And thanks to your shrewd move in telling him all about
     My family and wealth you've freed your own master from his chains.
Philocrates
     Yes, that's exactly how it went down. Good of you to remember my part in it.
     You truly deserve all I've done for you, Philocrates.   415
     It would take me all day and then some
     To recount all the good things you've done for me. You couldn't
     Serve me more obediently if you actually were my slave.
Hegio
                                                  By the gods,
     Such noble characters! They bring me to tears!
     It's obvious how much they care for each other—and for a slave   420

To so lovingly lavish such praise on his master!

Tyndarus

Really, he deserves

A hundred times the praise he gives me!

Hegio

You've already done so much for your master and now you have the chance
To top your prior service by doing this for him.

Philocrates

My desire to do it is surpassed only by the effort I'll put into it.   425
With Jupiter[27] as my witness, Hegio, I swear that I'll always be
Loyal to Philocrates—

Hegio

You are a true gentleman.

Philocrates

And always do to him just as I would want done to myself.

Tyndarus

I can only hope your actions will match your words.
It may be that I've said less than I wanted to about you.   430
Please don't be offended and listen closely:
Always keep in mind that you are returning home on bail,
At my risk, and it's my life here that's on the line.
And don't forget about me as soon as I'm out of your sight
And you've left me to be a slave here in your place.   435
Once you're free, don't break your promise and
Not bother to bring this man's son home and rescue me.
Keep in mind that you are being released on bail of twenty minae.
Stay loyal to someone who is loyal to you, and don't budge from that loyalty.
I am sure my father will do as he should.   440
Respect our friendship forever, and welcome this newly found friend.
As we shake hands, I beg you to swear again
You'll be no less loyal to me than I have been to you.
Go on, then: you are my master, protector, and father.
All my hope and safety rest with you.

Philocrates

Enough instructions.   445

Will you be happy if I convert all your instructions into realities?

Tyndarus

Yes.

---

27   Chief Olympian god (= Greek Zeus).

Philocrates

    I'll return fully equipped with what you both want.
    Is there anything else?

Tyndarus

                Just that you come back as quickly as possible.

Philocrates

                                      Yes, of course.

Hegio

    Come along to the bank and I'll get you some travel money,
    And we'll also get a passport from the praetor.[28]

Tyndarus

                         A passport for what?   450

Hegio

    For him to show to the army, so they'll let him go home.
    You need to go in the house.

Tyndarus

                Have a good trip.

Philocrates

                    Goodbye.

Hegio

                            What a great deal
    It was for me to buy those two at the quaestors'[29] auction!
    If the gods are on my side, I've freed my son from slavery!
    Hard to believe I ever hesitated to buy them.   455
    All right, you slaves: watch him closely inside, and make sure
    He goes nowhere without a guard. I'll be back home soon.
    I'm off to my brother's to see the other captives
    And find out if anyone knows this young man.
    But first we need to send you off. Follow me.   460

SCENE 5

Ergasilus returns from the forum.

Ergasilus

    It's sad to see a man searching so hard for a meal barely find it;
    Still sadder is to see him search hard and still find nothing; but the saddest
    Thing of all is when he's dying to eat and there's not a single morsel to be had.
    If I could, I'd scratch the eyes right out of this day, seeing that
    It's turned every living soul so spitefully against me.   465

---

28   Powerful Roman magistrate whose duties included administration of law.

29   Lowest ranking of the Roman magistrates.

Has any day ever been so stuffed with starvation, so full of hunger?
And I've never seen a day so bent on failure. What are
My stomach and gullet doing? Attending a Festival of Famine?
You can just kiss the parasitical profession goodbye once
The young men push us poor starving comedians away.   470
They haven't the time of day for us Spartans,[30] us champions of the
Uni-bench,[31] we who inherited only our ancestors' beatings, and whose only
Wealth is wit and words. No, they want guests who eat and then return
    the invite.
They even shop for food themselves—formerly the prerogative of us
    parasites—
Or march right up to the pimps and conduct their own business without
    a blush,   475
Just as solemnly as if they were handing down a guilty sentence in court!
They're so in love with themselves, they don't give a rat's ass for us parasites!
Why, just a little while ago I walked up to some young men in the forum
And I said: "Greetings, gents. So where are we having lunch?" Total silence.
"Did someone say 'follow me'?" Dead silence. Nobody even laughs.   480
"And what about dinner?" They just shake their heads.
I tell them one of my best jokes, the kind
That used to get me a month's worth of free dinners.
Not a single person laughs, and I realize it's all a set-up:
Forget about the laughs, not a single one of them   485
So much as bares his teeth like an angry dog.
I see I'm being mocked and so I leave them
And I go to one group, then another, and another—same old story:
They're all in cahoots, like the oil-dealers in the Velabrum![32]
I knew they were mocking me. So I'm back here again.   490
I wasn't the only parasite pointlessly on the prowl in the forum.
I know my rights, and even if I have to invoke some foreign law,[33] I'll have
My day in court against those who conspired to deprive me of life, liberty,
And the pursuit of food. Their fine? Ten dinners, I choose the menu,
And when prices are really high! That's my plan. But now I'm off to the
    harbor.   495

---

30   Males in the military state of Sparta were trained to endure hunger and hardship from an
     early age, and so the tag is ridiculously applied to parasites here.

31   Whereas Roman diners typically reclined on couches, guests of lower status, such as
     parasites, might have to sit on an *unisubsellium*, or "bench for one."

32   A flat space between the Capitoline and Palatine in Rome that became a central market for
     food, oil, and wine. For Ergasilus' propensity for Romanization, see Introduction, p. 20.

33   Literally "a barbarian (*barbaricus*) law," which by convention in Plautus means a Roman
     one. Cf. *Casina* 747 and n. 45 there.

That's the last port of call for my culinary voyage—if my prospects there
Have gone out with the tide, I'm right back here for the old man's harsh fare.

SCENE 6

Hegio returns from the forum with Aristophontes and guards.

(*SONG*)

Hegio

What ever could be finer than finishing up your
Personal business and doing a public service as well? That's just what
   I did
When I bought these men yesterday. People see me   500
And they have to run up with congratulations.
I'm utterly exhausted from the stopping,
   Staring, and shaking of my hand. Poor, pitiful me—
      I barely got away from it all!
   Finally, I get to the praetor, where I catch my breath   505
And get the passport, which I passed on to Tyndarus, who's now on his
  way home.
   So once that's done I head back home,
But first stop off at my brother's, who's keeping my other captives.
   I ask if anyone of them knows Philocrates of Elis,
   And this one says he's a good buddy of his.   510
   Once he hears I've got him, he begs and begs me
      To let him see him.
And so I gave the order to unchain him. Follow me now
(*to Aristophontes*),
     And I'll grant your request
      To see him.   515

SCENE 7

Tyndarus reacts to seeing Hegio and Aristophontes.

Tyndarus

With this development, I'm better off dead than alive!
There's nothing to hope for now, no one can help me.
This is the day that will do me in once and for all! There's no way
To escape destruction, no way to drive off the danger here,
Or just to cloak my elaborate fabric of lies. There's no chance of
  finding a   520

*   *   *

Sanctuary for all my fibs, no escape route for my schemes,
No accommodations for my machinations, no retreat from all my deceit!
What was covered has been discovered, our plot has been divulged
For all to see. What's left for me except to face untimely   525

Death, doom and destruction as my master's surrogate?
Aristophontes, the new arrival, has ruined me and my plan!
He knows me, and he's Philocrates's close friend and relative.
Salvation[34] herself couldn't save me now even if she wanted to.
My only chance is using my brain to devise some clever stratagem.   530
But what plan, what plot? Damn it! This is all
Just foolish chatter! I'm a fool–and I'm in a bind.

SCENE 8

Hegio and Aristophontes engage Tyndarus.

Hegio

Where'd that guy go who just rushed out of the house?

Tyndarus (*aside*)

That's the end of me. Prepare to face the enemy, Tyndarus.
What can I possibly say? Should I lie or deny it all? Just confess?   535
It's all so unclear, and there's nothing to give me any confidence.
I wish the gods had wiped you out before you ever left home,
Aristophontes, and wrecked my carefully planned out plan!
Unless I find some wickedly clever scheme, everything is lost.

Hegio

He's over there. Go over and speak with him.

Tyndarus (*aside*)

Is anyone more screwed than me?   540

Aristophontes

Tyndarus, why won't you even look at me?
Why do you pretend as if you don't even know me?
I may be just as much a slave as you are now, but back home I was free:
You've been a slave in Elis since your childhood.

Hegio

It's no surprise he avoids the sight of you, and even shuns you,   545
Since you insist on calling him Tyndarus instead of Philocrates.

Tyndarus

This man is considered to be raving mad back in Elis,
So pay no attention to his lies, Hegio.
He's chased his mother and father around the house with a spear.
He also sometimes has epileptic fits.   550
You should keep farther away from him.

Hegio

Yes, keep him away from me!

---

34   There were temples and shrines of *Salus*, "Salvation" or "Safety," in Rome and elsewhere.
Cf. n. 25 above.

Aristophontes

What? So I'm raving mad and chased my father with a spear
And I have epileptic fits? Why, you human punching bag!

Hegio

Now stay calm! That's a disease that afflicts many men,
And many of them have even been cured by being spat on. 555

Aristophontes

So you actually believe it?

Hegio

Believe what?

Aristophontes

That I'm insane.

Tyndarus

Just look at all that hostility on his face! You'd better leave now, Hegio.
It's just like I told you: watch out, there's a fit coming on!

Hegio

I realized he was insane right when he called you Tyndarus.

Tyndarus

Sometimes he doesn't even know his own name or who he is. 560

Hegio

And he also said that you were a close friend of his.

Tyndarus

Oh, right!

And I suppose Alcumeus, Orestes and Lycurgus[35] are
Old school-chums of mine too?

Aristophontes

Still slandering me,
You scumbag! I don't know you?

Hegio

Obviously you don't, when
You call him Tyndarus instead of Philocrates. 565
You don't even recognize the person right in front of your eyes.

Aristophontes

No, no he's claiming to be someone he isn't and denying who he really is.

Tyndarus

So your purpose here is to make a liar out of Philocrates?

---

35 In Greek myth, Alcumeus, or Alcmaeon, killed his mother Eriphyle to avenge the death
    of his father Amphiaraus and subsequently went mad; Orestes, who appears in various
    Greek tragedies, similarly avenged his father Agamemnon's death by killing his mother
    Clytemnestra and was driven to insanity by the Furies; Lycurgus foolishly attacked the god
    Dionysus (= Bacchus) and in an insane fit massacred his own family.

Aristophontes
No, the way I see it, your purpose here is to make
A mockery of the truth. But, damn it, look right at me.
Tyndarus

                                                                    Okay.

Aristophontes

                                                        Tell me now: 570
Do you deny that you're Tyndarus?
Tyndarus

                                            Yes.

Aristophontes

                                    And you say you're Philocrates?
Tyndarus
I do indeed.
Aristophontes
        And you believe him?
Hegio

                    More than I believe you—and as much as I believe myself,
Since the man you say he is left here today for Elis
To see this man's father.
Aristophontes

                        Father? What father? He's a slave![36]
Tyndarus

                                                Just as you are now.
You were free and I hope to be so again,   575
Once I've brought this man's son back to freedom here.
Aristophontes
You scumbag! I suppose now you're also claiming you're the freer of man? [37]
Tyndarus
No, I'm just claiming to be Philocrates—and a free man.
Aristophontes

                                            What?
This scum is making a mockery out of you now!
This man is a slave himself, and he's never owned any slave except
        himself.   580

---

36   According to a Roman legal fiction, slaves were said to have no parents. Cf. Introduction, p.
       21.

37   There is a pun here on *liber*, "free," and *Liber*, a title of Bacchus (= Greek Dionysus), who as a
       god of wine and inspiration provides welcome release for mortals.

Tyndarus

Just because you're poor back home and lack a decent livelihood
Doesn't mean everyone else has to be like you. That's nothing unusual:
Desperate people are spiteful and usually envy respectable folks.

Aristophontes

Hegio, you've got to stop blindly trusting this guy.
The way I see it, he's already scored a punch or two.   585
And his claim that he'll ransom back your son—that just doesn't sound right.

Tyndarus

Maybe not to you. But it's what I'm going to do—with the gods' help
    of course.
I'll restore this man's son to him, and he'll restore me to my father in Elis.
That's why I sent Tyndarus off to my father.

Aristophontes

                                                But that's who *you* are!
And you definitely are the only slave named that in Elis.   590

Tyndarus

Still needling me about being a slave, when it's only an accident of war?

Aristophontes

I don't think I can control myself!

Tyndarus

                                See! Did you hear that? You'd better run!
If you don't have him restrained, he'll be chasing us with stones!

Aristophontes

This is killing me!

Tyndarus

                                His eyes are flashing, Hegio! It's happening again!
Look at how his body is all covered with those horrible spots!   595
The black bile is taking hold of him again!

Aristophontes

                                Black pitch should be taking hold of you, damn it, and
Lighting up your head![38] If the old man had any sense, he'd take you right to
the executioner's.

Tyndarus

Now that's the craziness talking! The demons have control of him!

Hegio

Should I have him restrained?

Tyndarus

                                That would be the most sensible thing.

---

38 A gruesome form of Roman punishment in which the victim was smeared with pitch and
other flammable material and then ignited.

Aristophontes

This is killing me! If only I had a stone to bash in his brains!   600

This whipping post's jabber is driving me nuts!

Tyndarus

Hear how he's looking for a stone?

Aristophontes

I need a one-to-one with you, Hegio.

Hegio

Just say what you want from over there. I can hear you from over here.

Tyndarus

Don't go any closer to him or he'll bite your nose off your face.

Aristophontes

I'm not insane, Hegio, and I never have been,   605

And I've never had the disease he claims I do.

But if you're afraid of me, have me restrained—I don't mind

As long as you restrain him too.

Tyndarus

No, Hegio, don't restrain me—

Just restrain him since he's the one who wants it.

Aristophontes

Listen up, you phony Philocrates:

I'll prove right now that you really are Tyndarus.   610

Why are you winking at me?

Tyndarus

Winking at you?

Aristophontes

What would he do if you weren't so close?

Hegio

What if I just walk right up to this madman?

Tyndarus

You'd just get more nonsense and ridicule.

You won't be able to make heads or tails of his gibberish.

You'll think you're looking at an Ajax[39]—minus the costume.   615

Hegio

I don't care. I'm going right up to him.

Tyndarus (*aside*)

It's all over for me now!

---

39 Ajax went insane after losing the contest for the arms of Achilles to Odysseus, slaughtered
the flocks of the Greeks, and then killed himself (the subject of Sophocles' *Ajax*).

Stuck between a rock and a hard place[40]—I've got no ideas.

Hegio

I'm listening, Aristophontes. Say what you want.

Aristophontes

I want to tell you the honest truth, which you now believe to be a lie.

First, let me clear up one thing: I'm not insane   620

And there's nothing wrong with me at all, except that I'm a slave now.

May the king of gods and men keep me away from my native land forever

If this man is any more Philocrates than either you or I.

Hegio

                                      Well, who is he then?

Aristophontes

The very person I've been telling you from the start.

I hereby pledge to permanently surrender my liberty to you   625

And never see my parents again if you find out I'm lying.

Hegio

What do you have to say?

Tyndarus

                I am your slave and you are my master.

Hegio

                                  Not what I asked.

Were you a free man?

Tyndarus

           I was.

Aristophontes

                Nonsense! He most certainly was not!

Tyndarus

How would you know? How dare you be so bold!

I suppose you were my mother's midwife?

Aristophontes

               I saw you when we were both children.   630

Tyndarus

And I'm looking at you now that we're both adults, so right back at you.

Wouldn't it be smarter to stay out of my business? I stay out of yours, don't I?

Hegio

Wasn't his father Unmatchedmountainofmoneyides?

Aristophontes

No—and I've never heard that name before today.

---

40   The Latin proverb here is "between the sacrificial victim and the knife."

Philocrates's father is named Theodoromedes.
Tyndarus (*aside*)

That's it for me!   635
Can't you be still, my beating heart—or else just go hang yourself?
I'm so afraid I can barely stand and you're still jumping around!
Hegio

And so that is your absolute proof that this man was a slave in Elis
And he is not in fact Philocrates?
Aristophontes

Absolutely. Nobody'll ever prove I'm lying.
So where's Philocrates now?
Hegio

The last place in the world I should have sent him!   640
So then I've been ripped like a board, split down the middle like a cord
   of wood
By this scumbag who led me on with all the tricks of his trade!
But are you sure?
Aristophontes

Everything I've said is unimpeachable.
Hegio

Sure?
Aristophontes

Absolutely sure. Nothing could be more certain.
Philocrates and I have been close since childhood.   645
Hegio

What's your friend Philocrates look like?
Aristophontes

He's got a narrow face, a sharp nose, a fair complexion, dark eyes,
And wavy, reddish hair that falls down in little curls.
Hegio

That's him.

Tyndarus (*aside*)

And that's it for me: I really stepped into it today!
Alas for those poor rods, alas that they must die upon my back today![41]   650
Hegio

It's clear I've been bamboozled!
Tyndarus

Why, my shackles, do you tarry?

---

41   The rods are for beating him, a common punishment for slaves. Here and in 651-2 Tyndarus
      parodies tragic language.

Run to me and wrap yourself around my legs, so that I may protect you.

Hegio

So those two captives caught me in their web of deceit today,
The one pretending to be the slave, the other the master.
I've lost the nut and am left with just the shell as security.   655
They've really smeared egg all over my face today!
This one at least will never mock me again! Boxer, Killer, Banger!
Come on out from there—and bring the straps!

SCENE 9

The slaves emerge from the house to tie up Tyndarus.

Boxer

Want us to fetch wood or something?

Hegio

Clamp some handcuffs on this dirtbag.

Tyndarus

What's going on? What did I do?

Hegio

                                        You dare ask?   660
You're the germ, seed, and root of this mess!

Tyndarus

You left out "source, font, spring," etc.
Farmers need to water before they grow.

Hegio

The nerve of him, smarting off to me like this!

Tyndarus

An innocent slave who's done no wrong has every right   665
To be confident, especially in his master's presence.

Hegio

Tie up his hands now—and tightly!

Tyndarus

You might just as well have them cut off, since you own me.
But what's happening? Why are you so angry at me?

Hegio

Because all my hopes, plans, and prospects rested on you,   670
And you, your trickery and your
Perjurious plots have ruined me, ripped me to shreds,
And blown everything to pieces! It was just
That sort of deceit that cheated me out of Philocrates.
You led me to believe he was the slave, and you the free man: 675
That's what the two of you said, and you even
Exchanged names!

Tyndarus

I confess it all,

It happened just as you say. It was because of my

Deceitful plan and cunning that he got away from you.

But, please tell me: is that why you're so angry with me?   680

Hegio

You'll pay for what you did with extreme torture.

Tyndarus

I'm not afraid of dying, as long as it's not for an unjust cause.

If he does not return and I die here, at least

What I did will be remembered after my death,

How I restored my master to his freedom, father, and fatherland   685

After he had been captured and enslaved by the enemy,

And how, to save his life, I choose to expose

Myself to the ultimate danger.

Hegio

Then go ahead and reap the glory for your deed in Hades![42]

Tyndarus

He who dies courageously does not die entirely.   690

Hegio

I don't care if people say you're half-dead or entirely dead

Once I've dealt you the most exquisite tortures

And put you to death for your patchwork of lies!

As long as you're dead, they can say you're alive for all I care!

Tyndarus

I swear, if you do that, you do it at your own risk: 695

I'm quite confident that my master will come back here.

Aristophontes (*aside*)

By the immortal gods! Now I get it, now I see

What's going on! My friend Philocrates has been freed

And is back home with his father. Great!

There's no one I'd rather see doing so well.   700

But I cringe to think of the trouble I've caused him—

He's all bound up now because of me and my big mouth.

Hegio

Didn't I tell you not to lie to me today?

Tyndarus

You did.

---

42   The underworld of the dead.

Hegio

Then why did you have the audacity to do it?

Tyndarus

Because the person I was obligated to help would have been hurt by the
truth.   705

As it turned out, my lies helped him.

Hegio

Yes, and they will hurt you.

Tyndarus

Fine.

At least I saved my master and I'm glad for it,

Since my elder master had put me in charge of protecting him.

Do you really think I've done wrong?

Hegio

Terribly wrong!

Tyndarus

Well, I beg to differ with you: I say it was the right thing to do.   710

Suppose one of your slaves did the same thing

For your son: wouldn't you be very grateful?

Wouldn't you want to free that slave?

Wouldn't he be the most beloved slave in your house?

Please, tell me.

Hegio

I suppose.

Tyndarus

Then why are you so angry with me?   715

Hegio

Because you were more loyal to him than to me.

Tyndarus

Really? A prisoner just captured, your latest purchase—

In one day you really expected to train me

To serve you more loyally than someone

I've been together with since childhood?   720

Hegio

Then ask him for thanks for that. Take him off

And find him some thick and hefty shackles.

Then it's straight off to the stone-quarries.

There, while the others quarry their eight blocks,

You'll do twelve each and every day, unless   725

You want the nickname "Plaid-back."

Aristophontes

By all gods and men, Hegio, I beg you

Not to ruin this man!
Hegio
                              He'll be well taken care of:
At night he'll be chained to his cell and closely guarded;
In daytime he'll break rocks underground.   730
You see, I want his torture to last more than one day.
Aristophontes
Are you absolutely inflexible about this?
Hegio
                                        Inflexible as death.
Take him right off to Hippolytus the blacksmith
And have some sturdy shackles slapped on him.
Then lead him out through the city-gate   735
To my freedman Cordalus there at the quarries.
And convey my wish to Cordalus to see that
He gets no worse treatment than the worst-treated.
Tyndarus
Why ask for mercy when you won't grant it?
The danger you put me in puts you in danger too.   740
Once I'm dead, there's no evil in death to fear.
It's only for a brief span of time I'll endure your punishments—
Even if I live to a ripe old age.
Farewell and best wishes, though you don't deserve them.
And I wish you the farewell you deserve from me too, Aristophontes: 745
This all happened to me because of you.
Hegio
                              Lead him away!
Tyndarus
I have one last request: please give me a chance
To meet with Philocrates if he returns.
Hegio
I'll kill the whole lot of you if you don't take him out of my sight this instant!
Tyndarus
Talk about violence! I'm being pushed and pulled at the same time!   750
Hegio
There he goes off to the prison he so richly deserves.
This will serve as an example to the other captives
Of what will happen to them if they do the same.
If it hadn't been for this man who set me straight,
Those tricksters would still be taking me for a ride.   755
I'll never trust another human being again!
Once fooled is one time too many. I just wanted

To ransom my son out of slavery: all my
Hopes of that have slipped away. I already lost one son
When he was four years old. A slave stole him from me,   760
And there's been no trace of either him or my son since then.
My older son has fallen into the hands of the enemy—what is this curse?
Did I have children only so that I would be childless?
This way, right back to where you were. Since no one pities me,
Neither you nor anyone else will ever get any pity from me again.   765

Aristophontes

Getting out of my chains seemed like a good omen; now I think
I'd best get back into them and try my luck over again.

SCENE 10

Ergasilus returns from the harbor.

Ergasilus

Mighty Jupiter! My savior and supporter!
You bring me the richest, no make that the fattest prosperity:
Plaudits and profits, festivity and frivolity, holiday and leisure-day,   770
A festival of foodstuffs, plenty of potables—pure joy!
Never again will I have to grovel before any human being!
This lovely day has lovingly showered me with so much loveliness
That I can favor my friends and harm my enemies just as I please.
I've fallen into the fattest inheritance, free of all liens!   775
So it's full bore ahead to old Hegio here, to whom
I bring all he's ever asked the gods for—and more!
Here's my plan: I'll make my entrance just like the slaves in comedies do,
The ones who bring the latest news.[43] Cloak bundled around neck—there.
This is how I'll earn an everlasting legacy of chow.   780

SCENE 11

Hegio comes out of his house and eavesdrops on Ergasilus.

(*SONG*)

Hegio

The more I toss this business around in my head,
The sicker I get in my heart. To think
That I had my face rubbed in it today like that!
    And I never saw it coming!
When people find out, I'll be the laughingstock of the city.   785
The instant I arrive in the forum, everyone will say:

---

43   Ergasilus will play the role of the "running slave," a set Roman comedic routine in which a
     slave enters breathlessly with news. Cf. *Amphitryon* 984ff. and n. 54 there.

"There's that clever old man who got himself bamboozled."
But look, is that Ergasilus I see way over there with his
Cloak all bundled up? Now what's he up to?

Ergasilus

No slacking now, Ergasilus, you've got work to do!   790
I order, no, I *forbid* anyone to get in my way—
Unless someone thinks he's lived long enough! Anyone I find
In my way will find himself flat on his face.

Hegio (*aside*)

                                        This one's itching for a fight.

Ergasilus

I know what I'll do. So everybody just keep moving along
And keep your business out of this street.   795
My fist here is a missile-launcher, my elbow's a catapult,
My shoulder a battering-ram, and my knee will just plain knock you flat.
Any man who gets in my way will learn the true meaning of "toothpick."[44]

Hegio (*aside*)

How absolutely astounding! Why all this bluster?

Ergasilus

He'll never forget this day, this place, this man: 800
Whoever faces me will come face to face with his life.

Hegio (*aside*)

What business could be so important as to call for all this bluster?

Ergasilus

So that ignorance of the law may not excuse, I hereby decree:
Stay at home and shelter yourself from my wrath!

Hegio (*aside*)

Well, I'll be! Looks like someone is stuffed completely full of himself! 805
I pity the poor man whose table fattened up his confidence.

Ergasilus

As for the millers who feed their swine on bran
And create such a stench that the mill is off limits:
If I so much as see one of their sows on the street,
My fists will make crushed bran out of its owner!   810

Hegio (*aside*)

What royal pronouncements! Such authority!
He's full of it! Such a bellyful of boldness!

Ergasilus

As for the fishmongers who ride on clomping and jolting nags

---

44   I.e., his victims will have to collect their teeth off the ground after he has knocked them out.

To peddle their fetid fish to the people, fish so foul
That they drive all the loafers out of the basilica[45] and into the forum: 815
I'll pummel their faces with fish-baskets,
To give them a taste of their own foul medicine.
As for the butchers who deprive the ewes of their young
And sell you lambs for the slaughter for twice their price,
And who refer to an old castrated ram as a "prime breeder:"   820
If I so much as see that "prime breeder" on the street,
I'll serve both owner and breeder up a big fat slice of mortality.

Hegio (*aside*)

Outstanding! Issuing aedile's[46] edicts now!
Seems as if the Aetolians have appointed him Chief Market Inspector.

Ergasilus

No longer call me a parasite, but a king among kings: 825
The cargo my stomach has long awaited has arrived: chow!
But now I must deliver my load of joy to old Hegio.
There's no one alive as lucky as he is.

Hegio (*aside*)

What could this load of joy be he's serving up in heaps?

Ergasilus

Hey, is there anybody home? Is someone going to open the door?   830

Hegio (*aside*)

Back for his dinner from me.

Ergasilus

                                Open up both these doors,
Before I pound them into splintery oblivion!

Hegio

        I'll speak with him. Ergasilus!

Ergasilus

                                Who calls Ergasilus?

Hegio

Turn around.

---

45   A large Roman public hall with walkways, where various types of business were conducted.
      The earliest known basilica in Rome was built by Cato the Elder in 184 BCE, the year of
      Plautus' death. For Ergasilus's tendency to Romanize, see n. 32 above.

46   The Roman magistrate (cf. Introduction, p. 6) whose various duties included supervision of
      the markets.

Ergasilus

That's more than Lady Fortune does or will do for you.[47]

Who is it?

Hegio

Over here—it's Hegio.

Ergasilus

Ah, yes,   835

Nice timing, O finest of all human beings in the world!

Hegio

Guess you found yourself a dinner, and that's why you're so high and mighty.

Ergasilus

Give me your hand.

Hegio

My hand?

Ergasilus

Yes, your hand-right now!

Hegio

Here it is.

Ergasilus

Be happy!

Hegio

Why should I be happy?

Ergasilus

Because I say so—so be happy!

Hegio

Sorrow trumps happiness in my life these days.   840

Ergasilus

I am about to drain off every last drop of sorrow from your body.

Be happy—and be proud of it!

Hegio

Okay, I'm happy—though I have no idea why.

Ergasilus

Great. Now give the order—

Hegio

For what?

Ergasilus

For a great big fire to be made.

---

47   A brash insult (Ergasilus is still in the character of the running slave), i.e., Fortune wouldn't give him the time of day. *Fortuna* was worshipped in Rome and throughout Italy from an early date. For the personification, see n. 25 above.

Hegio
> A great big fire?

Ergasilus
>> That's what I said

Hegio
>>> Listen, you vulture,
> Do you expect me to burn my house down for your amusement?

Ergaslius
>>> Don't be angry. 845
> Now how about having the pots set on the oven, the dishes washed,
> Maybe some bacon, and a beautiful banquet boiling over the fire?
> And be sure to have someone go fetch some fish.

Hegio
>>> He's daydreaming.

Ergasilus
> And have someone else get pork, lamb, and farm-fresh chicken.

Hegio
> Good taste—if only you could afford it.

Ergasilus
>>> Ham, sea bream,   850
> Mackerel, the catch of the day, stingray, tuna, cream cheese.

Hegio
> An abundant feast of words, Ergasilus, but these items are scarce
> In my house.

Ergasilus
>> So you still think this is all about me?

Hegio
> You won't be served nothing today, but you will get next to nothing.
> So just bring your everyday appetite.   855

Ergasilus
> I'm going to make you want to spend lavishly—even I won't be able to
>> stop you.

Hegio
> Really?

Ergasilus
>> You will indeed.

Hegio
>> So you're my master now?

Ergasilus
>>> No, just a good friend.
> Can I make you happy now?

Hegio

That certainly beats being miserable.

Ergasilus

Give me your hand.

Hegio

Okay.

Ergasilus

The gods are on your side.

Hegio

Yeah, and harboring a grudge.

Ergasilus

You haven't been to the harbor like I have—that's why you're bearing
   a grudge.   860

So have the sacred vessels prepared for the sacrifice—and fast!

And have a fat lamb brought in, all according to my order.

Hegio

Why?

Ergasilus

For the sacrifice.

Hegio

To which god?

Ergasilus

Why to me of course! I am your almighty Jupiter—
As well as your Salvation, Lady Luck, Light, Gladness and Joy.[48]
And so you must propitiate the great deity with a full feast.   865

Hegio

You're on the hunt for a meal, I gather.

Ergasilus

No, *you're* hunting and gathering. *I'm* eating.

Hegio

As you like. I'm easy.

Ergasilus

Old habit from when you were a boy, huh?[49]

Hegio

May Jupiter and all the gods rain destruction upon you!

---

48   Cf. n. 25 above.

49   Ergasilus imparts a sexual spin to Hegio's words—*facile patior*, "I readily submit [to your
     wishes]"—by suggesting that he engages in passive homoerotic activity, acceptable in the
     ancient world in the case of a boy, whereas a free adult male who allowed himself to be
     sexually penetrated drew scorn.

Ergasilus

But you ... really should shower me with thanks
Because of the good news I'm harboring from the harbor.
Now your dinner seems appealing.

Hegio

Get lost, you idiot! You're too late.   870

Ergasilus

You'd be justified in saying that if I'd come earlier.
But as things are now, listen up to my good news: I saw
Your son Philopolemus just now in the harbor. He's alive and well.
He was on a ferry, along with that young Elean,
And your slave Stalagmus, the one who stole   875
Your little boy when he was four and ran off with him.

Hegio

Go to hell! You're mocking me.

Ergasilus

By our Holy Mother of Indulgence,[50] Hegio,
As sure as I pray for her everlasting presence deep within my gut,
I did see him.

Hegio

My son?

Ergasilus

Your son and my Guiding Spirit.

Hegio

And the Elean Captive?

Ergasilus

Yes, by Apollo![51]

Hegio

And that worthless slave of mine,   880
Stalagmus, the one that kidnapped my son?

Ergasilus

Yes, by Cora![52]

Hegio

I'm to believe that?

Ergasilus

Yes, by Praeneste!

---

50 *Sancta Saturitas* here is a deity of Ergasilus' own devising: cf. n. 25 above.

51 Olympian god of poetry, music, and prophecy.

52 This and the names that follow are towns in the region of Latium, just southeast of Rome.

Hegio

            He's actually come?

Ergasilus

                    Yes, by Signia!

Hegio

You're sure?

Ergasilus

     Yes, by Frusino!

Hegio

         Positive?

Ergasilus

            Yes, by Alatrium!

Hegio

Why are you swearing by these foreign[53] towns?

Ergasilus

                 Because they're all disagreeable—

Just as you said your dinners are.

Hegio

         Damn you!

Ergasilus

                  Right back at you,   885

Since you don't believe I'm telling the absolute truth.

Now what nationality was this Stalagmus when he took off?

Hegio

Sicilian.

Ergasilus

      Now he's a Gaul and he's got a rather galling yoke around his neck:[54]

He's married to it so he won't have to steal other people's children anymore.

Hegio

Tell me now, is everything you've told me the honest truth?

Ergasilus

                      Yes, all of it. 890

Hegio

By the immortal gods, it's as if I've been born again—if you're not lying!

Ergasilus

What? You still have doubts despite my sacred oath to you?

Well, Hegio, if you think so little of my oath, why not go to the harbor

And see for yourself?

---

53   "Foreign" here translates *barbaricus*: cf. n. 33 above.

54   I.e., he wears a device used to restrain those accused of crimes.

Hegio

Yes, definitely. Go inside and do whatever needs to be done.
Whatever you want—Take it, ask for it, or just grab it. You're Storeroom-
    Czar.   895

Ergasilus

Damn it, if I've lied, you can give me a make-over—with a club.

Hegio

If you really are telling the truth, I'll feed you to the end of time.

Ergasilus

And who's paying?

Hegio

My son and I.

Ergasilus

Do I have your promise on that?

Hegio

Yes.

Ergasilus

And I promise you that your son is at the harbor.

Hegio

Do your best to get things ready.

Ergasilus

Enjoy your walk—and the walk back here! 900

SCENE 12

Left alone onstage, Ergasilus addresses the audience.

Ergasilus

He's gone, and has left me in charge of all the edibles!
By the immortal gods! Now's the time to slice neck from tenderloin:
The times are hazardous for hams, bacon faces blight,
Sow's udder is utterly done for, pork rind will find its ruin, and
The pork-sellers and butchers are facing a lot of fatigue.   905
It'd take far too long to mention all the ways to stuff a stomach!
I must go perform my solemn civic duty: passing judgment on the bacon,[55]
And trying hams left hanging in suspense.[56]

---

55 Ergasilus's obsession with pork reflects Roman, not Greek, taste.

56 The Latin verb for "hanging" here is used of unresolved lawsuits. The word *ius* in the phrase
    "passing judgment" in line 907 can indicate either "judgment" or "sauce" (the two words are
    unrelated: cf. "justice" and "au jus"), and so there is a similar culinary/legal pun there.

SCENE 13

A young slave rushes out of the house.

Slave Boy

May Jupiter and the other gods blast you, Ergasilus, you and your belly,
And all parasites and whoever even thinks of feeding them again! 910
Our house has just been devoured by disaster and destruction!
There he was, like a hungry wolf. I was so afraid he'd lunge at me!
Then the grinding and gnashing of his teeth—so horrible!
In he came and pulled down the meat rack, carcasses and all.
He grabbed a sword and sliced off three huge tenderloins; 915
Then he smashed all the pots and dishes holding less than two gallons!
He even wanted the cook to use the water tanks for boiling!
Then he broke into the pantry and opened up all the cupboards.
Watch him now, you slaves. I'm going to go find the old man,
And tell him to do some shopping if he wants to eat: 920
The way this guy's going, everything's gone already, or soon will be!

SCENE 14

Hegio returns from the harbor with Philopolemus,
Philocrates, and Stalagmus.

(*SONG through 927*)

Hegio

I owe so many thanks to Jupiter and the other gods
For restoring you back to your father,
For taking me off this mountain of misery
I've borne every day I've been without you; and 925
For bringing this slave back under my control,
And for the unfaltering honor of this man.

Philopolemus

I've had enough pain myself, and am worn out by tears and anguish,
And you've told me more than enough about your own grief.
Can't we just get down to business?

Philocrates

Well? I've kept my promise to you 930
And brought back your son and restored his freedom.

Hegio

For what you have done,
Philocrates, I could never thank you enough,
On behalf of both myself and my son.

Philopolemus

You'll find a way
Father, as the gods will show both of us how to

Properly thank the person we owe so much.   935
Likewise, father, you'll give this man exactly what he deserves. (*points to*
    Stalagmus)

Hegio

What more can I say? I could never refuse anything you want.

Philocrates

What I want is for you to return the slave I left here as security
, Back to me. He has always treated me better than he treats himself,
And I want to reward him for all the good he's done for me.   940

Hegio

After what you've done for me, I'll gratefully grant your request—
This one and any other you make. And I hope that you won't
Be angry with me because of the way I treated him in my anger.

Philocrates

What'd you do to him?

Hegio

                After I found out how he tricked me,
I had him condemned to the stone-quarries.

Philocrates

                      Oh no, no!   945
Such a decent human being suffering for my sake!

Hegio

Because of that I'll give him back to you at no cost:
Take him, gratis. He's free.

Philocrates

             Thank you, Hegio,
For your kindness. Please have him brought here now.

Hegio

                       Will do.

Hey, you (*to slave*)—go get Tyndarus immediately!   950
You two go inside. I want to interrogate this human punching bag
And find out what's happened to my younger son.
In the meantime, go on in and clean up.

Philopolemus

               This way, Philocrates.

Philocrates

                    I'm right behind you.

SCENE 15

Hegio and Stalagmus are left onstage.

Hegio

Come over here, my good man, my charming little piece of property.

Stalagmus

When a man like you tells lies, what do you expect from me?   955
I used to be handsome and charming, but I've never been a "good man"—
And never will be. So you're mistaken if you think I'll do you any good now.

Hegio

You seem to have a pretty good sense of where you stand.
It's to your advantage to be truthful—you can make a bad situation a little
    better.
So out with the honest truth—though you've never been   960
Truthful or honest before.

Stalagmus

          Do you think you can make me ashamed enough to confess?

Hegio

Oh, I'll make you ashamed all right—you'll be beet-en red all over.

Stalagmus

I do believe you're threatening me with a whipping—as if that was
    something new.
Enough of this. Say what you've got for me, so you can get what you want.

Hegio

Such a sharp tongue! But how about putting a lid on it for now?   965

Stalagmus

Whatever.

Hegio

          Hard to believe he was so respectful as a boy.
But more to the point: pay close attention and carefully answer my questions.
As I said, you can make things a little bit better for yourself.

Stalagmus

What crap! You don't think I know exactly what I deserve?

Hegio

Well, you might avoid some punishment—or maybe all of it.   970

Stalagmus

I might avoid a little, but there'll be a lot more coming. And I have it coming,
Since I ran away, kidnapped your son and sold him.

Hegio

To whom?

Stalagmus

> To a Theodoromedes Polyplusius, in Elis,

For six minae.

Hegio

> By the immortal gods! That's the father of Philocrates here!

Stalagmus

Well, I know him better than you do, and I've seen him a lot more.   975

Hegio

Mighty Jupiter, keep me and my son safe!

Philocrates, come out here right now! I need to speak with you!

SCENE 16

Philocrates emerges from the house.

Philocrates

Right here, Hegio. Tell me what you want.

Hegio

> This guy claims

That he sold my son to your father for six minae in Elis.

Philocrates

How long ago was that?

Stalagmus

> Twenty years ago.   980

Philocrates

He's lying.

Stalagmus

> One of us is. But your father did in fact

Give you your own four-year old playmate when you were a young boy, right?

Philocrates

What was his name? If you're telling the truth, you'll remember that.

Stalagmus

His name was Paegnium, but you later renamed him Tyndarus.

Philocrates

How is it I don't know you?

Stalagmus

> Because people tend to forget, or not know   985

Those they can no longer expect to get anything from.

Philocrates

So was the boy you sold to my father the same one

Who was given to me?

Stalagmus

> Yeah, it's his son.

Hegio

Is he still alive?

Stalagmus

I got my money. The rest I don't care about.

Hegio

What do you think?

Philocrates

I think that Tyndarus himself is your son.   990

All this man's testimony points to that. We were together since childhood,

And I can assure you he had a proper and respectable upbringing.[57]

Hegio

Oh, this is bittersweet for me if what you say is true:

If he really is my son, I have done a terrible, terrible thing to him!

How much more—or less—than what is right I've done!   995

To have done what I did—it's torturing me. If only it could be undone!

Look, here he comes, dressed in a way someone like him doesn't deserve!

SCENE 17

Tyndarus is led in by guards from the country, still in chains.

Tyndarus

I'd seen lots of paintings of the tortures in the underworld,

But none of these can capture the living hell

I was in at the stone-quarries. Down in that place   1000

You're worked far beyond the point of total exhaustion.

You know how patrician children[58] are given

Jackdaws, ducklings, and quail to play with? Well, when I got there

They gave me just this crowbar to amuse myself with.

But there's my master in front of the door. And my other master

from Elis!   1005

Hegio

Hello, my long-lost son!

Tyndarus

Your son? What?

Oh, I see. You're pretending you're my father and I'm your son

Because, like a parent, you've brought me into the light of day.

Philocrates

Welcome, Tyndarus.

---

57 The assurance here that Tyndarus has not been "tainted" by his servile status is elsewhere in Plautus made regarding young women who have become the property of a pimp (by, e.g., exposure at birth) and subsequently revealed to be of free status.

58 The allusion to the children of Roman patricians here encourages the audience to consider Tyndarus' situation in terms of their own social structure.

Tyndarus

          Same to you—thanks again for all the misery.

Philocrates

    But now I'm going to make you a free man—and a rich one too.   1010
    This is your father, and this is the slave who kidnapped you
    And sold you for six minae to my father. And then my father gave
    You to me as my own personal property when we were just boys.
    We brought this man back from Elis and he told us everything.

Tyndarus

    What about Hegio's son?

Philocrates

          He's your brother—and he's right inside here. 1015

Tyndarus

    You know I now seem to have this foggy memory
    Of my father being called Hegio.

Hegio

    Yes, that's me!

Philocrates

       And about those chains: shouldn't your son's load be lightened,
    And this slave's increased proportionately?

Hegio

              Yes, that's the first order of business.
    Let's all go inside. I'll see that the blacksmith is called to   1020
    Take off your chains and give them to him.

Stalagmus

    Just the thing for someone who has nothing of his own.

EPILOGUE[59]

Spectators, this has been the chastest of plays:
No lewd titillation, no lascivious assignation,
No substitute child in swaddling clothes, no swindling of cash,   1025
No prostitute purchased by a lovesick lover behind his father's back.[60]
There are very few plays like this around for playwrights today,
Edifying plays that make good folks even better. If we have pleased
And not repulsed you, please do send us a sign:
If you think respectability should reap its due reward, then clap!   1030

---

59   It is unclear if the epilogue is delivered by the actor playing Stalagmus, who last spoke, or the leader of the troupe. Cf. n. 1 above.

60   Stock New Comedy situations. For the play's claim to purity here, see 53-8, n. 15 above, and Introduction, p. 19.

Pseudolus

Characters with Speaking Parts

PSEUDOLUS, *slave of Simo (and so also of his son Calidorus)*
CALIDORUS, *son of Simo*
BALLIO, *pimp and neighbor of Simo*
SLAVE, *slave of Ballio*
SIMO, *head of the household*
CALLIPHO, *friend and neighbor of Simo*
HARPAX, *slave and military assistant to the Macedonian soldier
    (Polymachaeroplagides)*
CHARINUS, *friend of Calidorus*
SLAVE BOY, *young slave of Ballio*
COOK, *cook hired by Ballio to prepare his birthday feast*
COOK'S ASSISTANT, *young assistant to the cook*
SIMIA, *slave of Charinus*

SCENE

*Athens: the action takes place in front of the houses of Simo,
Ballio, and Callipho.*

PROLOGUE

You'd best get up and stretch your loins:
A long play by Plautus is coming onstage next.[1]

---

1   This opening is uniquely brief among Plautine prologues, and the third person reference to
    Plautus further suggests that it was added for a revival performance after Plautus' death: cf.
    Casina 13 and n. 4 there. The opening exchange between Pseudolus and Calidorus outlines
    the dramatic situation and so functions as a prologue.

SCENE 1

*Pseudolus and his (younger) master Calidorus
emerge from Simo's house.*

Pseudolus[2]

    Master! If your silence could tell me what
    Terrible troubles are troubling you so terribly,
    I'd gladly have spared the two of us the trouble—   5
    Me of asking and you of answering.
    But since that is impossible,
    I now must ask you directly: why is
    This tablet your constant companion?
    You constantly cry on its shoulder,   10
    But leave me completely in the dark.
    Out with it: I need to know what I don't.

Calidorus

    I'm so, so very sad, Pseudolus.

Pseudolus

                    Jupiter[3] forbid!

Calidorus

    My case doesn't fall within Jupiter's jurisdiction:
    Venus[4] is my judge and jury, not Jove.   15

Pseudolus

    Any possibility you can tell me about it? You've always
    Considered me your closest confidante.

Calidorus

    And I still do.

Pseudolus

            Fill me in then. I'll provide whatever you need—
    Cash, a loyal accomplice, or just a good plan.

Calidorus

    Take this tablet and read for yourself   20
    Why I'm wasting away so woefully.

Pseudolus

    Glad to oblige. Hey what's this?

Calidorus

                  What's what?

---

2   Pseudolus means "Liar" in Greek.

3   Chief god among the Olympians (= Jove and Greek Zeus).

4   Goddess of sex/love (= Greek Aphrodite).

Pseudolus
These letters are looking to raise a family:
They're all over each other!
Calidorus
                              Hah, hah.
Pseudolus
No one in the world could possibly   25
Make this out—except a Sybil.[5]
Calidorus
How can you insult such sweet letters,
So sweetly written by such a sweet hand?
Pseudolus
Yikes! Since when do hens have hands?
This is complete chicken-scrawl!
Calidorus
                              I hate you.   30
Either read the tablet or return it to me.
Pseudolus
                              Okay, I'll read it.

Mind listening?
Calidorus
                    If I had a mind—
Pseudolus
                              Please find one.
Calidorus
I'll listen, but you must find my heart in that wax:[6]
That's where my heart resides—not in my chest.
Pseudolus
I see your girlfriend, Calidorus!
Calidorus
                              Where, where?   35
Pseudolus
Right there, stretched out on the tablet, winking at you in the wax.
Calidorus
Damn, I wish all the gods would just—
Pseudolus
                              Bless me, yes!

---

5   Generic name of the prophetess whose oracular centers were located throughout the ancient
    Mediterranean world.

6   This common form of ancient tablet was framed in wood and had an erasable wax surface
    that could be written on with a stylus.

Calidorus
> As the grass of summer, so brief is my life:
> Quickly did I rise, so quickly was I mowed down.[7]

Pseudolus
> Quiet, while I read over the tablet.

Calidorus
>   Yes, please do.   40

Pseudolus
> "My dearest darling Calidorus: through this wax,
> This wood, these letters (our go-betweens), I send
> My greetings and beg you: *please save my life.* I write
> With tears, trembling in my heart and soul."

Calidorus
> I'm screwed! I've got absolutely no lifesaver   45
> To offer her.

Pseudolus
>   Just what flavor do you need?

Calidorus
>   Silver, pure silver.

Pseudolus
> You're trading her silver for wood?
> What kind of deal is that?

Calidorus
> Read on. I'll guarantee you'll see
> Just how soon I need that silver in hand.   50

Pseudolus
> "My pimp has sold me to a foreigner, a
> Macedonian soldier, for twenty minae,[8] my love.
> Before leaving, the soldier put down fifteen minae,
> And now just five minae will seal the deal.
> So the soldier left a token here,   55
> His own portrait in wax, taken from his ring.
> The pimp has pledged to send me along with
> Whoever brings a matching token. The designated day
> For that is the one right before the Dionysia."[9]
> That would be today.

---

7   The lovesick Calidorus waxes poetically (and melodramatically) here.

8   A Greek form of currency, equivalent to one hundred ancient drachmas. In the late Classical period, a skilled Athenian laborer made one drachma per day in wages.

9   A festival in honor of the god Dionysus (= Bacchus).

Calidorus

                      And that'll be the end of me,   60

Unless you can help!

Pseudolus

                      Let me read on.

Calidorus

Please do. It makes me think I'm talking with her.

Read on: ah, it's a bittersweet mix for me!

Pseudolus

"All our lovers' trysts, our intimate rendezvous,

The fun, the frolicking, sweet talk and sweeter kisses,   65

Our tangled bodies' tight embrace,

The little nibbles of limber lips,

The delicate tickle of erect little nipples—

Over all these lovely delights of ours

Loom destruction, discord and devastation,   70

Unless you rescue me or I you.

I've taken care to tell you all I know;

Now to find out what's real and what's pretend. Love, Phoenicium."

Calidorus

It's a woeful letter, isn't it Pseudolus?

Pseudolus

                            Absolutely wretched!

Calidorus

Why aren't you crying?

Pseudolus

                    I've got eyes of pumice. I couldn't convince them   75

To spill out so much as one single tiny tear.

Calidorus

Why's that?

Pseudolus

              Oh, I descend from a long line of dry-eyes.

Calidorus

Won't you help me at all?

Pseudolus

                  What can I do for you?

Calidorus

Waah!

Pseudolus

        Waah? Oh, I've got plenty of those to spare.

Calidorus

This is so depressing! I can't get a loan anywhere.   80

Pseudolus

    Waah!

Calidorus

    And I don't have a penny in the house.

Pseudolus

                         Waah!

Calidorus

    And he's going to take away my girl.

Pseudolus

                    Waah!

Calidorus

    That's supposed to help?

Pseudolus

              I do what I can.

    And I happen to have a vault full of "waahs."

Calidorus

    That's it for me! But I could use a single drachma,[10]   85

    Which I'll pay you back tomorrow. Got one?

Pseudolus

    Hardly—not even if I mortgaged myself.

    What do you want the drachma for?

Calidorus

                 I want to buy a rope.

Pseudolus

    Why?

Calidorus

        To hang myself with.

    I'm to be a shade before this evening's shadows fall.[11]   90

Pseudolus

    Then how would I get my drachma back?

    Or is that why you want to hang yourself—

    You're planning to default on that drachma, aren't you?

Calidorus

    There's no way I can go on,

    If she's dragged off, no longer to be mine!   95

Pseudolus

    Stop crying, you fool. You'll live.

Calidorus

               Any reason I shouldn't cry?

---

10   Cf. n. 8 above.

11   Calidorus's lament parodies the language of tragedy.

I haven't a nickel to my name,
And no hope of finding so much as a penny.
Pseudolus
If I get the gist of this letter,
You'd better cry a river of gold.   100
As for your big showery show of tears:
You're just pouring water down the drain.
Fear not, lover-boy, I won't desert you.
I hope to find you some help of the silvery variety—
By some honest means, or perhaps in my usual way.   105
I have absolutely no idea where I'll get it,
But I know that I will: my twitching eyebrow says so.[12]
Calidorus
I only hope you can do what you say.
Pseudolus
You know full well what chaos I create
Once I've marked out my victim.   110
Calidorus
You're my only hope of help.
Pseudolus
Will you be happy if today I make this girl your
One and only—or if I give you twenty minae?
Calidorus
Yes, either way!
Pseudolus
                    Then ask me for the twenty minae,
So you know exactly what I'm promising.   115
Please, please ask me: I'm dying to promise!
Calidorus
Will you give me twenty minae today?
Pseudolus
Yes. Now stop bothering me. And so
There's no confusion, listen carefully:
If no other tool's around, I'm fleecing your father.   120
Calidorus
May the gods forever bless you! But look:

---

12   If Pseudolus' mask had an asymmetrical brow, an actor skilled in the use of masks could
     easily represent twitching through gesture.

Out of full respect for family duty, could you fleece my mother too?[13]
Pseudolus

You can rest insured about that.
Calidorus

"Rest insured" or "rest assured?"
Pseudolus

           My way is so less cliché!
And so there's no confusion, everyone listen up: 125
I hereby decree,[14] to all citizens assembled here, to the
Entire populace, to all my friends and all who know me:
Be wary of me today and, above all, DON'T TRUST ME!
Calidorus

Shh! Quiet!
Pseudolus

      What's the matter?
Calidorus

          The pimp's door cracked open.   129-30
Pseudolus

I'd like to crack open his knees!
Calidorus

Here he is, in the flesh—the President of Perjury himself!

SCENE 2

As Ballio enters from his house, together with his (male)
slaves, Pseudolus and Calidorus recede in order to eavesdrop.
(*SONG through 264*)
Ballio

Come on now, you slackers (*to slaves*). It was my bad to buy you,
My bad to keep you! Has it ever occurred to any of you
To actually do something without my having to do THIS
(*he cracks his whip*)?   135
Your ribs are so calloused, you're asses, not men!
It hurts me more to whack these whip-wasters than its hurts them!
Given just the slightest opening, they can only think: "steal, snatch,
      Grab, gobble, guzzle—and run!"
You'd be better off having wolves watch your flocks than to   140

---

13   Pseudolus and Calidorus brazenly flout the important Roman concept of *pietas*, which
     required absolute obedience and respect toward parents. Cf. Introduction, p. 17.

14   Pseudolus comically misappropriates the Roman practice of convening a public meeting
     (*contio*), a privilege restricted to magistrates and priests, and usually reserved for speaking on
     important matters of state. For the thorough Romanization here, see Introduction, pp. 2-3.

Let these men guard your home!
Their looks may be deceiving, but their work is brutally honest:
It stinks. Now listen up carefully to this decree:
If you don't this instant shake the sleep and sloth out of your eyes,
With these very whips I'll weave such a pattern of welts on you   145
That your striped hides could outsell Campanian[15] quilts
Or oriental rugs with the most beastly designs!
Did I not yesterday assign you all your tasks and stations?
But your shameless skulls are so thick,
The only way to get you to work is THIS!   150
So this is your plan: to wear out me *and* the whip?
Short attention span? Maybe you'll pay attention to THIS!
Point your ears in my direction, you human whipping-posts!
Do you really think your hard hides can outlast this rawhide enforcer
    of mine!
Now what? Hurts, eh? Well, THIS is what a disrespectful slave gets!   155
Now all of you fall in line and listen closely.
You with the pitcher: fetch water and fill the cook's cauldron.
You with the axe: you're now Head of the Ministry of Firewood.

Slave

But the axe is dull.

Ballio

                So what if it is? That's never stopped me from using you.
So the two of you have something in common.   160
You there! You're to make the house shine. Run along, inside!
And you! You're Caretaker-of-the-Couch. And you're to polish the silver.
When I return from the forum, I expect to find everything right—
Swept, prepped, rubbed, scrubbed, and clean with lots of sheen.
        Today is my birthday, and your duty is to celebrate it with me.   165
        I expect to see bacon, ham, tenderloin, sow's udder all in a pot.
        I'm feasting some important fellows and want them to think I'm loaded.
        Now hurry along inside and get things ready: we can't delay the cook!
I'm off to the market, to clean them out of their fish.
Lead the way, boy! And let's take care no one tries to tap into my wallet!   170
Wait! I have one last decree to deliver to this household,
And it's for the women: do you hear me in there? (*to the prostitutes inside,*
    who emerge)
Distinguished hookers of distinguished men, you who daintily pass the days
In grace and elegance! Today I'll find out who wants to be free

---

15   A region of west central Italy renowned for its fertility and wealth.

And who just wants free meals, who earns her keep and who just wants
   to sleep;   175
In other words, who'll cease to serve me and who of you'll go up for sale.
Your task: see that your lovers lavish me with loot today, a
Year's provisions to be precise—or you'll be out walking the streets.
You know it's my birthday, so where are all those young dudes who call you
   "Light of my life," "sweetie-pie," "kissy-face," "boobykins," "honey-
   buns?"   180
I want a whole army of gift-givers here in front of the house, double-time!
Why do you think I supply you with clothes, jewelry and all that you need?
And what have you done today except make trouble and guzzle wine?
You drown your bellies in that, while I have to stay stone cold sober.
The best thing to do now is to call you each out by name,   185
So none of you claims she wasn't given any orders.
            Listen up, all of you!
You first, hey Hedylium![16] You're the darling of all the grain dealers
Who maintain mountains of grain at their homes.
Your job's to see we're brought a year's supply, enough for me   190
And the whole household. I want to be swimming in grain,
So that I'll no longer be known in the city as Ballio the Pimp,
But as the Corn-King.

Calidorus (*aside*)
                Just listen to that dirtbag brag!
   He thinks he's so magniloquent!

Pseudolus (*aside*)
                    Malignant, more like it.
   But quiet now and listen!   195

Ballio
Listen up, Aeschrodora![17] Your specialty is the butchers, rivals of us pimps:
Our fellow flesh-peddlers who ply their trade in rotten meat.
I want three meat-racks replete with tasty tenderloins today.
Otherwise, I'm sure you know how Dirce[18] was tied
To the side of a bull—you'll find yourself riding just so   200
Right on top of a meat rack!

Calidorus (*aside*)
              Every word of his burns me up!

---

16   Her name means "sweet thing" in Greek.

17   "Shameful (or ugly) gift" in Greek.

18   In Greek myth, Amphion and Zethus brutally avenged Dirce's mistreatment of their mother
     Antiope by tying her to the horns of a bull.

Pseudolus (*aside*)

    To think the young men of Athens even let him live here!

Where are they, where are those young dudes who buy their lovin' from a
    pimp?[19]

Why don't they all assemble and rid our populace of this pestilence?

    Fat chance! I'm so naïve, so foolish!   205

    As if they'd rise up against the master

    Who keeps them enslaved to their passion!

Calidorus (*aside*)

    Be quiet!

Pseudolus (*aside*)

        Why?

Calidorus (*aside*)

             You're not helping me when I can't hear him over your noise.

Pseudolus (*aside*)

    Okay, I'm quiet now.

Calidorus (*aside*)

                I'd prefer you actually were and not just saying you are.

Ballio

Hey you, Xystilis![20] Your turn to listen up! You are the darling of those 210

        Whose houses ooze with olive-oil.

        If you don't deliver an orchard of oil

        To me by the bucketful,

I'll see you're promptly dropped on a street corner tomorrow!

There you'll get a mattress, but you won't get any sleep—   215

        And that will be exhausting!

        Do you catch my drift?

Admit it, you snake! You've got all these friends soaking in oil,

But have your efforts ever made anyone's head slicker

In this household, or seasoned just one of my salads?   220

Your problem is lack of respect for the value of oil,

        While you practically worship wine.

Now listen carefully: I'll settle our bill once and for all if you don't do

        Everything exactly as I say!

---

19   The direct appeal to the males in the audience here is signaled by the Plautine formula *ubi
       sunt*, "Where are the …?"

20   She is named after the *xystos*, or covered practice track for running in the Greek gymnasium,
       where men removed their clothes and coated their bodies with oil before athletic activity. Sex
       is often portrayed as vigorous exercise in Latin (a prostitute in Plautus' *Cistellaria* is named
       Gymnasium).

Now as for you, Phoenicium:[21] Your specialty is always being   225
On the verge of counting out cash for your freedom.[22]
You talk the talk, but can never seal the deal.
You are the sweetie-pie of the upper-crust; unless pies and other provisions
Pour in today, you and your sore, sorry, crimson cheeks are out on the
　　street tomorrow!

SCENE 3

Pseudolus and Calidorus engage Ballio.

(*SONG*)

Calidorus (*aside*)

　　Pseudolus! Do you hear what he's saying?

Pseudolus (*aside*)

　　　　　　　　　　　　　　　　Oh, he's got my full attention.　　230

Calidorus (*aside*)

　　How can I keep him from prostituting my prostitute?

Pseudolus (*aside*)

　　Don't worry. I'll do the worrying for both of us.

　　This pimp and I are old buddies and chums:

　　For his birthday today I'll give him one heaping helping of hell!

Calidorus (*aside*)

　　What's the use?

Pseudolus (*aside*)

　　　　　　　How about thinking about something else?

Calidorus (*aside*)

　　　　　　　　　　　　　　　　　　　　But, but …　　235

Pseudolus (*aside*)

　　Putt, putt …

Calidorus (*aside*)

　　　　　This is torture!

Pseudolus (*aside*)

　　　　　　　Harden your heart!

Calidorus (*aside*)

　　Impossible!

Pseudolus (*aside*)

　　　　　You must.

21　Her name means "Crimson" or "Phoenician" (indicating her native land).

22　Roman slaves were allowed to accumulate their own property and money, and were motivated
　　to work by the prospect of purchasing their freedom from their masters.

Calidorus (*aside*)

How?

Pseudolus (*aside*)

Control your emotions.
In a crisis, think creative and constructive thoughts.

Calidorus (*aside*)

What crap! What's the fun of being in love if you can't be a fool?

Pseudolus (*aside*)

Not letting up?

Calidorus (*aside*)

Pseudolus, my friend, let me be worthless! Please, please!   240

Pseudolus (*aside*)

I'll let you on the condition you let me go.

Calidorus (*aside*)

No, no, don't go! I'll be good.

Ballio (*aside*)

Time's wasting and I'm wasting time. Move it, boy.

Calidorus (*aside*)

Hey, he's leaving! Call him back!

Pseudolus

Yoo-hoo, birthday boy, birthday boy, yes I mean you, birthday boy!
Come back!   245
Over here! Certain people would like to have word with you.

Ballio

What the? Who dares to detain a busy man like me?

Pseudolus

A past supporter of yours.

Ballio

A past supporter's as good as dead. I need a present one.

Pseudolus

So arrogant!

Ballio

So pestilent!

Calidorus

Grab him!

Ballio

Move on, boy!   250

Pseudolus

Let's cut him off this way!

Ballio

Go to hell, whatever your name is!
This way now, boy.

Pseudolus

Can I have a word with you?

Ballio

I'd rather you didn't.

Pseudolus

Even if it's in your best interest?

Ballio

Will you or will you not let me go?

Pseudolus

Oh, please do stay.

Ballio

Let go!

Calidorus

Ballio, hear me out!

Ballio

I can't hear babble at all.   255

Calidorus

I paid when I had cash.

Ballio

I'm not interested in what you had.

Calidorus

I'll pay when I've got cash.

Ballio

When I get that, you'll get something.

Calidorus

Oh poor, poor me, I gave and I gave and now
I have nothing but a mountain of misery!

Ballio

Your cash is dearly departed, so you're as good as dead to me.   260

Pseudolus

Consider who this is!

Ballio

I've known for a long time who he was.
It's his job to figure out who he is now.
Let's move along, you!

Pseudolus

Just give us a minute, Ballio.
There's cash in it for you.

Ballio

You just bought yourself that minute! If I were in the middle   265
Of a sacrifice to mighty Jove and suddenly the chance to
Grab some cash arose—end of sacrifice right then and there!

Cash! Under any and all circumstances, that's my higher calling.

Pseudolus (*aside*)

He thinks absolutely nothing of the gods we all revere!

Ballio (*aside*)

I'll speak to him. (*to Pseudolus*) Good morning to you, Athens's worst
slave![23]   270

Pseudolus

It's my wish and his that the gods bless you;
Or if you deserve otherwise, that they curse you.

Ballio

How's it going, Calidorus?

Calidorus

I'm madly in love and my cash is utterly gone.

Ballio

How pitiful—if only I could feed my family on pity.

Pseudolus

Very funny, but we already know exactly what you are—no need to
broadcast it.   275
But do you know what we want most?

Ballio

Pretty much—my destruction?

Pseudolus

Yes, of course—and there's another reason we called for you. Listening?

Ballio

Yes,
But I'm quite busy, so keep it short.

Pseudolus

He's very ashamed about what he promised you for his girlfriend,
And that the payment date for the twenty minae has passed.   280

Ballio

Better something causes him shame than that it be a crying shame for me;
He's a bum because he hasn't paid. It bums me out because I haven't been
paid.

Pseudolus

He'll get it and he'll pay. Just give him a few days.
He's really afraid you'll sell her out of spite.

---

23   Although some emphasis is placed on Pseudolus's Greekness (cf. 339), he and his actions
are frequently associated with definitively Roman institutions in the play: cf. 125-8 and n. 14
above, 586-91 and n. 41, and 1232 and n. 65 below.

Ballio

He's had a chance to pay me for a long time if he really wanted to.   285

Calidorus

What if I didn't have it?

Ballio

A true lover would have taken out a loan,
Found a loanshark, paid some interest—or you could have
Ripped off your father.

Pseudolus

Ripped off his father? That's bold!
As if you'd ever give good advice!

Ballio

Now that's simply not in the Pimp's Code of Ethics.

Calidorus

Just how could I rip off a suspicious old man like my father?   290
And besides, even if I could, my filial duty prohibits it.

Ballio

I hear you.
So curl up in bed with that filial duty instead of Phoenicium.
And now that I know you put filial duty above love,
Is everyone in the world your father? There's no one else you can
Ask for a loan?

Calidorus

A loan? That word doesn't exist anymore.   295

Pseudolus

That's for sure! Those jowly bankers rise up from their tables in the forum
Right after gobbling up their loans, but serve their creditors nothing!
The result: everyone's full of caution when it comes to loans.

Calidorus

Poor, poor miserable me! Not a penny to be found anywhere!
I'm dying from both lack of cash and lack of love.   300

Ballio

Two words of advice: "olive oil," purchased in futures and sold for cash.
And presto! You'll have as much as two-hundred minae in hand!

Calidorus

I'm still screwed by the law against making loans to minors.[24]
No one will dare to give me credit.

---

24   A Roman law (*lex Plaetoria*) prevented young men under twenty-five from entering into
contracts on their own. For the very precise Romanization here, cf. Introduction, pp. 2-3.

Ballio

I have a similar law of my own: no credit for you.

Pseudolus

No credit? You're not happy with the profit you've already made off him? 305

Ballio

The only true lover is the one who keeps paying me forever.

Let him pay and keep paying! When that ends, love ends.

Calidorus

You have no pity?

Ballio

Not when you've just got words—they don't "ca-ching".

But I do hope you're alive and well.

Pseudolus

Oh, you think he's already dead?

Ballio

Yes, quite dead for my purposes when he talks like that. 310

A lover's declared dead the instant he pleads with a pimp for mercy.

Don't bother coming to me with a complaint unless it's silver-plated.

Regarding your current lack of funds: complaining to me is

Like complaining to your stepmother.

Pseudolus

What? You married his father?

Ballio

Disgusting!

Pseudolus

Please, Ballio, if you don't trust him, at least trust me. 315

Within three days, I'll find that money, whether by

Land or sea—or maybe from somewhere else.

Ballio

I trust you?

Pseudolus

Why not?

Ballio

I might just as well

Tie up a starving dog with lamb-sausages.

Calidorus

This is the kind of thanks I get from you after all I've done? 320

Ballio

Just what do you want?

Calidorus

For you to wait just six days or so before

You sell her and kill the man who loves her—me.

Ballio

Cheer up! I'll even

Wait six months.

Calidorus

Fabulous! You delightful man!

Ballio

That's nothing. How'd you like for me to make you even happier?

Calidorus

How?

Ballio

It's like this: Phoenicium is not currently up for sale.   325

Calidorus

She's not?

Ballio

That's the absolute truth.

Calidorus

Pseudolus, fetch

The sacrificial animals! Call the butchers, let's sacrifice to
Almighty Jupiter here! This Jupiter of mine is mightier than Jove!

Ballio

No sacrifices, please. But you'd win me over with some choice lamb.

Calidorus

What are you waiting for? Get the lambs! Jupiter has spoken!   330

Pseudolus

I'll be back soon, though I need to run outside the city gate first.

Calidorus

Why there?

Pseudolus

That's where I'll get the two butchers with bells,[25]
Along with two herds worth of elm-rods[26] as well.
That way this Jupiter can receive even more than he deserves.

Ballio

Go to hell!

Pseudolus

Precisely where this King of Pimps is heading.   335

* * * *

* * * *

---

25   Roman executioners had bells that became symbolic of their profession.
26   Used to beat Roman slaves.

Ballio

My death's not in your best interest.

Pseudolus

Why not?

Ballio

Because once I'm dead, you'll become the most worthless man in Athens.

Calidorus

Please tell me the truth and no more joking around: 340
My girlfriend Phoenicium is currently not for sale?

Ballio

Absolutely not! I swear—seeing that I sold her long ago.

Calidorus

What? How?

Ballio

Minus her accessories, but with all her organs intact.

Calidorus

You sold my girlfriend?

Ballio

Absolutely, for twenty minae.

Calidorus

For twenty minae?

Ballio

Right. Or for four-quintuple-minae if you prefer,   345
To a Macedonian soldier, who put fifteen minae down.

Calidorus

What are you saying?

Ballio

That your girlfriend has been converted into cash.

Calidorus

How could you?

Ballio

I felt like it. And I owned her.

Calidorus

Hey, Pseudolus!

Go get me a sword.

Pseudolus

What for?

Calidorus

To kill him—and me!

Pseudolus

Why not just kill yourself? He'll die of starvation soon enough.   350

Calidorus
Tell me, O most perjurious man in human history:
Didn't you swear you'd never sell her to anyone except me?
Ballio
True.
Calidorus
                And in formal and binding terms?
Ballio
                                                More like fabricated and winding ones.
Calidorus
That's perjury, you scum!
Ballio
                                Yes, and it's also money in my pocket.
And this "scum" has a vault-full of that at home.   355
You, on the other hand, are pious, pedigreed—and penniless.
Calidorus
Pseudolus, stand on the other side and bury him with insults![27]
Pseudolus
                                                                Sure.
I'll be there sooner than it'd take me to sign my emancipation papers.
Calidorus
Begin the attack!
Pseudolus
                Time for a verbal assault, you degenerate!
Ballio
Got that right.
Pseudolus
                Bag of crap!
Ballio
                                Ain't that the truth.
Pseudolus
                                                Human punching-bag!   360
Ballio
Of course.
Calidorus
                Tomb-robber!
Ballio
                Right on.

---

27 A comic version of the ancient Italian practice (*flagitatio*) of publicly shaming a debtor into
    payment follows. Cf. 555-6 below.

Pseudolus
                              Dirtbag!
Ballio
                                   Well-put.
Calidorus
     Traitor!
Ballio
               My specialty.
Pseudolus
                         Murderer!
Ballio
                                   Continue.
Calidorus
     Blasphemer!
Ballio
                 Can't deny it.
Pseudolus
                            Perjurer!
Ballio
                                   Now that's fresh.
Calidorus
     Scofflaw!
Ballio
               Absolutely.
Pseudolus
                            Corrupter of youth!
Ballio
                                      How stinging.
Calidorus
     Thief!
Ballio
          Oh-la-la.
Pseudolus
                         Runaway slave!
Ballio
                                Bravo.
Calidorus
                               Danger to public safety!
Ballio
                                            Well, duh.   365
Pseudolus
     Cheater!

Calidorus

> Garbage!

Pseudolus

> Pimp!

Calidorus

> Raw sewage!

Ballio

> All music to my ears.

Calidorus

Father-and-mother-beater!

Ballio

> Correction: father-and-mother-killer.

Better than having to feed them. Now, was that wrong?

Pseudolus

This is a complete waste of time and effort!

Ballio

Anything else you'd like to add?

Calidorus

> Have you no shame whatsoever?   370

Ballio

I'd be ashamed to be a hollowed-out nut of a lover like you.
But even though you've showered me with insult after insult,
If the soldier fails to pay the five minae he owes me
(today being the absolute deadline for that payment)—
If he doesn't bring it, I think I can do what is expected of me.   375

Calidorus

Which is?

Ballio

> If you pay me the money, I'll break my deal with him.

That's what everybody expects of a pimp anyway. I'd love to chat more,
If there were something in it for me. But as I like to say,
"Pity has its price"—and you're flat broke. So do what you must.

Calidorus

You're leaving?

Ballio

> So much to do right now.

Pseudolus

> And so much more to be done to you soon!   380

I've got him now, unless all gods and men desert me.
I'll fillet this fellow, just as a cook slices up an eel!
Now, Calidorus, I need your attention.

Calidorus

What do you need?

Pseudolus

My plan is to lay siege to this town and capture it[28] today.
This plan requires someone clever, cautious, crafty and cunning,   385
Who's able to carry out orders, someone who won't sleep on the job.

Calidorus

So what's the plan?

Pseudolus

You'll know in good time. I don't want
To have to repeat myself: plays are long enough as it is.

Calidorus

All right, fair enough.

Pseudolus

Hurry off and get my helper.

Calidorus

We have no shortage of friends—just of reliable ones.   390

Pseudolus

I know. First muster our very best troops.
Then pick out the one person we can completely rely on.

Calidorus

He'll be here in no time.

Pseudolus

Shouldn't you be off? The more talk, the more delay!

SCENE 4

Pseudolus is left alone onstage.

Pseudolus

He's gone and you're all on your own, Pseudolus.
You laid it on thick for your young master and now   395
It's time to bring home the bacon, wherever that is.
Let's see: you haven't got the least bit of a plan, just as
Much money, and no idea what to do at all either.
Where to start weaving your web of deceit,
Or how to bring that design to completion?   400
But just like a poet[29] takes up his tablet and though
He looks for what doesn't exist at all, he still finds it, and
Makes complete fiction seem like the truth.

---

28   I.e., the pimp.

29   The word *poeta* is used of poets in general and playwrights in particular.

That's it! I'll become a poet and find
The twenty minae which are nowhere!   405
I had promised to give it to him a long time ago,
And wanted to launch an attack on our old man,
But he somehow scented it out first.
It's time for me to stop talking:
Here comes my old master Simo approaching   410
This way with his next-door neighbor Callipho.
I'll dig out twenty minae from this ancient tomb to
Give to our young master today!
I'll just slip over here and listen in on them.

SCENE 5

Simo and Callipho enter from the forum.

Simo

If the bankrupt and lovesick young men   415
Were to appoint a dictator[30] for themselves here in Athens,
I have no doubt my son would win hands down.
He's all the talk of the town right now, how
He wants to free his girlfriend and how he's
Hunting down the cash for that. That's what I'm told,   420
Though I already had gotten wind of it myself and had my suspicions.
But I played dumb.

Pseudolus (*aside*)

      He's right on the scent of his son.
That's the death of our plot! Very sticky business!
The road I'd planned to take to financial freedom
Is now completely blocked. He's clairvoyant: 425
The prey has been snatched from the predators.

Callipho

If it were up to me, all the people who spread
Rumors and all who listen to them should be hung—
The gossips by their tongues, their audience by the ears!
Now the things that you're told about your son,   430
That he's in love and wants to con you out of the cash—
It may very well be that they're all lies.
But even if it's all true, given today's moral climate,
Big surprise if a young man is in love and wants to free
His girlfriend. What's new about that?

---

30 A reference to the Roman practice of appointing a *dictator* to deal with a military or domestic
emergency. Note the placement of a distinctly Roman institution in Athens.

Pseudolus (*aside*)

What a wonderful old man! 435

Simo

Well, I'm an old man and I object.

Callipho

Stupidly in my opinion,
Or else you shouldn't have been doing the same thing at his age.
A father had better be righteous, if he requires his
Son to be more righteous than he was himself!
As for all your debts and disgraceful acts back then: 440
There was more than enough of them to distribute to everybody on welfare!
Big surprise if the son inherited the sins of the father!

Pseudolus (*aside*)

Oh Zeus,[31] how few men are this sensible!
Now that is exactly the sort of father a son should have!

Simo

Who's talking there? Ah, it's my slave Pseudolus. 445
He's the one corrupting my son, he's the root of all evil,
He's the ringleader, he's the rottenest role model—and he's
The one I want tortured.

Callipho (*aside to Simo*)

Now it's downright foolish
To make a show of anger. It makes better sense
To approach him calmly and then ask him whether 450
Or not the rumors you've heard are true.
In a crisis, keeping a positive attitude is half the battle.

Simo

I hear you.

Pseudolus (*aside*)

They're coming at you, Pseudolus.
Prepare for a war of words with the geezer.
First I'll serve up a greeting for master, and then 455
Share any leftovers with the neighbor.

Simo

Hey, what's up?

Pseudolus

I'm up, as you can see here.

Simo

Just look at his attitude, Callipho! So high and mighty!

---

31 See n. 3 above and n. 35 below.

Callipho

Yes, no lack of confidence there.

Pseudolus

And why shouldn't an innocent and upstanding   460
Slave stand proud before his master?

Callipho

We've heard some hazy rumors and there a few things
We'd like you to clear up for us.

Simo

You're about to be overwhelmed by his words:
You'll think you're speaking with Socrates,[32] not Pseudolus.   465

Pseudolus

So that's how it is? You've always had a low opinion of me.
I know how little trust you put in me. You actually
Want me to be bad—but I'll frustrate that wish of yours.

Simo

Keep open the gateway of your ears, Pseudolus,
And allow my words to enter as I wish them to.[33]   470

Pseudolus

I'm quite angry with you. But say what you want.

Simo

You, my slave, are angry with me, your master?

Pseudolus

                                        Do you find that
So surprising?

Simo

                        The way you put it,
I need to be on guard against your anger. You're planning
To whip me—and somehow differently from the way I whip you.   475
What do you think?

Callipho

                        I think he has every right to be angry
When you put so little trust in him.

Simo

                                        That's just fine.
He can be as angry as he wants: I can protect myself.
Now what about my question?

---

32 Famous Greek philosopher executed by the Athenians in 399 BCE, representative of
    intelligence and verbal dexterity here.

33 Mock-tragic language.

Pseudolus

Ask me whatever you want.
Consider my response your personal Delphic oracle.[34]   480

Simo

Pay close attention and keep your promise then.
Tell me: are you aware that my son is in love with
A music-girl?

Pseudolus

I am indeed.[35]

Simo

And he wants to free her?

Pseudolus

Yes, I'm aware of that too.

Simo

And you're planning to
Cheat me of twenty minae, through all that   485
Trickery of yours?

Pseudolus

I'd do that to you?

Simo

Absolutely! You'd give it to my son to free his girlfriend.
Confess! Tell us that's the plan.

Pseudolus

"That's the plan."

Callipho

He's admitting it.

Simo

What was I just telling you, Callipho?

Callipho

I remember.

Simo

Why wasn't I informed the instant you found this out?   490
Why was I kept in the dark?

Pseudolus

I'll tell you why.
I didn't want to be the one to establish the terrible precedent
Of having a slave accuse his master before his master.

---

34   Prophetic center of Apollo at Delphi on Mt. Parnassus in Greece, where the Pythia (the
     inspired priestess of Apollo) delivered oracles to pilgrims for centuries.

35   Pseudolus here and in the lines following peppers his speech with Greek phrases, as
     apparently was done in colloquial Latin. There is also humorous irony in having a nominally
     Athenian character drop such phrases in what should be his native tongue.

Simo (*to Calliphos*)
> Wouldn't you have had him dragged straight off to the mill?[36]

Callipho
> Really, what harm has been done?

Simo
>   Oh, plenty!   495

Pseudolus
> It's all right, Callipho. I can fight my own battle.
> I did do wrong. And here's why:
> I didn't inform you about your son's love affair,
> Since I knew I'd land smack-dab in the mill if I did.

Simo
> And you didn't know the same thing would happen to you   500
> If you kept quiet?

Pseudolus
>   I knew.

Simo
>   So why wasn't I informed?

Pseudolus
> One punishment was very near, the other a ways off:
> It was either "off to the mill" or a short grace period.

Simo
> What'll you do now? Now that I'm on to you,
> No money is going to be stolen from me!   505
> I'll publicly proclaim: "let no one loan Pseudolus a penny!"

Pseudolus
> I'll never beg anyone for money as long as
> You're alive: I guarantee you'll be giving me that money!
> Or, to be more precise, I'll be taking it from you.

Simo
>   You'll take it from me?

Pseudolus
>   For sure.

Simo
> You can poke out my eye if I give it to you.

Pseudolus
>   You will.   510
> I'm telling you so you'll be on guard.

---

36   Slaves were sent to mills to do difficult and tedious labor there as a punishment. Cf.
       Introduction, p. 21.

Simo
                                        I know one thing for sure:
If you pull it off, your achievement would be absolutely amazing!

Pseudolus
   I will.

Simo
            What if you don't?

Pseudolus
                        Then flog me with rods.
   But what if I do?

Simo
                  As Jupiter is my witness,
   You'll spend the rest of your life in peace.

Pseudolus
                                     Don't forget that!   515

Simo
   You don't think I can watch out for myself when I've been forewarned?

Pseudolus
   I'm forewarning you to watch out. I'm telling you straight out: WATCH
      OUT!
   The money will come to me right out of your hands today!

Callipho
   He's the very picture of human perfection if he keeps his word!

Pseudolus
   Cart me off to be your slave if I don't.   520

Simo
   How clever! Aren't you already my property?

Pseudolus
   Want to hear something even more amazing?

Callipho
   Yes, absolutely—it's my pleasure to listen to you.

Pseudolus
   Before I wage my war with you, there's another battle to fight,
   One that will become famous and unforgettable.   525

Simo
   What battle's that?

Pseudolus
                  The one against your neighbor here, the pimp.
   A little combat of cunning and cleverness.
   I'll trip up and trick that pimp out of the music-girl
   Your son loves to death.

Simo

How's that?

Pseudolus

I'll win both battles by this evening.   530

Simo

If you accomplish both as you predict,
Your valor will surpass King Agathocles'.[37]
But if you don't, is there any possible reason why
I shouldn't consign you to the mill instantly?

Pseudolus

No, and not just for a day, but for every last day of my life.   535
But if I succeed, will you freely agree to give me the money
To give to the pimp?

Callipho

Pseudolus makes a good case.
Say you will.

Simo

But something just occurred to me.
What if these two are conspiring together, Callipho,
And have patched together some scheme   540
To cheat me out of some cash?

Pseudolus

Who in the world
Would attempt such a scheme? Listen to me, Simo:
If we ever have conspired, schemed, or consulted,
You may write all over me with elm-rods
And inscribe me with letters, just as if I were a book!   545

Simo

Let the games begin!

Pseudolus

Callipho, please do me a favor today by
Not involving yourself in any other business.

Callipho

Well, I had already planned to go to the country.

Pseudolus

How about taking down the siege-engines you've set up?[38]   550

---

37   Tyrant and king of Sicily (died 289/8 BCE).

38   A grandiose way (typical of Pseudolus) of saying "How about changing your plans?"

Callipho

    Okay, I'll stay for your sake, Pseudolus.

    It's a pleasure to be a spectator at your games.

    And if I see him not handing over the money as he promised,

    Rather than see you go off empty-handed, I'll hand it over myself.

Simo

    I'll keep my word.

Pseudolus

                    You bet you will! If you don't,   555

    I'll call you out to pay, loudly and clearly![39]

    Move along now, go inside you two:

    It's time to give my tricks a little breathing room.

Callipho

    All right, as you wish.

Pseudolus

                 But I want you to stay

    Right at home.

Callipho

            Yes, you've got my full cooperation in this.   560

Simo

    Well, I'm off to the forum. I'll be back soon.

Pseudolus

                      Yes, very soon.

    I have a sneaking suspicion that you all suspect

    I've only promised to do these daring deeds

    In order to entertain you during this play,

    And there's little chance I'll do what I promised.   565

    I'll keep my word. To the best of my knowledge,

    I don't know exactly how I'll do it, but I do know

    That I will. Now, it's the duty of every actor to be original

    Enough to bring something original on stage:

    If he can't, let him step aside for someone who can.   570

    I'd like to slip inside for a while,

    To privately muster my army of tricks.

    I'll be right back after just a short delay.

    Meanwhile, the piper is here to play for you.   573a

---

39   As a slave, Pseudolus would not have recourse to *flagitatio* (see n. 27 above) in real life.

SCENE 6

After a short time, Pseudolus emerges from Simo's house.

(*SONG*)

Pseudolus

Holy Jupiter! How everything I do turns out with such finesse and success!

No need for fear, no cause for dread, when there's a plan in my head!   575

How stupid it is to entrust a daring deed to a faint-hearted man!

It's what you do, it's the goal you choose to pursue,

        That makes things as they are.

       How in my head I've marshaled my troops!

Two lines of tricks, three lines of lies, so wherever I meet the enemy   580

    Victory is mine, and my prey is ensnared in my web:

    My confidence rests on the valor of my ancestors,[40]

    As well as on my own diligence and diabolical deceit.

    As for this common foe of yours and mine:

    Just watch, while I deftly de-ball Ballio!   585

    I'll storm and sack this town today!

Here is where I'll lead my legions. Once he's defeated (an easy feat for my

    fellow citizens),

It's straight on with my army to this ancient citadel! (*points to Simo's house*) From there

I'll cram my troops with booty, load them down with loot, leaving only fear

    to our foes.

Such is the line from which I descend: I am destined for deeds   590

    Of distinction that bring me fame and lasting renown![41]

But who's this that I see? Who's this stranger my eyes espy?

I'd like to know what he's up to and why he has a sword.

I'll set a trap for him right over here.

---

40   A bombastic claim in that, according to Roman law, slaves had no parents or ancestors. Equally ridiculous is Pseudolus's claim in 587 to be a citizen. Cf. Introduction, p. 21.

41   Pseudolus takes on the airs of a Roman aristocratic general here, who after a noteworthy military success might publicly and boastfully lobby for the right to celebrate a triumph, i.e., a formal, lavish triumphal procession to the temple of Jupiter on the Capitoline. Cf. Pseudolus' claim to a triumph at 1051.

SCENE 7

Harpax enters from the harbor.

(*SONG to 604*)

Harpax

    This is the place he told me about,   595

    If I can trust my eyes. The soldier, my master,

    Said that the pimp's house was the seventh from the city-gate.

        I'm to give him the token and the money. It'd be nice

        To have someone tell me for sure which house is his.

Pseudolus (*aside*)

        Shh, quiet now! Unless all gods and men fail me, he's mine!   600

        This new and sudden situation calls for a new and sudden solution.

    First order of business: all my previous plans just flew out the window!

    Now I'll launch a full-scale assault against this military messenger.

Harpax

    I'll knock on the door and call someone out here.

Pseudolus

    Whoever's there, would you please stop pounding on the doors?   605

    I'm coming out to plead and intercede for them.

Harpax

    Are you Ballio?

Pseudolus

        No, I am in fact Vice-Ballio.

Harpax

    Meaning what?

Pseudolus

        I put things in and pull them out: I'm procurator of the pantry.

Harpax

    So you're like a backdoor man?

Pseudolus

        Actually, I'm on top of the backdoor man.

Harpax

    So what are you? Slave or free man?

Pseudolus

        At the moment I'm a slave.   610

Harpax

    That's obvious. And it's clear you don't deserve to be free.

Pseudolus

    Ever take a look in the mirror when you're insulting others?

Harpax (*aside*)

    This guy must really be trouble!

Pseudolus (*aside*)

                  The gods really do love me!

Here's my own personal anvil, to forge a fort of fraud on.

Harpax (*aside*)

    Why's he talking to himself?

Pseudolus

               Say, young fellow!

Harpax

                       What?   615

Pseudolus

Are you or are you not the slave of that Macedonian soldier,

The one who purchased the woman from us?

He gave my master, the pimp, fifteen minae for her

And owes five more.

Harpax

          That's me. But how in the world do you know who I am?

I've never seen you or spoken with you before. I've never been   620

To Athens and I never laid eyes on you until today.

Pseudolus

You just look like you were sent by him. When he left a while back,

Today was set for payment—and it hasn't arrived yet.

Harpax

Oh, yes it has now.

Pseudolus

           You've brought it?

Harpax

                     Sure have.

Pseudolus

                       So hand it over.   624-5

Harpax

To you?

Pseudolus

       Yes, of course. Who else? I handle all my master's accounts.

Accounts received, accounts paid—I manage it all.

Harpax

I sure as hell don't care if you're the accountant of almighty Jupiter!

I wouldn't trust you with a single penny.

Pseudolus

                 In the time it'd take you to sneeze,

We could wrap up this business.

Harpax

            I think I'll just keep it wrapped up right here.   630

Pseudolus

How dare you insult my integrity! As if I didn't
Handle accounts a thousand times bigger than this all by myself!

Harpax

Perhaps other people put their trust in you. I don't.

Pseudolus

You're practically saying that I intend to cheat you.

Harpax

Correction: you're saying it, I'm assuming it.   635
What's your name, by the way?

Pseudolus (*aside*)

The pimp has a slave named Surus.

I'll say that's me. I'm Surus.

Harpax

Surus?

Pseudolus

That's my name.

Harpax

Enough chitchat. Whatever your name is, how about calling your
Master out, so I can finish the job I was sent to do?

Pseudolus

If he were home, I would. But the deal can be sealed easier   640
With me now than with him in person.

Harpax

Here's the real deal:
I'm here to pay, not to be played. You're starting to
Sweat because you can't sink your claws into the cash.
No one gets a penny from me except Ballio in the flesh.

Pseudolus

I'm afraid he's occupied at the moment—with a legal matter.   645

Harpax

Good luck to him with that! I'll return when I think
He'll be home. Take this letter from me and give it to him.
That's the token[42] there our masters agreed on.

Pseudolus

I know it well. Yours said to send the woman with the guy
Who brought us the cash along with his portrait seal.   650
He left a copy of it here.

---

42   For the soldier's portrait on his signet ring, see 55-8.

Harpax

You're on top of it all.

Pseudolus

Why shouldn't I be?

Harpax

Give him the token then.

Pseudolus

Okay.

But what's your name?

Harpax

Harpax.[43] But you can call me "Steele."

Pseudolus

Get away!

You won't be allowed in our house! We don't need you stealing around there!

Harpax

I got the name from how I steel myself for battle.   655

Pseudolus

More likely from stealing stainless steel from people's houses!

Harpax

Hardly. But do you know what I need from you, Surus?

Pseudolus

I will if you tell me.

Harpax

I'm staying outside the city-gate. Third inn, run by an old lady named
Chrysis—she's big, built like a brickhouse, has a bad limp.

Pseudolus

And?

Harpax

Come get me there when your master returns.   660

Pseudolus

Of course, as you wish.

Harpax

I'm beat from traveling,

And I want to rest up.

Pseudolus

That's a fine plan.

Just make sure I don't have to hunt for you when I come.

Harpax

I've no plans beyond lunch and a nap.

---

43   The Greek root of Harpax's name means "snatch."

Pseudolus

                                    Excellent.

Harpax

   Is that it?

Pseudolus

         Go have a nice nap.

Harpax

                          I will.

Pseudolus

                          One more thing, Harpax: 665
   Cover up well! There's nothing better than a full sweat on a full bed.

SCENE 8

Pseudolus, alone onstage once again,
addresses the audience.

Pseudolus

   By the immortal gods! His arrival is my salvation!
   I'm back in business and he's bankrolling me.
   Opportunity[44] herself could not appear as luckily
   As this lucky letter appeared to me!   670
   My cornucopia has come, complete with all I need:
   It's brimming with trouble, treachery and trickery,
   Not to mention money and a tryst for my lovesick master!
   I've earned the right to boast and bluster:
   I'd already planned how I'd steal the little lady from the Pimp.   675
   I had every last detail drafted and drawn up
   Just as I wanted. But here's how it is: the work of
   One single goddess trumps the plotting of a hundred men!
   Her name is Fortune.[45] And this holds true as well:
   It's how you make use of Her that makes you successful and wise in
      men's eyes.   680
   When someone's plan succeeds we pronounce him clever;
   When things turn out badly, we call him a fool.
   But we're the real fools when we ignorantly pursue what we desire,
   As if we could possibly know what's best for us!
   We shun what we have, we chase what we don't,   685
   And despite all our pain and strain, death creeps up on us all the while.

---

44 The personification of *Opportunitas* here is Plautus' own doing. Cf. n. 45 below.

45 One of many abstractions that were personified in Roman religion; there were temples
    dedicated to *Fortuna*, a goddess of "luck" in Rome and throughout Italy from an early date.

Enough philosophizing! I digress and delay our plot.
By the immortal gods! That improvised lie of mine
Just now—that I belong to the pimp—was worth its weight
In solid gold! This letter will be my trifecta of trickery: 690
I'll deceive my master, the pimp and the guy who gave it to me!
But look! Fantastic! Calidorus is coming, along with someone else.
Another stroke of luck, just as lucky as the last one!

SCENE 9

Calidorus returns from the forum with Charinus.

Calidorus

You've heard it all, both the bitter and the sweet: You know
What I'm desiring, you know how I'm perspiring, *you know* what I'm
   requiring!   695

Charinus

I've got it all. Just tell me what you need from me.

Calidorus

Pseudolus told me to bring him someone sharp who's
On our side.

Charinus

           You've done your job:
I'm a friend and an ally. Pseudolus, however, I don't know.

Chalinus

He's the very picture of human perfection—and my mastermind!   700

Pseudolus (*aside*)

I'll address him in highfalutin' style.[46]

Calidorus

                 Whose voice doth resound?

Pseudolus

'Tis thee, thee, Sire, that I seek, O thou who commandeth Pseudolus.
To thee I bring triple joys in treble manners three times over,
Threefold pleasures taken thrice from a triumvirate by skill in triplicate!
A triumph of trickery, treachery, and downright roguery!   705
All this I have brought to you in this tiny sealed envelope.

Calidorus

That's our man!

Charinus

          This dogmeat can really ham it up!

---

46   I.e., in the style of tragedy, as is Calidorus's question in 702 (contrary to the expectations of naturalistic dialogue: cf. *Amphitryon* 180 and n. 20 there).

Pseudolus

Tread forth, tread near,
And boldly put forward your hand in welcome.

Calidorus

Well, Pseudolus, should I welcome you with salutations or beg you for my
salvation?

Pseudolus

Um, both.

Calidorus

Greetings, "Both." What's going on?

Pseudolus

Stay calm!   710

Calidorus

I managed to catch this guy.

Pseudolus

Huh, "catch"?

Calidorus

I meant to say "fetch".

Pseudolus

Who is he?

Calidorus

Charinus. He's quite the charmer.[47]

Pseudolus

Excellent. I'm charmed to meet you.

Charinus

At your service—just say the word.

Pseudolus

A charming offer, but no thanks.
We don't want to bother you, Charinus. Good luck to you.

Charinus

You bother me? Really, it's no bother at all.

Pseudolus

Okay then, hold on for a second. 715

Calidorus

What's that?

Pseudolus

A letter and a token I just happened to intercept.

---

47 Pseudolus plays extensively on Charinus's name: *charis* in Greek means "grace" or
"gratitude."

Calidorus

A token? What token?

Pseudolus

                              One that just arrived from the soldier.
His slave brought it, along with five minae,
To get your girlfriend. He'll be wiping egg off his face!

Calidorus

How so?

Pseudolus

Need I remind you this play is being performed for the spectators? 720
They saw exactly what happened. I'll bring *you* up to speed later.

Calidorus

What do we do now?

Pseudolus

                         You'll be wrapping your arms around a free woman today!

Calidorus

I will?

Pseudolus

You most certainly will! If yours truly makes it through the day,
And if you find me a man fast.

Charinus

                         What sort of man?

Pseudolus

                                        Someone unscrupulous,
Clever, devious and smart, a quick study   725
Who has the natural talent to finish what he's started.
And, of course, someone who's not well-known here.

Charinus

                                             Does it matter
If he's a slave?

Pseudolus

           Not at all: I'd prefer a slave to a free man.

Charinus

I think I have just the man. He's unscrupulous and smart.
My father sent him here from Carystus.[48] He hasn't left the house   730
And had never set foot in Athens until yesterday.

Pseudolus

Perfect! I'll also need a loan of five minae, which
I'll pay back today. That's what his father owes me.

––––––––––

48   A city on Euboea, a large Aegean island.

Charinus

It's yours. No need to ask anyone else.

Pseudolus

Oh, what luck to have met you!

I also need a cloak, a sword, and a traveler's hat.

Charinus

I've got those, too.   735

Pseudolus

By the immortal gods! This charming fellow's no slacker. I'm rich!

But about that slave from Carystus: does he have a sharp sense about him?

Charinus

Yes—the sharp scent of goat in his armpits.

Pseudolus

Well, then, he'll need a long-sleeved tunic.

Anything else sharp about him?

Charinus

He has a heart of acid.

Pseudolus

Has he anything sweet in the mix, if we need that?

Charinus

You have to ask?   740

There's sweet wine, raisin wine, honey wine, anything

Sweet—all bottled up in his heart! He could open up a market there.

Pseudolus

Lovely, Charinus! You beat me at my own game.

But what's this slave's name?

Charinus

Simia, aka "The Monkeyman."

Pseudolus

Can he twist his way out of a bad situation?

Charinus

Like a tornado!   745

Pseudolus

Is he tried and tested?

Charinus

Oh, he's been tried *and convicted* many times.

Pseudolus

What if he's caught red-handed?

Charinus

He turns into an eel and slips away.

Pseudolus

Is he astute?

Charinus

        He's his own institution!

Pseudolus

    From what you say, he sounds like a great guy!

Charinus

                      You'll find out for yourself.

    One glance at you and he knows exactly what you want.   750

    So what's the plan?

Pseudolus

            I'll tell you. Once I have him in costume,

    I want him to fill in for the soldier's slave.

    Then he's to take the token and the five minae to the pimp,

    And then take the woman away with him. That's the entire plot.

    The rest of the details I'll tell him myself.   755

Calidorus

    Why are we still standing here?

Pseudolus

              Bring the man

    In all his get-up to Aeschinus the banker's place.

    And do it fast!

Calidorus

        We'll beat you there.

Pseudolus

             Get along then!

    All my doubts and fears have melted into thin air;

    My mind is cleared, the path is open.   760

    Time to lead my legions with their standards all in order:

    The omens are favorable, all looks auspicious for my plan!

    I'm confident I can conquer my enemies!

    I'm off to the forum to saddle Simia with my instructions.

    For the scheme to succeed, he can't slip up at all.   765

    Let the siege of Pimp-city commence!

SCENE 10

A young slave comes out of Ballio's house.

Slave Boy

    It's bad enough that the gods make a boy slave it

    For a pimp. But to make him ugly to boot

    Is, in my humble opinion, to double

    His trouble and triple his pain!   770

    Take my case: my life is a mountain of misery,

    All types of trouble, both little and large,

And I can't find a single fellow to love me, and
To bring me just an ounce of care and concern.
Now today's the pimp's birthday.   775
He threatened us all, highest and lowest:
"Either lavish me with exquisite gifts today,
Or suffer lavish and exquisite torture tomorrow!"
What's someone in my situation supposed to do?
How's a have-not to get what the haves have?   780
If I don't come up with a gift for the pimp today,
I'll be force-fed urinal cakes tomorrow![49]
Oh god, how terribly my master terrifies me!
And then there's always that thing[50] I'm just too small for:
Although the cash can sure stretch out the wallet,   785
They say it's all grunts and groans—
Perhaps I'll learn how to just grin and bear it.
But look: here comes master along with a cook.
I'd better bite my lip and give him the slip.

SCENE 11

Ballio returns from the forum with a cook and his assistants.

Ballio

How stupid to call that place "Cooks' Corners!"   790
It's really should be called "Crooks' Corners!"
Try as I might, I could not possibly find a poorer
Specimen of a cook than the one I've brought here!
He's a babbler, a bragger, a fool and a slacker!
Orcus[51] closed the door to hell in his face,   795
So there'd be someone left alive to cook for the dead:
That's just the sort of lifeless feast he alone can cater.

Cook[52]

If that's really what you think of me,

---

49 The boy says, "I'll have to drink fuller's fruit [i.e., the stale urine used by ancient fullers to
    treat cloth]." The meaning is obscure. Scholars have taken it as a reference to either physical
    beating or forced fellatio.

50 I.e., sexual penetration as a male prostitute.

51 God of the underworld (= *Dis* and Greek Plutus), a dull and gloomy place to the ancients.
    Ballio jests that the cook is prevented from dying, so that the dead, whose tastes are far from
    exacting, will have someone to provide them with appropriately bland fare.

52 While many scholars have viewed the lengthy cook's scene here as an "inorganic" comic
    interlude, some see the figure of the cook—who combines and "spices up" disparate elements
    in novel ways to please diners—as analogous to a successful Roman comic playwright. For
    metatheater in Plautus, see Introduction, pp. 8-9.

Why'd you hire me?
Ballio

Labor shortage. I had no other choice.
But if you really are a cook, why were you sitting   800
All alone in the forum?
Cook

I'll tell you why since you ask.
It's a fault of human nature, not my own,
That makes me unpopular.
Ballio

How so?
Cook

I'll expound on that.
When people set out to hire a cook, they don't
Seek out the best and priciest.   805
No, they settle for the cheapest and worst.
That's why I was haunting the forum alone today.
Those losers will slave for a dollar a day. It takes
Twice that to budge my butt an inch.
I don't season my meals the way other cooks do: 810
They proudly present their guests grasslands
Peppered on plates, and pile on even more greens
As if they were feeding cows, not guests.
They give them sorrel, cabbage, beets, spinach,
Add cilantro, fennel, garlic, and parsley,   815
And pour on a pound or so of Asafoetida.
Then dread mustard is grated in, the kind that
Makes the graters cry even before it's grated.
When these cooks cook and spice their meals
With this, it's as if they're letting loose   820
Screech owls to gnaw on their guests' guts!
And when stomachs are stuffed with such stuff
(scary even to talk about, let alone eat!),
Is there any wonder the life of man is so short?
Men must chew the greens that cows eschew!   825
Ballio
And what about you, O high critic of condiments?
Am I to assume you use celestial seasoning,
To lengthen man's life?
Cook

Let it hereby be known:
Someone who dines on my spicy concoctions

Can expect to live for two hundred years!   830
When I've sprinkled on some cookidrum[53]
Or onionmeg or clownonia or headwoundorim,
The plates themselves instantly feel the heat.
Such are my spices for Neptune's flocks;[54]
On creatures of the Earth I sprinkle castoroilium   835
Or mushmeatsis or sluiceia.

Ballio
                    Argh!
To hell with you and your entire rack of
Spices, along with your pack of lies!

Cook
Allow me to continue.

Ballio
               Go right on talking—and then go to hell!

Cook
When everything's ready I remove the lids: 840
The scent flies to the sky with outstretched hands.

Ballio
"A scent with outstretched hands?"

Cook
                   Oh, my mistake.

Ballio
Huh?

Cook
      I meant to say "with a scent out of hams."
Jupiter feasts daily on that scent.

Ballio
Really? What does he eat on the days you're not cooking?   845

Cook
He goes to bed hungry.

Ballio
             And you should just go to hell!
This is what I'm supposed to be paying you for?

Cook
True, my cooking services are very costly.
But wherever I'm hired to cook, I guarantee
A good value.

---

53   The names of this and the other spices are comic coinages by Plautus.

54   Mock-tragic language for "fish;" Neptune (= Greek Poseidon) was god of the sea.

Ballio

      I guarantee anyone who values his goods won't hire you! 850

Cook

 Have you ever known a cook without
 The claws of a kite or an eagle?

Ballio

 Have you ever known a cook who shouldn't
 Have his claws clipped wherever he works?
 Hey you! Yes, you, my private property! (*to slave*) Your orders 855
 Are to stow away all our stuff pronto,
 And then keep your eyes focused on his!
 If he so much as glances at something, you glance at it too;
 If he so much as takes a step, you step with him;
 If he so much as raises his hand, raise yours with his. 860
 If he grabs anything of his own, let him grab it;
 If he grabs something of ours, grab him at once!
 He moves, you move; he stops, you stop too;
 And if he bends over, you must bend over too.
 I'll likewise assign guards to his thieves-in-training. 865

Cook

 Now just settle down here!

Ballio

       The only thing settled here
 Is that I'm letting a thief into my house.

Cook

 But listen to what I've got cooked up for you:
 Remember how Medea boiled old Pelias[55]
 In a stew of her special herbs and potions, 870
 And made him a tender and juicy young man again?
 What Medea did for Pelias,
 I'll do for you today!

Ballio

     Oh? So you're a sorcerer too?

Cook

 Goodness, no! I'm the savorer of mankind.

---

55 The cook undercuts his claim here by confusing Greek myths. Medea used her magical
 powers to rejuvenate Jason's father Aeson by cutting him into pieces and boiling him in a
 pot with special herbs. By contrast, Medea tricked the daughters of Pelias into attempting
 the same method of rejuvenation on their father, but without her magic herbs, he was simply
 killed.

Ballio

Hah, hah!

How much will you charge to give me that recipe?   875

Cook

Which one?

Ballio

The one that'll save me the expense of a robbery.

Cook

The going rate if you trust me. It's not for sale if you don't.
Now about this dinner you're hosting today: is it for friends
Or for enemies?

Ballio

For my friends of course!

Cook

How about inviting your enemies instead of your friends?   880
The sumptuous feast I'll serve today
Will be so sweetly seasoned with sauce
That your guests will gorge on their fingers
And literally lick them to the bone!

Ballio

Please do then take a taste yourself, and share with your   885
Sous-chefs before serving my guests,
So you'll all lick away your larcenous claws!

Cook

I have a sense you don't believe what I say.

Ballio

Now you're annoying me. Stop chattering and just shut up.
There's my house. Go inside and cook dinner!   890
Move it!

Cook's Assistant

Take your place at the table and call your guests.
Dinner's all but ready.

Ballio

Well, the fruit doesn't fall far from that tree!
Already a scumbag, and his master's mouthpiece, and at his age!.
I really don't know what to guard first:
A house full of thieves or the robber next door.   895
Now a little while ago in the forum, my neighbor,
Calidorus's father, warned me in no uncertain terms
To be on guard against his slave Pseudolus,
And not to trust him at all. Word is he's on the prowl today,
To see if he can swindle me out of the woman.   900

He solemnly swore to my neighbor
That he'd fleece me out of Phoenicium.
I'm going inside to deliver this decree:
"No one of this household is to trust Pseudolus at all!"

SCENE 12

Pseudolus returns from the forum with Simia.

(*SONG through 950*)

Pseudolus

If the immortal gods ever help mortals at all,   905
Then they're for rescuing Calidorus and me and for wrecking the pimp!
How else to account for the creation of this cunning and clever fellow to
    help us?
But where'd he go? How silly of me to stand here talking to myself!
    Damn, I've been fooled, as I now see! You'd think I'd be
    Smart enough to keep close tabs on someone as wicked as me!   910
I'm finished if he's given me the slip—and fat chance of finishing this
    scheme!
Oh look! The spitting image of a human punching bag! Look at him strut!
Hey, I was looking all over for you! I was afraid you'd hit the road.

Simia

    That would be perfectly in line with my line of work.

Pseudolus

Where'd you stop?

Simia

    Where I wanted to.

Pseudolus

    Oh, that old tune!

Simia

    Then why'd you ask?   915

Pseudolus

I have some advice for you.

Simia

    I'd advise you to hold on to that advice.

Pseudolus

    Try not to be so disrespectful!

Simia

    Why not? Isn't disrespect expected
    Of a celebrated military man like myself?

Pseudolus

Yes, but let's proceed with the matter at hand.

Simia

Isn't that what I'm doing?   920

Pseudolus

Walk faster then.

Simia

Sorry. Slower is my preference.

Pseudolus

Here's our chance: while he's sleeping I want you to beat him to the punch.

Simia

Easy now. What's the hurry?

I hope to god that the soldier's man,

Shows up exactly at the same time I do.   925

You can be damn sure I'll be a better Harpax than he is! So stay calm!

I'll work all the kinks out of this plan for you nicely.

My tricks and lies will so terrify our visiting soldier

That he himself will deny that he is who he is,

And solemnly swear that I'm him!

Pseudolus

How's that possible?   930

Simia

Your questions kill me!

Pseudolus

Oh, you delightful fellow!

Simia

And just so you know, my dear teacher: with my

Tricks and lies I can beat you any day!

Pseudolus

May Jupiter watch over you—for me!

Simia

No, for me!

But look here: is this costume right for me?   935

Pseudolus

It's perfect!

Simia

All right!   935a

Pseudolus

May the immortal gods grant you everything you desire;

If I desired them to grant you what you truly deserve—you'd get

Less than nothing! I've never known anyone more wickedly wicked than you!

Simia

You mean me?

Pseudolus

I don't mean anything.

But just think of what I'll do for you if you pull this off!   940

Simia

Could you shut up? Pestering a person with a perfect memory makes him forget.

I've got the scam right in here (*points to his chest*)—fully rehearsed and remembered.

Pseudolus

What a fine fellow!

Simia

You can't mean either of us.

Pseudolus

Just don't slip up.

Simia

Could you just shut up?

Pseudolus

I call upon all the gods—

Simia

To ignore you. Now a flood of fiction will follow.

Pseudolus

Oh, Simia! I love, cherish, and honor your dishonesty!   945

Simia

That's the sort of fluff *I'm* famous for: don't bother trying to stroke me!

Pseudolus

Oh, the plums and perks you'll get from me when you pull this off!

Simia

Hehee!

Pseudolus

Delightful delicacies, hors d'oeuvres, perfumes, liqueurs—and

A delightful lady to smother with kisses of course!

Simia

Sweet!

Pseudolus

Oh, you'll be saying "sweeter" if you succeed.   950

Simia

If I don't, I deserve to be crucified! But hurry up and point me to the pimp's hovel.

Pseudolus

It's the third one here.

Simia

Shh! The doors are gaping open.

Pseudolus

I'm guessing the house isn't

Feeling so well.

Simia

Why?

Pseudolus

Because it's puking out the pimp himself right now!

Simia

That's him?

Pseudolus

Sure is.

Simia

He's as crooked as a three-dollar bill!

Pseudolus

Yes, look at

How he slides sideways, just like a crab!   955

SCENE 13

*Ballio enters from his house and Simia engages him while
Pseudolus eavesdrops.*

Ballio

I do believe he's less wicked than you'd expect from a cook.

So far he's only stolen a cup and a ladle.

Pseudolus (*aside*)

Hey, it's now or never!

Simia (*aside*)

Agreed!

Pseudolus (*aside*)

Make your way slyly. I'll be lying in ambush over here.

Simia (*wanting to be overheard*)

I've got the number exactly right. This is the sixth street straight   960

From the gate, the one he told me to turn into.

But I'm not quite sure how many houses down he said it was.

Ballio (*aside*)

Who's the guy in the cloak? I wonder where he's from and what

He wants. Looks like a foreigner—I sure don't know him.

Simia

There's someone who can clue me in on what I'm after.   965

Ballio (*aside*)

He's coming right my way. Where in the world could he be from?

Simia

Hey you there, you with the goatee! I need to ask you something.

Ballio

No "Hello" first?

Simia

To hell with your Hello!

Ballio

Same to you!

Pseudolus (*aside*)

That's a nice start.   969-70

Simia

Tell me: do you know anyone on this street?

Ballio

I know myself.

Simia

Few human beings can make that claim.

There's probably one man out of ten in the forum who knows himself!

Pseudolus (*aside*)

Glory be! He's a philospher!

Simia

I'm looking for a really rotten guy:

A scofflaw, a degenerate, a filthy liar.

Ballio

He must be looking for me,   975

Since those are my aliases. If only he'd mention my real name.

What's the man's name?

Simia

Ballio the Pimp.

Ballio

Do I know him?

Young man, I'm just the man you're looking for.

Simia

You're Ballio?

Ballio

I most certainly am.

Simia

But you're dressed like a burglar.

Ballio

Yes: you probably wouldn't want to meet up with me in a dark alley.   980

Simia

My master sends warm greetings to you

And told me to hand you this letter.

Ballio

And your master's name is?

Pseudolus (*aside*)

> Damn! That muddies up the water!

He doesn't know the name! Now we're stuck!

Ballio

> So what do you say his name is?

Simia

Check out the seal: *you* tell *me* his name,   985

So I can be sure you're really Ballio.

Ballio

Give me the letter.

Simia

> Okay. Now identify the seal.

Ballio

Oh, it's Polymachaeroplagides![56] I'm one-hundred percent certain!

Yes, Yes, I see it's Polymachaeroplagides!

That's the name.

Simia

> Now that you've said "Polymachaeroplagides"   990

I can be sure I gave the letter to the right person.

Ballio

What's he doin' these days?

Simia

> Exactly what every bold and beautiful warrior must do.

But I'm in a big hurry, so please read this letter now.

Take this payment and give me the girl.

I've got to be back in Sicyon[57] today or I'll be dead tomorrow!   995

My master is very domineering.

Ballio

> Yes, I've met him.

Simia

So hurry up and read the letter then!

Ballio

> I will if you'll shut up.

"To Ballio the Pimp: Here you will find the letter

I have written and sealed with the portrait-seal

We both agreed on some time ago."   1000

---

56   A grandiose comic name, probably made up by Plautus (cf. Introduction, p. 5), meaning "Son of many blows by the sword."

57   Sicyon is a city near Corinth on the Greek mainland where the Macedonian soldier currently is (cf. 1174), though it is unclear how Simia knows this.

Simia

The token is right there on the letter.

Ballio

Yes, I can see that. But does he always
Write letters without a proper greeting?

Simia

That is the way of the soldier, Ballio.
In battle, he warmly welcomes his friends;   1005
In battle, he rains down blows upon his foes.
But continue reading and see for yourself
What the letter says.

Ballio

                    Listen up then!
"This is my aide-in-combat Harpax ..."
Are you Harpax?

Simia

                Yes, but you can call me "Steele."   1010

Ballio

"... who comes before you with my letter. Take the money
From him and send him off together with the woman.
It's proper to wish the worthy well; if you weren't so worthless,
I'd wish you well as well. Polymachaeroplagides."

Simia

Well?

Ballio

          Give me the money and I'll give you the girl.   1015

Simia

And just who's holding that up?

Ballio

                  Follow me in then!

Simia

                       Right behind you.

SCENE 14

Pseudolus, alone onstage, addresses the audience.

Pseudolus

Never, ever have I seen a worse human being,
A more deviously wicked fellow than this Simia!
He so awfully damn good he scares me!
What if, just when things are going well,   1020
He turns his wily weapons against me
As soon as he gets the chance?

Since we're on the same side,
I don't want that—and I need him as an ally!
Now I'm absolutely terrified for three reasons: 1025
First, I'm afraid my comrade here will go AWOL
And maybe even join up with the enemy;
Second, what if my master returns from the forum
And catches us thieves with our booty?
Finally, the other Harpax may get here before   1030
Our Harpax gets away from here with the girl.
Damn, they're taking way too long in there!
My heart has packed its bag and is all ready
To seek exile right out of my chest,
If he doesn't come out with the girl right now! (*he spots Phoenicium*) 1035
Ah, sweet victory! I have vanquished my vigilant foes!

SCENE 15

Simia exits from Ballio's house with Phoenicium.

Simia

Don't cry, Phoenicium! You don't know
What's happening, but you will soon enough—
Just about dinner time.
I know why you're weeping, but I'm not   1040
Taking you to that Macedonian monster.
I'm taking you to the man you want to be with:
In the blink of any eye, you'll be in Calidorus' arms.

Pseudolus

How could you linger in there for so long?
My beating heart has taken quite a beating!   1045

Simia

Listen, you punching-bag!
This is no time for questions,
When we're surrounded by the enemy like this!
How's about we march out of here, double time?

Pseudolus

That's great advice coming from a bum like you!   1050
Onward, troops! It's time to toast our triumph![58]

---

58   For a slave's bombastic claim to a grand Roman triumph, see n. 41 above.

SCENE 16

Ballio comes out of his house and addresses the audience.

Ballio

    Hehee! That's a load off my mind, now that
    He's gone and taken the woman with him!
    Let's see that ringleader Pseudolus
    Come and try to trick me out of her now!   1055
    There's one thing I know for sure:
    I'd rather solemnly perjure myself a thousand times
    Than let him make a laughingstock out of me once!
    I'll have the last laugh, the next time we meet—
    Which, I do believe, should be in the mill.[59]   1060
    I'd really love to run into Simo now,
    So he might have a half-share of my happiness.

SCENE 17

Simo returns from the forum.

Simo

    Now to see what my Ulysses has accomplished:
    Has he seized the Palladium[60] from Pimp-citadel?

Ballio

    Oh, you lucky fellow! Give me your lucky hand, Simo!   1065

Simo

    What's up?

Ballio

          Now—

Simo

             Now what?

Ballio

               Your fears are over.

Simo

                     What?

    Did he come to you?

Ballio

           No.

---

59   See n. 36 above.

60   The Palladium was a statue of Athena which ensured the safety of Troy, as long as it remained
    in Trojan hands. Odysseus (= Ulysses) and Diomedes stole the Palladium and thereby made
    the fall of Troy to the Greeks possible. Extravagant mythic comparisons—especially those
    made by triumphant slaves—are a distinctive feature of Plautine comedy.

Simo
> Then what's the good news?

Ballio
Those twenty minae you and Pseudolus bet on today
Are now safe and sound for you!

Simo
I only wish!

Ballio
> I swear you can take the twenty minae out of my pocket.   1070
If he gets possession of the girl today,
Or hands her over to your son as he promised!
Please, please make me swear! I'm dying to,
And just want you to know your money's safe!
And you can even have the girl as a gift for yourself.   1075

Simo
I like those terms. There's no risk here that
I can see. So you'll give me the twenty
Minae?

Ballio
> I will.

Simo
> This isn't a bad deal!
But did you meet him?

Ballio
> Yes, I met both of them together.

Simo
Well, what did he say? What did he tell you?   1080

Ballio
Typical theatrical blather, the usual abuse heaped on
Pimps in the comedies. Kid's stuff, really—
How I'm a nasty scumbag, a liar, etc.[61]

Simo
He got that right!

Ballio
> Yes, I wasn't upset at all.
What's the use of bad-mouthing a man   1085
Who doesn't mind the abuse and doesn't deny any of it?

Simo
But why don't I have to be afraid of him anymore?

---

61   Ballio refers to 357ff. Cf. Introduction, pp. 29-30.

Ballio

Because he can't ever possibly cheat me out of the girl.
Remember how a while back I told you
That she'd been sold to a Macedonian soldier?   1090

Simo

Yes.

Ballio

Well, his slave brought me the money
And the token—

Simo

Yes, and?

Ballio

Which the soldier and I had agreed upon.
He took the girl away with him just a while ago.

Simo

Are you telling me the honest truth?

Ballio

Now just how could *I* do that?   1095

Simo

How can we be sure he hasn't put some scheme together?

Ballio

For me the proof is in the letter and the seal.
Why, he's on his way to Sicyon with her right now!

Simo

Excellent! Now I should sign up Pseudolus
To be the first citizen of the colony of Millstonia.[62]   1100
But who's this guy in the cloak?

Ballio

I sure don't know.
Let's watch where he goes and see what he's up to.

SCENE 18

Harpax returns from his nap at the inn.
(*SONG through 1133*)

Harpax

How wicked and worthless is the slave who ignores his master's
Orders, or can't remember to do his duty without being reminded!
Then there are the ones who declare themselves free men   1105
The instant they're out of their masters' sight:

---

62   See n. 36 above.

Living it up, wasting what little they have in whorehouses!
    Little chance they'll ever be free!
  The only skill they can boast of is
  Surviving their own shameless deeds. 1110
  I choose neither to meet
    Nor to greet such slaves.
Once I've got my orders I do them whether master's present or absent.
  I fear master even when he's not around, so I won't have to be afraid
  When he's here![63] And now to the matter at hand. 1115
  I waited at the inn for Surus (the one I gave the token)
  Just as we had agreed. He said he'd summon
  Me the minute the pimp got home.
  But he didn't come or call, so I've come on my own
To see what's up and see if he's just toying with me. 1120
I'd better knock on the door and call someone out. I need to pay off
  The pimp, get the girl, and get out of here!

Ballio

Hey, you!

Simo

    What?

Ballio

      This guy's all mine.

Simo

How so?

Ballio

     He's the usual prey I hunt:
He wants a whore, I want his money. That's a beast I love to sink my
  teeth into. 1125

Simo

    Planning to devour him right now, eh?

Ballio

           Yes, it's my duty
When he's fresh, warm, and full of the spirit of giving.
Mighty moral giants like you may enrich the state,
But it's the degenerates that enrich me.

Simo

    And the gods will pay you back in kind for that! 1130

---

63   The "good slave" speech here is a commonplace in Plautus, where, as here—seeing that
Harpax fails to carry out his master's orders—such claims to dedicated service are usually
ironic. Cf. *Amphitryon* 590-1 and n. 44 there.

Harpax

No reason why I shouldn't just knock
And see if Ballio is home.

Ballio

It's Venus who blesses a profiteer like me with these bankrupt fools!
What a life they lead! Eating, drinking, loving my ladies—and their debt!
    They're
A far cry from you! You deny yourself pleasure and envy others people's. 1135

Harpax

Hey! Anybody here?

Ballio

He's coming right to me now.

* * * *

The omens look good: I just know this one will be easy prey.

Harpax

Will someone open up here?

Ballio

Hey, you in the cloak? What's your business here?

Harpax

I'm looking for the master of the house, Ballio the Pimp.   1140

Ballio

Whoever you are, young man, you can stop searching.

Harpax

Why?

Ballio

Because you are looking right at him, in the flesh.

Harpax (*to Simo*)

So you're Ballio?

Simo

Hold it right there, soldier boy, unless you're looking for a fight!
Point your finger right over here: he's the pimp!

Ballio

And he's a true gentleman.
And you, good sir, would be hounded by your creditors in the forum   1145
Without a penny to your name, if a certain pimp didn't always bail you out.

Harpax

How about talking to me?

Ballio

Fine. What do you want?

Harpax

I want you to take this money.

Ballio

There's nothing I want more. What took you so long?

Harpax

Here's five minae, solid silver, all counted out for you.

My master Polymachaeroplagides ordered me   1150

To close his account and bring Phoenicum back with me.

Ballio

Your master?

Harpax

That's right.

Ballio

The soldier?

Harpax

That's right.

Ballio

The Macedonian one?

Harpax

Precisely.

Ballio

So it's Polymachaeroplagides who sent you?

Harpax

That's the truth.

Ballio

And you're supposed to give me this money?

Harpax

Yes, if you really are

Ballio the Pimp.

Ballio

And you're supposed to take the girl away?   1155

Harpax

Right.

Ballio

He said Phoenicium, right?

Harpax

You've got it all right.

Ballio

Wait a second.

I'll be right back.

Harpax

Well, make it snappy! It's late in the day

And I'm in a hurry.

Ballio

                              Yes. I just need to consult my friend.
        Wait right there—I'll be right back. Well, now what, Simo?
        What should we do? I've caught him and the money red-handed!   1160

Simo

        Come again?

Ballio

                        Don't you see what's up?

Simo

                                              Like a blind man.

Ballio

        Your Pseudolus recruited him to play the part of the
        Soldier's aide.

Simo

                        Have you got his money?

Ballio

                                              Here: ask your own eyes.

Simo

        Hey, don't forget to give me half of the loot.
        We really should share it.

Ballio

                              What the hell? It's all yours anyway.   1165

Harpax

        Over here! Any time now!

Ballio

                              We'll get right to you. What's your plan, Simo?

Simo

        Let's have some fun with this phony messenger
        Until he figures out for himself that the game's up.

Ballio

        Follow me! So you are of course the soldier's slave?

Harpax

                                              Obviously.

Ballio

        What'd he buy you for?

Harpax

                              His unvanquished valor won me in war.   1170
        I was the leading general back in my native land.

Simo

        Oh, so he sacked the prison back in the old homestead?

Harpax

        If you insult me, I'll insult you back!

Ballio

How long
Did it take you to get here from Sicyon?

Harpax

A day and a half.

Ballio

Very impressive!

Simo

Oh, yes, he's as nimble as can be.   1175
And look at those calves: they could carry quite a load of chains!

Ballio

Tell me: did you used to lie in a cradle as a little boy?

Simo

Of course he did.

Ballio

And did you used to lie in your own—Oh, you know what I mean.

Simo

Of course he did.

Harpax

Are you two insane?

Ballio

Let me ask you this:
At night, when you and the soldier were out patrolling,   1180
Did his sword fit snugly up inside your sheath?

Harpax

Go to hell!

Ballio

Just where you're heading in due time.

Harpax

Either send out the girl or give me back the money!

Ballio

Now wait a minute.

Harpax

Why?

Ballio

Tell us how much the cloak rental set you back.

Harpax

What?

Simo

How much was the sword?

Harpax

You two need help!

Ballio

                                  Hey—   1185

Harpax

    Let go of me!

Ballio

                What's the owner of the hat raking in today?

Harpax

    What do you mean "owner?" Are you dreaming?
    These are all mine, purchased with my own private funds!

Ballio

    You mean with your own private parts, don't you?

Harpax

    You old men are so slick! I think you need a good old-fashioned rubbing
        out!   1190

Ballio

    Please just answer this one question. Seriously now:
    How much did you cost? What did Pseudolus hire you for?

Harpax

    Who's Pseudolus?

Ballio

                Your tutor, the one who trained
    You to trick me out of the girl.

Harpax

    What Pseudolus? What trick? I have no idea   1195
    Who or what you're talking about.

Ballio

                      Why don't you just come off it?
    There's nothing left for you thieves to steal today. Tell Pseudolus
    Someone else already captured his prey, someone
    By the name of Harpax.

Harpax

                But I swear I'm Harpax!

Ballio

                           I swear you wish you were.
    You are one hundred percent pure scam-artist.

Harpax

                      I gave you the money,   1200
    And when I arrived here a while back I gave your slave
    A token—the letter sealed with my master's portrait.

Ballio

    You gave my slave a letter? Which slave?

Harpax

                         Surus.

Ballio

This trickster is no lightweight.
What a wicked scheme! That punching bag Pseudolus   1205
Has planned and plotted so carefully!
He gave this guy exactly what the soldier owed
And dressed him up to steal the girl.
Now the real Harpax has already brought the letter to me.

Harpax

My name is Harpax and I'm the slave of the Macedonian soldier!   1210
I'm not here to swindle or diddle you,
And I have no idea who in the world this person Pseudolus is!

Simo

Barring a miracle, pimp, I'd say you've lost that lady!

Ballio

The more I hear, the more I'm afraid that you're right!
That Surus, the one that took the token from him,   1215
Sent quite a chill down my spine! Barring a miracle,
I'd say it's Pseudolus! What did the guy look like?

Harpax

Let's see: red hair, pot belly, thick calves, dark complexion,
Large head, bug-eyed, ruddy face,
And absolutely enormous feet.[64]

Ballio

                         Oh those feet! That's murder!   1220
It was Pseudolus! That's it for me, Simo. You can pronounce me dead!

Harpax

Oh, no you're not! At least not until I get my
Twenty minae back!

Simo

                         And I also get another twenty minae!

Ballio

You wouldn't really collect on that bet I was only kidding about?

Simo

From a degenerate like you? You can bet I'll collect—and loot you
   to boot!   1225

Ballio

At least hand over Pseudolus to me!

---

64   Harpax here provides what is our fullest description of a clever slave's costume and mask.

Simo

Why should I?
What's he done wrong? Didn't I tell you a hundred times to watch out
    for him?

Ballio

He's ruined me!

Simo

And he's cheated me out of twenty minae too.

Ballio

What should I do?

Harpax

Give me the money—and then go hang yourself!

Ballio

Oh, screw you! Well, follow me to the forum so I can pay you.

Harpax

Right behind you.   1230

Simo

And what about me?

Ballio

Today I settle with foreigners; tomorrow, fellow citizens.
Pseudolus sought the death penalty for me today in the assembly[65]
When he recruited that guy to steal the lady.
You! follow me! And you: don't expect me to return home by this way.
The way things are going, I think I'll stick to the alleys.   1235

Harpax

If you walked as much as you talk, we'd be in the forum already.

Ballio

I might as well rename my birthday my "deathday."

Simo

I've fleeced him well, as has my slave Pseudolus!
Now I think I'll wait right here for Pseudolus, but not
With whips and chains like in other comedies: 1240
I'll go in and get the twenty minae I promised
If he pulled it off, and just wait here to hand it over to him myself.
What mortal is more clever, cunning and crafty?
He's got it all over Ulysses[66] himself and the Trojan Horse!
I'm off to get the money inside and then lie in wait for Pseudolus.   1245

---

65   Another striking instance of Romanization, as the assembly referred to here is the large and
    powerful *comitia centuriata*, whose many important functions included passing the sentence
    of death on citizens. Cf. Introduction, pp. 2-3.

66   I.e., Odysseus. Cf. n. 60 above.

SCENE 19

Pseudolus enters from Simo's house.

(*SONG*)

Pseudolus

    Hey feet, what ya' doing? Care to stand up—or not?

    Is that what you want—for me to fall and be dragged offstage?

   Damn! It's all your fault if I fall! Still stumbling?

   Time for me to get tough with you now!

    The worst thing about wine? Easy: 1250

   It trips up the ol' feet like some tricky wrestler!

   Damn straight! I've got absolutely the best buzz going on!

 And inside, dishes done so deliciously, every kind of elegance, a perfectly

    Festive setting and reception, fit for the gods!

   I won't beat around the bush: this is what   1255

     Makes a man love life!

   Here are all delights, here is all we like,

     The best thing on this side of heaven!

 Whatever could be finer than a lover hugging a lover—

    Tongue tied up with tongue, lip locked to lip,   1260

 Breast pressed to breast, skin right on skin,

 A cup in a milky white hand, the toast of a lover to his beloved!

    There you'll find no nasty nattering,

    No obnoxious bores or tedious talk.

    Nothing but perfumes and perfumed oils,   1265

    Wreathes everywhere, garlands galore—

    As for the rest—don't ask me any more!

 That's how Young Master and I spent this merry day,

     To celebrate my feat and

     Our enemy's defeat!   1270

   I left them reclining there, wining and dining

   Their whores just as I had mine, consigning their hearts to joy!

  As I got up to go, they begged me to dance.

   I showed them a few steps I'd expertly learned at

   The Ionic Academy of Dance.[67] I hitched up my cloak and frolicked

    like this.   1275

   They clap and shout "more, more," so I do an encore.

   Not wanting to be a bore, I start over like this, to win some more lovin'

    From my honey. I made a full turn—flat on my face,

---

67 The Ionic style of dance, which Pseudolus performs here, was condemned as lewd by Roman moralists.

> And that was the sad end of my romp!
> I struggled to rise and—Plew!—I sort of soiled my cloak.   1280
> Oh, the fun they found in my fall! I'm handed a drink,

And I trade in that cloak for a clean one. I came out here to shake off my hangover.

Now it's time to remind my older master of our earlier deal.

Hey, open up, somebody, and tell Simo I'm here!

SCENE 20

Simo answers Pseudolus' call to open the door of his house.
(*SONG*)

Simo

> I'm being called outside by the worst human being alive.   1285
> But what's this? Huh? What do I see?

Pseudolus

> Your very own Pseudolus, wreathed and wasted!

Simo (*aside*)

> And proud of it! Look at the attitude!
> Not an ounce of respect in him on my account!
> Let's see: should I be nasty or nice with him?   1290

This wallet here rules out violence, if there's any hope of getting anything out of him.

Pseudolus

> The worst of mankind
> Gives greeting to the best.

Simo

> God bless you too, Pseudolus. Phew! Get the hell away!

Pseudolus

Why the rejection?

Simo

> Why? When you're drunk and burping in my face?   1295

Pseudolus

> Hold me up gently now, so I don't fall. Can't you see
> How stinkin' drunk I am?

Simo

> The impudence! Walking around drunk
> In the middle of the day wearing a wreath!

Pseudolus

> I felt like it.

Simo

> You felt like it? And still burping in my face!   1300

Pseudolus

Leave me alone, Simo—it's a lovely belch.

Simo

You scum! I think you could swill
Mount Massicus'[68] four finest harvests
In one single hour!

Pseudolus

Make that a winter hour.[69]

Simo

Touché! But do tell me: 1305
Where exactly did you load up on this cargo full of wine?

Pseudolus

I had more than a couple drinks with your son.
But, Simo, look how Ballio was conned.
Every last detail done as I promised you!

Simo

You are a horrible, horrible person!   1310

Pseudolus

It's the girl's fault. She's on the couch with your son—and a free
woman now.

Simo

Yes, I know every last detail of what you've done.

Pseudolus

Then why don't I have my money?

Simo

Fair enough—here it is.

Pseudolus

You said I'd never get it.
Load me up and follow this way!

Simo

Load you up?

Pseudolus

Ah, hah.   1315

Simo

What should I do with him? He takes my money and mocks me too!

---

68   A fertile Italian mountain spur (between Latium and Campania in Italy), famous for the fine
     wine produced from its vineyards.

69   Pseudolus takes Simo's jest a step further: the Romans divided the day into twelve hours, and
     so the midwinter hour was briefest (c. three-quarters of our hour).

Pseudolus

"Woe to the vanquished!"[70]

Simo

Then turn your shoulder this way.

Pseudolus (*accepting the bag of coins*)

Right there.

Simo

I never envisioned this—
Humbling myself like this to you!
Oh, Oh, Oh!

Pseudolus

Now stop that!

Simo

It hurts.

Pseudolus

One of us has to be hurting.   1320

Simo

You're really going to take this from your master, Pseudolus?

Pseudolus

With absolute pleasure.

Simo

You won't give me back just a part of the money?

Pseudolus

No. Call me greedy if you want, but you'll never be a penny richer for that.
How much pity would you have given my back if I had failed today?

Simo

I swear I'll have my revenge.

Pseudolus

Swear all you want. I've got a strong back.   1325

Simo

Go ahead then.

Pseudolus

Come on back.

Simo

Why should I?

Pseudolus

Just come on back—no tricks.

---

70   This proverbial Latin phrase was thought to have originated with the Gallic chieftain
     Brennan, who led the capture of Rome in 387 BCE; it becomes delightfully bombastic in
     Pseudolus' mouth here.

Simo

I'm here.

Pseudolus

Let's you and I have a drink together.

Simo

You and I go for a drink?

Pseudolus

Yep, do what I say!

If you join me, I'll see you get half or more of this cash back.

Simo

Okay then. Lead the

way.

Pseudolus

Tell me, Simo: you're not mad at me

And your son about all this, are you?   1330

Simo

No, not at all.

Pseudolus

This way.

Simo

Right behind you. How about

Inviting the audience to join us?

Pseudolus

Oh, hell! They never

Invite me out and so I return the favor.

But if you'd like to show your approval of the

Play and cast by applauding now, I'll invite you for tomorrow.[71]   1335

---

71   I.e., he perhaps means to the performance of another play at the festival.